Eva's Uncommon Life

Eva's Uncommon Life

Guided by Miracles

Eva Perlman

Reseda, California, USA

EVA'S UNCOMMON LIFE: GUIDED BY MIRACLES
by Eva Perlman

Copyright © 2019 by Eva Perlman

Published by: Perlman Publishing

Cover and Design: Pedernales Publishing
Cover butterfly image via iStock by Getty Images, credit stereohype

Cover author photo: Larry Estrin / Eugene Photography

All photographs are the property of the author, with the exception of the following which are public domain:

3.1 Map of France Divided 1940
Eric Gaba [CC BY-SA 4.0 (https://creativecommons.org/licenses/by-sa/4.0)]

14.1 Routes of deportation to Auschwitz
Jorge Láscar from Australia [CC BY 2.0 (https://creativecommons.org/licenses/by/2.0)]

ISBN: 978-1-7333835-2-3 Paperback Edition
        978-1-7333835-3-0 Hardcover Edition
        978-1-7333835-1-6 Digital Edition
        978-1-7333835-0-9 Audio Edition

Library of Congress Control Number: 2019910833

Author services by Pedernales Publishing, LLC
www.pedernalespublishing.com

Printed in the United States of America

This book is dedicated to

My parents, Rodolphe and Charlotte Gutmann z"l, of blessed memory, whose wisdom and bravery saved us during the war and to Mel Perlman z"l, of blessed memory, the love of my life.

TABLE of CONTENTS

FOREWORD

After twenty years as a Holocaust educator, leading thousands of Jewish teens and adults on the March of the Living, what happened during the Holocaust remains incomprehensible to me. I have found that perhaps the closest way to truly understand this atrocity is through the lens of the survivors, or more aptly put, the storytellers who were there. The life story of Eva Perlman is profound in every sense of the word – not only in how she and her family survived the horrors they did, but also in Eva's dogged commitment to telling her story, so that all the stories that were not given voice, will never be forgotten. Most astounding to me is Eva's "joie de vivre," her zest for life, and her sense of continued hope. I feel so grateful for the miracle that brought Eva into my life. She is a role model in every sense of the word – living life to the absolute fullest. I have had the privilege of traveling on the March of the Living with Eva for nine years, and I know one thing for certain, she has enriched not only my life, but the lives of all the people she has encountered and will continue to encounter on the way, and all the people who will be lucky enough to read this remarkable story.

Monise Neumann
International March of the Living
National Consultant

PREFACE

"There are only two ways to live your life. One is as though nothing is a miracle. The other is as though everything is a miracle."
Albert Einstein

Throughout my life, I have often thought of writing down my memories for my three children and six grandchildren. Perhaps even my great-grandchildren will one day read my story.

I feel fortunate to have lived a long and interesting life. But writing down one's life story is a bold undertaking, and I did not know if I was up to the task. As luck would have it, I was invited to a life story writing class, which I ended up attending weekly for over twelve years. My life, spanning more than eight decades, was filled with miracles.

There are many books of Holocaust survivors available today, each more interesting than the next. While most of them focus on survival during the war years, my book is not only about our survival, but also about the many years thereafter. To this day I am fortunate to continue to lead, well into my eighties, an amazing and forever evolving adventure.

I begged my mother many times to write her memories of the war years for my children and grandchildren. The thought of having to relive those traumatic years, in order to write about them, was too painful for her. Fortunately, she finally agreed to write down one story which she called *"Un jour pas comme les autres"* (a day unlike others), referred to in our family simply as "the bicycle story" of August 31, 1944. I have included it in her own words.

As a child in hiding, I actually have many of my own memories—when you live in turbulent times, you tend to recall the events better. To supplement my memories, I have relied upon various documents such as certificates, scrapbooks, letters, diaries, videos and photos. In addition, my daughter Ilana and son-in-law Mark managed to make a family video, interviewing my mother in 1990 on the occasion of her 80th birthday trip to Los Angeles. We were so excited to get her talking! Steven Spielberg had many survivors interviewed for the Shoah Foundation, including my mother in

October 1995. I have relied on that interview for information and have also incorporated several family memories that I found in my maternal grand-mother's handwritten diary in formal German script, written in 1976, just months before she died. Later memories about Uganda are supplemented by a chapter written by my husband, Mel Perlman, *of blessed memory,* in the college textbook *Marginal Natives: Anthropologists at Work,* 1970.

I mention many events and places in my book, but my explanations may be very succinct for lack of space, so I encourage you, the reader, to do your own research whenever you would like more information or clarity. In order to protect copyright, I have not included pictures of the art I mention, but you can find many good pictures on the Internet.

The butterfly on the cover symbolizes survival, overcoming obstacles, change, growth and transformation.

ACKNOWLEDGMENTS

I wish to thank my whole family, my daughters, Ilana and Tamar, and granddaughters, Diane and Myra, who encouraged me for years to write my story, and also helped me get in touch with some vital people from my past. It was their curiosity about my life and our family history that inspired me to write my autobiography. My brothers, Ernest and Raymond, and my son, David, also gave me constructive criticism and advice, and made important suggestions.

I wish to thank Lee Barnathan, the first to edit my manuscript; Jeanette Shelburne, a professional writer, teacher and featured speaker, and her class, who initially gave me needed direction and offered invaluable constructive criticism; and Monise Neumann, who made important comments and suggestions for the March of the Living chapter.

My deepest gratitude goes to Martina Gruber, who became my main editor. We met regularly to restructure and reorganize the manuscript, turning individual stories into a real book. Her research was invaluable in setting the war chapters into the historical events of the times. Martina brought passion and significant attention to detail to enhance character development.

I am extremely grateful to Jennifer Croslow (Jen), who served as my second editor, and whose support has been essential in bringing this manuscript to conclusion. Jen brought skill, enthusiasm, and sensitivity to deepen the insights. She focused primarily on the reader's perspective, and was important in turning my life into a meaningful story.

Also, a word of thanks to Ed Addeo and several friends who reviewed the whole manuscript for grammar and punctuation, and to Jose Ramirez of Pedernales Publishing for transforming the manuscript into this book.

Lastly, my deepest gratitude goes again to my eldest daughter, Ilana Meskin, for her extensive project management, technical assistance, and brainstorming partnership. Without her limitless support, I have no idea how I could possibly have completed this journey to publication.

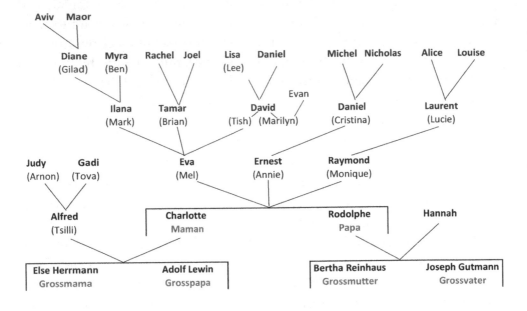

Eva's Family Tree

CHAPTER 1

FAMILY ROOTS: GERMANY

My grandfather's name was Adolf. Had his parents known what that name would come to symbolize later, I'm sure they would have chosen differently. But it was a popular name for German boys in the 19th and early 20th centuries. Adolf Lewin married Else Herrmann in Ulm in 1909, and settled in Driesen, a small village, then part of Prussia and now Poland. The village was surrounded by lakes and forests and some 5,000 people lived there, including thirty Jewish families. Berlin was only a three-hour train ride away. Adolf opened a jewelry store in the central square, close to the courthouse and across from a *Brenkenhof* memorial sculpture. Aside from selling jewelry, he also repaired watches and clocks. Times were tough, unemployment high and food scarce. His wife Else, a beautiful, elegant and rather quiet woman, helped in the store. At home they kept strictly kosher and observed all the Jewish holidays. Adolf ruled the household with an iron fist. He was an irascible man, and, I am sure, difficult to live with. A year after they married, the couple was blessed with their first child, my mother Charlotte, in September 1910, and two years later they had a son, Alfred.

In July 1914, the First World War broke out. Charlotte was only four that summer when her father and many other men were drafted to fight for Germany and the women were left to fend for themselves. Thankfully Else's father Moritz Herrmann, a retired baker, was too old to be drafted. Since he lived with them, he helped to take care of the two children so his daughter Else could run the store. Charlotte loved her grandfather.

One day Adolf came home unexpectedly in the middle of the war. The clock of the courthouse tower had stopped working and he was given a one-week furlough to repair it, as most residents depended on that clock to tell time. Only the wealthy could afford wristwatches. Every day Adolf took

Charlotte and Alfred with him until the clock was repaired. Because they were such good children he rewarded them with a special treat: a tiny piece of marzipan.

When Charlotte was five, her mother Else fell very ill. She decided at that moment to become a doctor so she could take care of her family. She loved tending to her "sick" dolls and nursing them back to health.

The winter of 1917 was particularly cold and tough. Temperatures fell to minus 20 degrees Celsius. Charlotte's mother walked with her children to a small town to sell some of her earrings so she could buy food. On the way, Charlotte's foot froze and began to swell. She was in such pain she could no longer walk. Thankfully, her grandfather Moritz came to the rescue and carried her home. For quite a while, her little brother Alfred had to pull her to Hebrew school on a sled.

Passover came and the war was still raging. The only men left in town were Russian prisoners of war who were being kept at the local sawmill. Among them were several Jewish men. Suspecting they were homesick, Else and her father invited them over for the Passover Seder. She served them a nice meal and they sang Jewish songs. When they left that night, they thanked her profusely. Finally, in 1918, the war came to an end and Adolf returned with a chest wound and an Iron Cross for bravery. Millions of lives had been lost, and many returned wounded. Two of Adolf's brothers, Moses and Gustav, had been killed.

My grandfather and his brothers were among 100,000 German Jews who proudly served in military uniform as soldiers, sailors, airmen and administrators. But far from an improved public opinion of German Jewish citizens, there was instead, after Germany's crushing loss, a significant rise in anti-Semitism. Among the common myths circulating at the time were assertions that Jews were war profiteering at home. It was also rumored that Jews were evading military responsibilities or "war shirking," in spite of statistics showing that the percentage of Jewish casualties was no smaller than that of the non-Jewish population. The potent mix of prejudices and stereotypes quickly led a battered post-WWI German people to pin all their troubles on a perennial scapegoat: the Jews.

Upon Adolf's return from the war, life began to run its normal course again — at least at first. In 1920, at the age of ten, Charlotte chose to learn Latin because it was a prerequisite for medical studies, and English two years later. Driven by her desire to become a doctor, Charlotte gained acceptance to a *gymnasium* (like a U.S. high school) so she could eventually attend university. However, every day she had to ride the train for two hours each way, because the closest school was in Landsberg on the Warta River, southwest of Driesen.

In school, Charlotte began experiencing hostility and discrimination just because she was Jewish. This was her first personal encounter with anti-Semitism. One day, the teacher asked her to collect the students' papers, and when she placed them on his desk, her eyes fell on *Der Stürmer*, an anti-Semitic newspaper first published in 1923. On the front page the Jews were depicted with ugly cartoons. When her teacher noticed her looking at the paper, he quickly put it into the inner pocket of his jacket. As he did this, Charlotte noticed a swastika on the underside of his lapel. Soon most of the girls in her class ignored her and she was not invited to birthday parties or other events. She began to feel different, ostracized.

Nevertheless, she made one friend, her desk partner, whose father was a wealthy Protestant land owner in Landsberg. When this girl asked him if she could invite her Jewish friend over, her father said, "There are nineteen girls in your class. Can't you find a non-Jewish friend?" Although he was not happy with his daughter's choice of friends, he allowed her to bring Charlotte over after school. At the dinner table, he asked her many questions about her beliefs and Charlotte explained the strict dietary laws to which she adhered.

"I am also a traditionalist and believe in certain laws," he finally said. "A girl who sticks to her tradition I find remarkable." He turned to his wife and said, "Please buy some special dishes and cutlery just for Charlotte. When she comes over again we'll have fish or an omelet for her so that she can eat with us without having to disrespect her laws." Charlotte was relieved and grateful.

One day this wealthy Protestant landowner invited her to a ball at the local parish with his daughter and his wife. Charlotte, now in her teens, was not your typical dark-featured Jewish girl. Her eyes were a striking blue and her hair had a pretty light brown shade. A young man noticed her immediately and invited her to dance, assuming that she was a member of that family. He was so enchanted with her that he insisted on dancing with her all evening. Charlotte would have liked to dance with others as well, but she did not have the courage to tell him.

The following week they went on a date and he asked to meet her parents. Charlotte was not particularly attracted to him, and besides, he was not Jewish, but she did not know how to break it off. The next time she got on the train to go back home after school, he insisted on accompanying her. During the ride, he began to talk about love and marriage.

"I feel honored, sir," Charlotte finally said, "and I am flattered by your attention. But there is something I must tell you — I am Jewish."

When he heard this, his face flushed to the roots of his red hair. He immediately got up, took his hat from the rack above his seat, and walked away, leaving her sitting there, without another glance or another word. Charlotte was crushed, not because she cared for him, but because it was such a cruel blow to her self-esteem.

In 1929, shortly before Charlotte turned nineteen, she was accepted at the Friedrich Wilhelm University in Berlin (now Humboldt University). Her dream of studying medicine had become a reality. She was immensely grateful as she was well aware of the financial sacrifices her parents were making to support her. Fortunately, her grandfather Moritz now lived in Berlin and she could live with him rent-free. Charlotte lived on a tight budget—at times she had to save just to buy toothpaste, and to buy meals at a reduced price at the kosher cafeteria on campus and to get free admittance to the medical library to borrow books, she joined a socio-democratic student group.

Charlotte also joined a Jewish singles group. On a lovely summer Sunday a few weeks later, the group met for a picnic at a lake in one of Berlin's suburbs. A tall, handsome man caught her attention. "This will be my husband one day!" she thought.

His name was Rudolf Gutmann. Since Charlotte and Rudolf were the only ones who had brought their bathing suits, they swam and frolicked, laughed and kibbitzed in the water while the others stood there in their best Sunday clothes and looked at them with great envy from the shore. At the end of the day Rudolf invited Charlotte to a paddleboat outing for the following weekend and suggested she bring her swimsuit. Charlotte was excited. He was eight years older, smart and well-educated, and already an established patent attorney working as a partner with Alfred Bursch.

They began dating regularly. Rudolf still lived with his parents, Joseph Gutmann (my *Grossvater*), born in 1865, and Bertha née Reinhaus (my *Grossmutter*) born in 1867, both in Germany. They lived in an apartment that belonged to the school Joseph directed. Joseph was about to retire in 1931 from a long and successful career as a scholar and educator. For many years he had been the principal of several Jewish private schools in Berlin and was very involved in Berlin's Jewish community. He and Bertha had four children, but in those days, infant mortality rates were high and only one child survived, my father. Another was stillborn, one boy died at two and a half months, and a little girl, Hanna, died at two years of tubercular meningitis.

It did not take Rudolf long to be certain that he wanted to marry Charlotte. She had completed her fifth semester and had just passed her exams when he asked her to marry him.

"But what about my studies?" she asked, concerned.

"Of course you'll continue with your studies," he assured her, and so Charlotte accepted.

Rudolf invited her over to meet his parents, Joseph and Bertha, who welcomed her warmly into the family.

Charlotte's father, on the other hand, was not too happy when he found out that his daughter had gotten engaged.

"You are only twenty-one and I haven't even met this gentleman," he remarked angrily. "How could you get engaged without asking for my blessing first?"

Engagement of Rudolf and Charlotte

Adolf then made a special trip to Berlin to meet Rudolf. The three went to a concert together and spent an enjoyable evening. When they went to the bus stop to take their respective buses home, Rudolf boarded his bus quickly and waved goodbye. Adolf was shocked.

"This young man should have waited for us to get on our bus first," he mumbled. However, once Adolf and Else got to know their future son-in-law, they realized he was a prize. They learned to love him like a son and appreciated him for his integrity and the great love he had for their daughter.

On August 6, 1931, about a year after Charlotte and Rudolf had first set eyes on each other, they were married. It was a very hot day. During the ceremony Charlotte was wiping the sweat off her brow, when she overheard an old lady say, "How touching to see a young bride cry on her wedding day!"

Now that Rudolf's father was retiring, he had to move out of the school's administrative apartment. After some searching, he found a place to live along the Spree River at *Hansa Ufer 8*. The apartment was large enough to be divided into two smaller living quarters, so he let Rudolf and Charlotte share the place and they accepted. Soon thereafter, when the Gutmanns learned Charlotte was pregnant, they were thrilled. Joseph and Bertha offered to help take care of their soon-to-be-born grandchild, so that Charlotte could continue to focus on her medical studies.

Eva four months old in 1932

Nine months after the wedding, on May 18, 1932, Rudolf rushed Charlotte to the hospital in Berlin Charlottenburg. The doctor took forever to fill out the papers.

"Please doctor, take me to the delivery room right away. The baby is coming!" Charlotte pleaded. A few minutes later, at 5 a.m., I was born. Apparently by 6 a.m. I was already sleeping peacefully on the hospital's balcony, and my mother remembered that it was a beautiful day. I was given the names Eva Hanna, but I never liked the name Eva. My mother would say to me later, "Eva! You are named for the first woman!" I was given Hanna as a second name after my father's little sister who had died. While my father was at work and my mother at university, my grandparents were the best caregivers. Grossmutter Bertha was delighted. On sunny days she happily pushed me in my stroller along the Spree River.

On January 30, 1933, when I was just eight months old, life changed forever for the Jews of Germany. German President Paul von Hindenburg appointed Adolf Hitler as the new chancellor of Germany. That same night the Nazi party celebrated its victory with a massive torchlight parade. Nazi soldiers proudly carried flags with swastikas through Berlin's Brandenburg Gate while the rest of the world looked on with confusion and alarm.

In Berlin the change in leadership was felt almost immediately. New regulations were implemented, restricting all aspects of Jewish public and private life. Jews were excluded from state service and labeled "politically unreliable" civil servants. By April 1933, German law restricted the number of Jewish students at German schools and universities as well as "Jewish activity" in the medical and legal professions. Jews were denied admission to the bar. The city of Berlin forbade Jewish lawyers and notaries to work on legal matters, the mayor of Munich forbade Jewish doctors to treat non-Jewish patients, and the Bavarian interior ministry denied new Jewish students admission to medical school. Government agencies started to prevent Jews from earning a living. Jewish officers were expelled from the army, and Jewish university students were not allowed to sit for doctoral examinations.

No one cared that the Jews had fought for Germany as good citizens during the Great War.

By September 1, 1933, my father (Papa) could no longer earn a living in Germany. In the official Gazette of the German Patent Office his name was erased from the list of patent attorneys. Papa had worked for several years patenting inventions in France with his non-Jewish French colleague, Mr. Plasseraud. Mr. Weissman, a Jew, and Mr. Plasseraud were two of the three partners in the Paris patent firm Cabinet Weissman. Mr. Plasseraud valued Papa's work greatly and told him he was always welcome to join his firm in Paris if the situation grew worse for the Jews of Germany.

This was Papa's extraordinary chance. He decided to accept Monsieur Plasseraud's offer, and suggested his partner, Alfred Bursch, consider leaving as well. Bursch decided to stay, reasoning that things could not possibly get worse. He was tragically wrong. A few years later, Bursch and his wife Lina were murdered in Auschwitz.

In September 1933, Papa went to Paris. It was very difficult for him to leave his elderly parents. Nevertheless, he left and started working in France. My mother (Maman) stayed behind with me to organize our move. For the time being, she continued to attend classes at the university. Almost immediately, the first two rows in the lecture halls were reserved for SS students, who proudly wore their brown uniforms with swastikas. They shouted *"Juden raus!"* (Jews get out!) when the Jewish students and professors walked in, and everyone clapped. Maman was terrified.

As part of her medical studies, she accompanied doctors on their daily rounds and assisted them. One time she followed the doctor and the nurse into the delivery room. A woman was moaning and groaning. She had been in labor for hours with her twelfth child. While the doctor and the nurses were waiting for labor to advance, they openly talked about the Jews in the most despicable way, not suspecting that the blue-eyed Charlotte could be Jewish. "Let's hang them all from the lamp posts and skin them raw!" one of them suggested.

"Put salt and pepper in their wounds," another added.

Maman got so frightened that she began to shake. The doctor noticed her distress.

"I think you need to go home and get a little rest, Mrs. Gutmann," he suggested. "Let's give our patient a break so she can rest before the final push. I am expecting you back by six a.m. to administer the shot to start the woman's labor again."

The next morning a baby boy was born.

"Let's name him Adolf after our new chancellor," the excited parents exclaimed in unison.

When Maman was alone with the doctor she said frankly, "I understand that you don't like Jews, but the way you talk about them really upsets me!"

"Are you Jewish?" the doctor asked, surprised.

"Yes, I am."

Soon after, as of October 3, 1933, all Jewish professors, doctors, nurses, lab assistants and students were no longer allowed to work in their professions, attend schools or universities.

"We can't just abandon our patients on the operating table!" the Jewish surgeons protested.

"Germany would rather see the patients 'croak' than have them be treated by Jews! You have twenty minutes to pack your belongings and leave!" was the response.

That same month Maman found a letter in the mail signed by the director of the Friedrich-Wilhelm University.

Sie werden vom weiteren Studium an der Universität Berlin ausgeschlossen, weil Sie sich im marxistischen Sinne betätigt haben.
Der Rektor

You are no longer permitted to continue your studies at the University of Berlin because you participated in Marxist activities.
The President

Maman was devastated. In eighteen months she would have graduated. It was the death of her dream. She had only joined the socio-democratic Jewish student group to buy discounted meals and gain free admission to the medical library and she was certainly not a political activist. Everyone was in shock, especially Maman. She felt she had been robbed forever of her potential to be a doctor.

At the same time, Maman's 21-year-old brother Alfred had a new bride and was an apprentice to a big land owner. In November his boss received a letter from the National Socialist Labor Party:

17 November 1933

Ortsgruppe Gollnow

After our last conversation with you mid-October, I told you to dismiss your apprentice, the 21-year-old Jew, in a few weeks. Now I have been informed that you have not done so. This Jew even had the nerve to speak back to me.

It is unacceptable that a Jew should now be able to work on a farm while our German workers are suffering from need and hunger, as they are unable to find work in their own country. You are herewith ordered to dismiss this Jew, or else I will have to take more drastic measures against you.

HeilHitler
Walter
Ortsgruppenleiter
Deutsche Arbeiter-Partei

Uncle Alfred and his wife, Aunt Tsilli, left Germany in 1934 on a ship to Palestine (which was to be under British rule until 1948). They were part of the early wave of emigration, years before there were massive numbers of people seeking refuge from Europe. After almost 2000 years, during which the Jews had lived as an oppressed minority, suffering expulsions and massacres, a movement was born to support the return to their ancestral land. Alfred and Tsilli were our family's first pioneers, returning to the Jewish homeland.

CHAPTER 2

ESCAPE TO FRANCE

By December, the situation had grown even worse for the Jews. My grandparents, the Gutmanns and the Lewins, all seniors now, stayed in Berlin and Driesen respectively for the time being, hoping the situation would improve. They could not imagine living anywhere but in Germany. It was painful to even think about living in a foreign country, especially at an advanced age. But Maman and I had to move. She said goodbye to her parents-in-law next door, took one last look around her empty apartment at *Hansa Ufer 8*, and locked the door behind her. We boarded the train to Paris. In the dining car I sat quietly and was well-behaved. I ate everything I was given without complaining. Travelers complimented Maman on my exemplary table manners. I was only 18 months old and made my mother proud.

When the train pulled into the Paris train station Gare du Nord, Papa was already waiting on the platform. He had missed us very much during the two months he had been alone. For the time being we all lived in a hotel. Every day Maman looked through the local ads, hoping to find an apartment to rent. It was not easy because many other Jewish refugees were also looking for shelter in France. The first three weeks I stopped eating and lost weight fast. Papa and Maman were very worried. Then one evening Papa returned from work with a large, round pumpernickel bread. My eyes lit up as I grabbed the bread and devoured half of it. I had been completely uprooted, and the taste and smell of that bread brought back memories of home. After that I started eating normally.

About six weeks after we arrived, Maman found an apartment that was large enough for all our furniture and pictures that had arrived by then. Among the pictures, I clearly remember an elderly man lighting the *havdalah* candle and a group of people studying Torah under a very dim light. The apartment was on the second floor of a multi-story apartment building on 8, *rue St. Guillaume* in Courbevoie, a suburb of Paris, close to the Seine River and a fifteen-minute train ride to Papa's work.

Life in a foreign country was not easy. Maman had learned some French in high school and she had read Balzac and Victor Hugo, but to buy a kilo of meat at the butcher shop or necessities at the pharmacy was a challenge. Taking care of every day chores and getting settled helped her keep her mind off the fact that she could no longer study medicine. She decorated my bedroom by drawing animals on the walls.

It turned out that many tenants in our building were also refugees from Germany, such as Claire and Serge Levier and their two daughters, twelve-year-old Michèle and seven-year-old Maggy. Their mother, Tante Claire as I soon called her, had a very gentle face and full lips. She was quiet and shy — just the opposite of Maman, who had a strong and outgoing personality.

More refugees kept moving in. Fritz and Edith Simson became neighbors and Fritz changed his name to Fred just as Papa had changed his name from Rudolf to Rodolphe. Papa and Maman invited them for tea. They noticed that Edith was very reserved, while Fred, on the other hand, was a lively, passionate and worldly man. He, too, had left Germany because he was no longer allowed to work as a judge. Instead, in France, he became a journalist and started writing for a Swiss newspaper. Fred and my parents had spirited discussions about politics. Naturally, I had no idea what they were talking about.

On May 17, 1935, one day before I turned three, my brother Ernest was born in Neuilly-sur-Seine, just outside of Paris, making me proud to be a big sister.

While the Jews were losing rights in Germany, those who lived in France in 1937 still lived a fairly normal life. I was five when I started kindergarten. When Maman dropped me off on my first day, she said to the teacher, "Please be lenient with Eva. We moved here from Berlin just a little over three years ago and we only speak German at home, so Eva does not understand or speak any French." But she stopped worrying a week later when she overheard me scolding my doll in French, "*Zut alors! Place de la Concorde! Tu as de nouveau fait pipi dans ta culotte* (Darn! You peed in your panties again).

Papa and Maman stayed in touch with their parents in Berlin by mail, telegrams and phone calls. They were worried, yet their elderly parents continued to pray the situation would improve. After all, how could things possibly get worse for the Jews? Grossmama Else wrote that they had closed their jewelry store and moved to Berlin because anti-Semitism had even reached small towns like Driesen. They thought that in a metropolis they would be more anonymous and therefore safer. In Driesen, on the other hand, everyone knew they were Jewish and they had very few customers left. The only jewelry items still selling were wedding bands, as many young men wanted to marry their sweethearts before they were drafted, should war break out. Now Grosspapa Adolf was trying to make ends meet by buying and reselling silver items from Jews who wanted to leave Germany and needed cash.

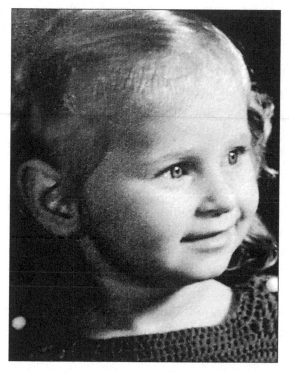

Eva at age five

After four years in France, in February 1938, Papa and Maman could apply for French citizenship. It was to be a very difficult process because the French were hostile towards all refugees — particularly the Jews. My father applied and needed references attesting to how valuable his work was to his employer and to France, and how important it was for him to become a French citizen. Mr. Plasseraud and Mr. Weissman gave my father exceptional references; they really valued him highly. One day an official letter arrived from City Hall informing my parents that their citizenship documents were ready to be picked up and they needed to stop by with two French witnesses who could testify that they were honorable people and would make good French citizens. Maman thought the butcher, from whom she regularly bought meat, would help out.

"I am very sorry, Madame," he said. "I cannot help you. I am Polish."

So Maman went to the neighborhood pharmacy.

"I would love to help you, Madame," the pharmacist said, "but I am alone in my pharmacy and I can't leave it. Try the hotel across the street. I'm sure the owner will be more than happy to help you."

Sure enough, the owner of the hotel was not only willing to help, he brought a friend with him as the second witness. So on February 23, 1938, my parents and the two witnesses, whom my parents had just met, went to City Hall together, signed the papers, and walked out, duly certified to be honorable. They offered the witnesses a glass of wine, and then found out that some older men always sat outside City Hall, waiting to be of service to new citizens-to-be so that they were rewarded with a glass of wine. To their astonishment they also found out the so-called hotel across the street was a one- or two-hour hotel for "couples!" Their new status as French citizens, humor aside, was an extraordinary achievement as it was to help them greatly when France declared war on Germany in 1939. If not for their French citizenship, they would have been interned as "enemy foreigners." The new naturalization document included my name along with my parents', showing my place and date of birth, and, since I had no other, I used it in France until after the war as my birth certificate.

Hitler wanted to reunite Austria and Germany to create a Great German Reich, so that all German-speaking people should live in one nation and under one and the same leadership. In March 1938, Germany marched into Austria. England and France were concerned that this might lead to a world war. To appease Hitler, they agreed, during the Munich Conference, to let him take over part of Czechoslovakia, the Sudetenland, hoping he would not invade further. They were wrong. Six months later the Nazis invaded the whole of Czechoslovakia. Every time they invaded another country, refugees got frightened and packed their suitcases, just in case they had to leave in a hurry.

In the summer of 1938, Maman became pregnant again. "How can you have a third child when war may break out at any moment? Isn't that irresponsible?" Maman's friends commented in disbelief. None of them had more than one child.

"Well, with three children we will have to be three times more careful. What else can I say?" was Maman's answer.

Now that Maman was expecting again and the family was growing,

Papa started looking for a bigger place for us. Soon he found a three-story villa for rent with six bedrooms at *15 bis, avenue Maurice Berteaux* in Le Vésinet, a pleasant suburb west of Paris, about six miles west of Courbevoie. We soon moved and I attended school in Le Vésinet.

Our villa in Le Vésinet

Avenue Maurice Berteaux, a small street, ran parallel to the railroad tracks. Every ten minutes an electric train passed by. It took some time to get used to the noise, but soon these trains regulated our lives and served as our clock. In fact, when there was a train strike, life seemed strange and uneasy because it was hard to tell time. The two rooms on the third floor became my brother Ernest's and mine, while Papa and Maman moved into one of the three bedrooms on the second floor. Now there was room for Papa's parents to come and live with us. There was also a basement where we stored coal and food staples.

My parents loved art. News swept across the border in July 1937 about two art exhibitions in Germany. The Great Art Exhibition showed pictures of representative art of which the *Führer* approved. Meanwhile, he called modern or abstract art 'Degenerate Art,' but still allowed it to be exhibited. More than a million people visited these exhibitions in Germany.

At that time, the Jeanne Bucher Gallery in Paris was exhibiting works of an abstract Jewish sculptor and painter of German descent, Otto Freundlich, in honor of his 60th birthday. The artist had moved to Paris in 1924 to be able to freely express himself through art. In Paris he was able to become a member of the *Union des Artistes Allemands Libres* (Union of German Free Artists) founded in the autumn of 1937. Papa and Maman loved his art, befriended him and bought two of his paintings.

Now that we lived in a big house, my parents loved to invite guests over for Sunday afternoon tea. I got to meet Otto Freundlich and his non-Jewish, common-law wife Jeanne Kosnick-Kloss, who came wrapped in a colorful, extravagant fabric. With her turban on her head covering lots of curls, she looked very exotic to me. While the adults chatted, I sat quietly and listened. Otto and Maman excitedly reminisced and recited a German nursery rhyme *Der Wunderbaum* (The Wonder Tree) from their kindergarten days in Germany.

In meinem Garten steht ein Baum,	In my garden stands a tree,
Und das ist ein Wunderbaum.	And that is a wonder tree.
In dem Baum ist ein Zweig,	In the tree there is a branch,
Und das ist ein Wunder Zweig.	And that is a wonder branch.
Auf dem Zweig ist ein Nest,	On the branch there is a nest,
Und das ist ein Wunder Nest.	And that is a wonder nest.
In dem Nest liegt ein Ei....	In the nest lies an egg ….
In dem Ei ist ein Schlüssel....	In the egg there is a key ….
Dieser Schlüssel öffnet eine Laube....	This key opens a gazebo....
In der Laube steht ein Tisch....	In the gazebo stands a table....
Auf dem Tisch liegt ein Buch....	On the table lies a book....
In dem Buche ist geschrieben	In the book it is written
Du sollst Deinen Nächsten lieben.	You shall love your neighbor as yourself.

"Charlotte, I am going to paint the *Wunderbaum* for you!" Otto exclaimed.

A month later, when Otto Freundlich came for tea again, he brought Maman the *Wunderbaum* painting. Maman loved it and thanked him profusely.

"I can no longer display my art," he said, concerned. "In fact, the Nazis seized some of my work in Germany. To them free thinkers are a threat."

Grossmama wrote that they had moved again, this time to the lively *Grosse Frankfurter Strasse*, just around the corner from their old place. Again their apartment was above a store, but it was smaller. Even so, most people were not buying anything from Jews and my grandparents were finally convinced they needed to leave Germany. Grossmama was trying to get passports, which was very difficult because so many people were applying at the same time.

President Franklin D. Roosevelt had hoped to find a solution to the refugee crisis at the conference in Evian, France. Delegates from 32 countries, including the United States, Great Britain, France, Canada and Australia, got together to discuss what to do with the increasing number of Jewish refugees who were fleeing the Nazi regime. There were only a few places that would accept Jews such as South Africa, Argentina and China. My parents were very concerned for my grandparents at this point.

By October 1938, the letter "J" was required to be stamped into all foreign Jewish passports in France. Almost every day the newspapers were filled with terrible news from Germany and the news on the radio was no better. Jews had lost all rights and protection. They were no longer permitted to have a retail store, practice a trade or sell any products or services. They were ordered to sell their real estate and surrender all assets.

In November 1938, news spread to France that the Nazis had destroyed Jewish stores and had set synagogues on fire all over Germany. Jewish homes were vandalized and looted, Jewish properties confiscated, and storefront windows smashed all over the nation. This became known as *Kristallnacht*, the Night of Broken Glass. More Jews than ever before were applying for visas, hoping to be granted permission to leave Germany. One of the few places that accepted them without a visa was Shanghai. If a Jew had a ticket to get on a ship to Shanghai, he was permitted to leave Germany. After *Kristallnacht*, Papa was adamant about getting his elderly parents and in-laws out of Germany.

Worried, Maman called her parents in Berlin.

"Have you been able to get your passports?"

"Yes," Grossmama replied. "We had to add Israel and Sarah to our names.

"The *Trinton* is leaving for Shanghai from the port of Marseille on March 9 (1939). Can you get to France in time to board that ship?" Maman asked.

"We'll do our best," Grossmama replied.

As soon as Maman hung up, Papa purchased the tickets from the Worldaround Transport & Shipping Company and sent them to his parents-in-law. In a telegram Grosspapa informed Maman that she would receive, for safekeeping, two trunks filled with old clothes, which they could not take with them.

A few weeks later Maman received a letter from the Paris central railway station. Two trunks needed to be cleared through customs and picked up. The next day Maman went to the station, even though by this time she was eight and a half months pregnant and voluminous. The customs official detected her German accent and ordered her to open those trunks while grumbling about all the foreigners who were invading France. "How can you be so callous and insensitive? How would you feel if your elderly parents had to leave everything behind — their home, their business and their friends — to save their lives in a foreign country?" Maman fired at him. She got so furious that the customs official must have feared she might deliver her baby right then and there.

"OK, lady! Take your junk and get the hell out of here!" he bellowed.

Maman hailed a taxi and back at home in Le Vésinet she opened the trunks. Underneath the old clothes she found much of my grandparents' sterling silver — three pairs of tall candlesticks and many other items such as an old silver kettle that Grosspapa had treasured. Inside, neatly wrapped were several beautiful jewels.

"Thank goodness I did not know what was in those trunks when I passed customs!" she said, hugely relieved. "Sometimes it pays to be ignorant."

I went with Maman to run some errands. The baker's wife was standing by the store entrance and when Maman walked by her, pushing Ernest's stroller, the baker's wife looked at my 4-year-old brother and admired him. Pointing at Maman's belly I said proudly, "There's a baby in there." The woman seemed shocked, and pushed her own young daughter aside. We found out why: French women in those days told children that a baby boy was found in a cabbage and a baby girl in a rose.

On April 13, 1939, my second brother, Raymond, was born in a Catholic clinic in Saint-Germain-en-Laye, two train stations from Le Vésinet. That was where my mother's doctor delivered his patients. When the nun walked into Maman's room, she found her crying.

"Why are you crying, Madame?" she asked. "You just gave birth to a beautiful baby boy. Rejoice!"

"I can't," Maman replied. "My parents left on a ship to Shanghai over a month ago and I still don't have any news from them. I am terribly worried."

"Oh, that Hitler!" the nun said. "I would like to be his nurse."

"What?" Maman exclaimed, outraged. "You would like to take care of him?"

"No, I would give him a suppository of dynamite!"

"You are a religious person, how can you speak this way?" Maman asked.

"For Hitler I'd make an exception!"

The next day Papa arrived at the hospital with incredible news.

"Your parents have made it safely to Palestine and they are reunited with Alfred!" he exclaimed.

"They were on their way to China. How did they end up in Palestine?" Maman asked, confused.

"In Marseille they found out that another illegal ship was leaving for Palestine, so they chose to board that ship instead. They were on the water for forty days. It was a very difficult journey." (We did not have more detailed news about how they made it until years later).

In mid-July 1939, my paternal grandparents, Joseph and Bertha Gutmann, my Grossvater and Grossmutter, finally got their visas to leave Germany and came to live with us in Le Vésinet. We had not seen them for five years.

The French government labeled my grandparents "enemy foreigners." Every week they had to make an appearance at the police station with their passports. By September 1939, approximately 282,000 Jews had left Germany.

Papa and Maman stayed in touch with our old neighbors from Courbevoie, the Leviers and the Simsons, and invited them for Sunday tea. Fred loved to tell jokes and when he did, I was all ears. Jokes were a great way to release tension.

"A Jew and a non-Jew are sitting in a train, facing each other," he began. "They start chatting and eventually the non-Jew asks, "What makes you Jews so intelligent?"

The Jew replies, "We eat herring, all of it – the head, the tail, the scales, everything." Lunchtime comes and the Jew takes his herring out of the newspaper it was wrapped in. The non-Jew says, "I'll give you $20 for your herring."

"I can't sell you my intelligence," the non-Jew replies.

"$50 I'll give you."

"No, thank you."

"I'll pay a hundred dollars for your herring!"

At that offer the Jew reluctantly says, "Okay."

He hands over the herring and the other guy starts eating it.

"It's gross," he says.

After a while he comments, "With a hundred dollars I could have bought a barrel of herring." Hearing that, the Jew exclaims, "You see? It's working already!"

Even at age seven, I loved seeing how jokes cheered people up. I learned that finding some humor in dark times is essential to life. We needed all the cheering possible; the situation was worsening every day.

Grossvater and Grossmutter August 1939

I was happy to get to know Grossvater and Grossmutter. Since I was only 18 months old when Maman and I left Berlin, I did not have any recollection of the days we used to live next to one another when they took care of me. Maman did her best to keep a kosher home, and did everything to make sure that her in-laws were well cared for.

Grossmutter Bertha was sweet, rather shy and soft-spoken. She minded her own business or helped Maman in the kitchen. Grossvater loved to tell anecdotes from his teaching days. I was a willing listener and an attentive student. Amongst ourselves we spoke German. "One day I was standing at my office window when I spotted two of my students hiding behind a bush, smoking cigarettes," he told me. "I ordered them to my office. There I handed each one a cigar and forced them to inhale deeply. They began to cough immediately. Well, *Evchen* (little Eva, in German), they never smoked again," Grossvater chuckled.

"Another time a student was looking intently at a large photograph of Michelangelo's Moses that hung over the stairs leading to my office," he continued. "Who do you think this is?" I asked him. The student looked puzzled and, shrugging his shoulders, replied, "Well, a former director of this school, I suppose."

I soon found out that Grossvater was a strict disciplinarian as well. "For years I forced your father to eat beans for lunch on Mondays," he said. "He hated them with a passion. When he turned twenty-one, lo and behold, lunch came on the following Monday, and... no beans! 'How come we don't have beans today?' your father asked. Well, now that you are twenty-one, you do not need to eat them anymore. It was a matter of discipline, and now you are grown up. By the way, I hated them too, all these years."

Once an educator, always an educator. "*Wer viel spricht kann Fehler nicht vermeiden*" (He who talks a lot cannot avoid making mistakes) and "*Wer viel fragt kriegt viel Antwort*" (He who asks a lot of questions gets a lot of answers). Many times he quoted these two proverbs to me, probably because I talked too much and asked too many questions.

Grossvater loved to tell jokes. "The teacher says to the children in the classroom, 'The weather is so nice today. I will ask you one question and if one of you knows the answer, you can all go outside and play for twenty minutes. How many hairs does the school janitor's dog have?' A boy in the back row raised his hand and said, 'I know! Two million four hundred sixty-eight thousand six hundred and twenty-two.' Astonished, the teacher asked, 'How did you know?' 'Well sir, that's the second question,' the boy replied."

"One day I told this joke to a friend," Grossvater continued. "As soon as I got to the number of hairs he stopped me, pulled out a paper from his pocket and said, 'Wait a minute! I want to write this number down. I've always wanted to tell this joke but I could not remember the exact number of hairs!"

I credit Grossvater with my lifelong love of joke-telling. My parents, although they enjoyed hearing jokes, never told any.

Grossvater brought me two wonderful books, the Grimm and Andersen Fairy Tales, which he soon started reading to me. I loved the fairytales so much that I forced myself to learn to read the old German script, so I could read them myself. I developed a passion for those tales, and became a true romantic. I especially loved *The Travel Companion*. A young man loses his beloved father. He soon sees two men quarreling on his father's grave, because the dead man owed them money. The young man pays off his father's debt with all the money he has and decides to go off into the world, seeking his fortune. On his way he meets an old woman and helps her carry her heavy load. To show her gratitude, she gives him a few things. She is actually a fairy and her gifts will eventually help him to win the love of a beautiful princess who had been turned into a mean woman by her wicked, jealous stepmother. He was able to remove her spell and they got married and lived happily ever after.

I enjoyed the suspense and the love story. I learned that love always seems to be the answer. I learned about romance and started to hope that one day I, too, would find my prince. I learned about compassion and that obstacles are there to be overcome with courage, determination and perseverance in spite of fear and hardship. I was happy when good people prevailed over evil ones.

CHAPTER 3

THE WORLD AT WAR:
LIFE IN HIDING

The following chapter is dedicated to the incredible bravery and generosity of the Plasseraud, Giron, Ravaud, Mégoz and Menthonnex families who helped save my family. We owe our survival to them all.

Six weeks after Grossvater and Grossmutter Gutmann moved in with us, on September 1, 1939, Nazi Germany invaded Poland. France and the United Kingdom declared war against Germany. Fortunately, Papa was only inducted as a reservist and could continue to live at home and work for Monsieur Plasseraud.

In May 1940, the Germans launched their offensive in the West. Fearing defeat, the French National Assembly gave Maréchal Philippe Pétain full power, and he quickly established the Vichy Régime, which collaborated with the Nazis.

On June 14, Parisians woke up to a voice with a German accent informing all citizens via loudspeakers that a curfew was being imposed for 8 p.m. that evening. By the time German tanks rolled into Paris, two million Parisians had already fled south and the German Gestapo went to work; arrests, interrogations and spying became the new order of the day, and a gigantic swastika flew beneath the *Arc de Triomphe*.

Following the Franco-German Armistice of June 1940, a demarcation line was drawn dividing France in two — the northern zone, occupied by the Germans, and the free southern zone governed by the Vichy régime that supported Nazi Germany.

The French police started organizing raids to capture Jews and other "undesirables," at first only in the northern zone. The Nazis took control of all the northern radio stations including Radio-Paris.

France Divided 1940

Concerned about the archives of the Cabinet Weissman, Mr. Plasseraud urged Papa to take the archives from the Paris office to Massay, a village three hours south of Paris. He completely trusted my father to do this as he held him in the highest esteem. Those archives needed to be sheltered to prevent seizure by the Nazis, because they contained numerous files relating to French national defense. Employees could still work as attorneys, while employers could not. Therefore my father was put in charge of those archives, and could continue to make a living, even though it was well known that it was against the law for the French to help Jews. He would in fact be paid half of his salary all through the war, partly because the Cabinet was grateful to my father for saving the archives, and partly because they were hopeful that my father would come back to Paris after the war to work for them again, as both Mr. Plasseraud and Mr. Weissman valued Papa's exceptional professional and moral qualities. So Papa took me, eight, and Ernest, five, and left behind my mother, my grandparents and my baby brother. They would follow us later.

In Massay, Papa found a small castle for rent, with turrets and a large, bright patio with a glass roof where Papa set up his desk and chair. He hired an older French lady to take care of us and we stopped speaking German. A few days later, we heard a terrifying sound.

"Sirens!" Papa shouted. "Into the cellar! Quick!"

Papa and our caretaker rushed us downstairs. Shortly thereafter we heard airplanes passing overhead, then a terrible crash and the cellar began to shake. Bombs were whistling and exploding overhead. Sometime later the sirens sounded the all clear.

"It's over. We can go back upstairs," Papa said, relieved.

Bomb alerts became part of our daily life. One day Papa went back upstairs after one of those bombings and found broken glass everywhere on the patio. A piece of a bomb had come through the glass roof and through his chair.

"What a miracle that I did not remain at my desk! Surely an angel watched over me," he said.

Papa had no way to contact Maman, and she had no way to contact him. They were both terribly worried about each other.

One morning I woke up with violent abdominal pains and high fever. The doctor diagnosed me with acute appendicitis. Papa rushed me immediately to Issoudun, the nearest city with a hospital. One of the best surgeons from Paris happened to be there that day and could operate on me immediately.

"Fortunately you managed to get here right away," the doctor said to Papa. "Twenty-four hours later I may not have been able to save your daughter." Here was the first time I felt that my life had been in immediate danger. I felt personally touched by a miracle.

After the surgery I was moved to a large ward lined with beds, packed with patients. One morning my neighbor, a young soldier, was making strange sounds. Then I saw him sit up suddenly and vomit blood. The nurse rushed over and drew the curtains around his bed immediately. Even at the young age of eight, I knew something terrible had happened. I heard from someone later that he had died. Almost 80 years later, I remember this as if it were yesterday. I was relieved when Papa came to take me home.

In September 1940, German occupation forces published the First Ordinance, defining "who is a Jew." One month later the Second Ordinance was made public, imposing even more restrictions on Jews. By then, every family received food stamps.

In October 1940, the Vichy government passed anti-Jewish measures prohibiting Jews from moving and limiting their access to public places and most professional activities. The measures, published in the *Journal Officiel* on October 18, targeted primarily foreign Jews. Papa and Maman were not really affected because they were French citizens, but Grossvater and Grossmutter were. A 'J' had been stamped into their passports to identify them as Jews.

After almost a year in Massay, Papa, my brother and I were forced to move again, another three and a half hours southeast, to stay ahead of the Germans who kept advancing. Papa rented an office at *Rue des Quatre Chapeaux* in Lyon, still in the free zone, and an apartment in Caluire at *2, Chemin des Petites Brosses* (2 Little Brushes Lane), a small road off the main street, in a suburb just north of Lyon. Every day Papa took the streetcar to the Lyon office. Monsieur Weissmann was also in Lyon now, seeking safety, and the office secretary, Madame Mégoz, came from Paris to work for them.

Papa again hired an older lady to take care of us. Maman was planning to join us as soon as she arranged for our furniture to be sent and for my grandmother to receive the special permit to cross the demarcation line. What we did not yet know was that Grossvater had died suddenly in January 1941 of pneumonia, and Maman had been unable to reach Papa with the sad news.

When Maman arrived at the *ligne de démarcation* with my little brother and Grossmutter, the French official of the pro-Nazi Pétain regime checked their papers. He said to Maman, "You can go with the baby, but the old woman stays behind." "I am not leaving without her!" Maman shouted. "If you don't let her through, you force me and the baby to stay behind as well, and if we get killed, our deaths will be on your conscience!"

She made such a fuss that the officer finally let them pass. I was so glad to see Maman, Grossmutter and my brother Raymond. He had grown a lot during the year we had not seen him.

"Where is my father?" Papa worried.

"Rodolphe, I am so very sorry to tell you that your father passed away on January 23," Maman broke the news. "He caught pneumonia and fell into a coma. I could not reach you, so I purchased four plots in the Le Vésinet cemetery and buried him."

Papa was devastated and Grossmutter inconsolable. I had become very fond of Grossvater and I was grieving too. He had taught me a lot. We were grateful that the rest of us were together again, but it was a huge loss.

Our new apartment was located in a big yard with lots of wooden planks, next to a carpentry shop and up some stairs. Now we lived above our landlords. Mr. Giron, the carpenter, and his wife, a middle-aged couple, turned out to be very kind. To feed six people on food stamps was a challenge so Madame Giron allowed Maman to plant a vegetable garden behind the house next to hers. One day Maman managed to come home with three slices of salami. It was so rare to get meat that she did not care what animal it came from. It was no longer possible to keep kosher.

Soon Grossmutter developed abscesses in her breasts. She was in such pain that the doctor had to stop by weekly to drain them. It was horrible. I heard her suffer. There were no antibiotics yet!

Our friends from Courbevoie, Serge and Claire Levier and their daughters Michèle and Maggy, followed us to Lyon. Nevertheless, life in the "free" zone was becoming more dangerous every day. Still, we celebrated the Passover Seder together. Michèle had become an extremely attractive 18-year-old and Henri, the 30-year-old son of another émigré, fell madly in love with her.

Papa and Maman were not too surprised when Michèle and Henri announced their engagement soon thereafter. On the day of the engagement Maman dressed Maggy and me up like the painter Rubens' angels and tied wings to our backs. We were up high on ladders, and she hid our bodies up to our arms behind a curtain. Maman instructed us to look down on the newly engaged couple, wishing them well from up in the heavens, reciting a poem in German she had written especially for them. Michèle and Henri were grateful, moved, and very happy.

When Papa read *Le Journal Officiel du Commissariat de la République* one morning he was shocked. In June 1941, many naturalized French citizens, of whom 40% were Jewish, lost their French citizenship, even Jews who were born in France! This meant not only Papa, Maman and I, but also my brothers, who were born in France, were classified as illegal aliens, even

Raymond who was born in France to French parents. Papa was even more shocked when he found our names on the *Journal* list.

On August 31, 1941, the Vichy régime confiscated all radios from French Jews. They were forbidden to use public telephones and were no longer allowed to leave their homes between 8 p.m. and 5 a.m. Jews were barred from public places and music of Jewish composers was banned. Every week, new restrictions, prohibitions and decrees were issued. On the subway Jews were allowed to ride only in the last carriage. Although I was only ten, I understood that the Jews were in terrible danger.

Otto Freundlich, my parents' artist friend and his non-Jewish companion Madame Kosnick-Kloss had left Paris in May of the previous year and were now hiding in the Pyrénées, the mountains between France and Spain. The winter of 1941 was bitterly cold. Worried about their friend Otto, Maman wrote to him to find out if she and Papa could help in any way.

"If you could spare a little money for firewood, some paint and some brushes, we would be eternally grateful!" Freundlich replied.

Papa sent him some money immediately. Soon thereafter, Maman received a package. Enclosed was a letter and a colorful abstract painting on a 15- by 18-inch wooden board from Otto Freundlich. He wrote that he had painted this abstract for her birthday, on a small flat board that he found among the pieces of firewood he had purchased with their money, as a thank you for supporting him in these difficult times.

After Grossvater died, Grossmutter was never the same. The abscesses continued to cause her major pain. Then, on January 1, 1942, she passed away, just before it became obvious that we were going to have to go into hiding. Now with three young children, my parents had plenty of responsibility as it was. Although my father was terribly sad to lose both his parents, I feel as though my family was clearly being protected from above. My mother had difficulty at the border with one elderly parent — how would she have made it with two? We were no longer safe in Caluire, as the Nazis kept moving further south.

"Our children would be safer in a *pension d'enfants* in the mountains somewhere above Grenoble," Papa said to Maman. In France, before the war, I heard of many of those *pensions* as large homes in the mountains that took in children for a few weeks, while their parents could enjoy a much-needed vacation by themselves. The altitude was about 3,000 feet above sea level, the air was pure, the food excellent, and the children were well cared for. It was like a summer camp, but in large homes, not tents. Some children stayed there through the year and were schooled. Papa added: "The Vercors region with its narrow valleys, speckled with secluded little farming villages, is difficult to access and safer."

Maman thought it was a great idea. Grenoble was 72 miles southeast of Lyon, so within two days Maman took the train there, then traveled up the mountains by bus. She went from village to village, hoping to find a *pension* that would take my brothers and me. The answer was always the same.

"Sorry, Madame. We cannot take any more children. We are at maximum capacity."

Many families, especially those who lived in the big cities, had already sent their children there for more security and more food. After having visited about thirty of these children's homes, Maman was getting discouraged, but she decided to make one last stop in Autrans. To get there, she had to cross another mountain. The village population, about 1,000 inhabitants before the war, had grown to 2,000. Half the population was in hiding. A mile from the center of the village, she found *Clairfontaine*. It belonged to Geneviève and Roland Menthonnex.

Clairfontaine

A kind and caring woman and her husband, a robust and strong-looking Frenchman, had already accepted about thirty children, but somehow they were willing to take us in as well. Maman was so grateful. She noticed a crucifix on the wall.

"Madame, I see that you are a devout Christian," Maman said, concerned. "I am grateful that you are willing to accept my children, but I hope that you are not going to convert them."

"I promise you I won't," Madame Menthonnex replied, and so Maman left, relieved.

For about nine months from the fall of 1942 to the spring of 1943, *Clairfontaine* became home for my brothers and me while Papa and Maman remained in Caluire. I was ten, Ernest seven and Raymond almost four. We called the Menthonnex couple 'Parrain' and 'Marraine' (godfather and godmother). I really liked their eleven year-old son Jean, a slender and handsome boy. A few times a week he guarded their two cows, Marquise and Piloune, and some goats in the hills. When I asked if I could come along, he was delighted. After we brought the animals home to the stable, we stopped by the vegetable garden. There we dug up two carrots, washed them and ate them with delight. After eating rutabaga and tripe, which smelled awful, they tasted divine. Marraine did her best, given the circumstances, to keep all of us fed.

Every day a pretty young nurse took us on a walk, regardless of the weather. She talked about all kinds of things, even how the male organ penetrates the female organ to make a baby. That scared me to death.

During our walks, I did my best to distract Raymond so he could walk long distances without complaining. I would say, *"Regarde la vache! Regarde les moutons!"*(Look at the cow! Look at the sheep!) Ernest, being four years older, was fine. On Sunday mornings all thirty-three children went to the church in the center of the village for mass, and learned the catechism. Like many others, I learned and wanted to become Catholic. We missed our parents terribly, and I was obviously searching to belong somewhere in what had become a scary and lonely world.

While we were more or less safe in Autrans, life for the Jews and even for the French people in the rest of the country kept getting worse. Every week a new ordinance came out, restricting their lives further. Since we were in the mountains, we escaped having to wear a yellow star.

In the spring of 1943, Maman came to visit us at *Clairfontaine*. Just as she was about to return to Lyon that evening, she received an urgent telegram from Papa that said, "Stay up there. I'm coming." Maman had planned to come to see us for two days and was not prepared to stay. Luckily she found a hotel room. A few days later Papa arrived with two suitcases.

Just about two miles from *Clairfontaine*, on the main road that passed through Autrans, stood a nice yellow house with a 'for rent' sign. It was surrounded by fields and belonged to the Ravauds, a non-Jewish French couple in their fifties. They had two girls. Colette was my age and Georgette was eight years older. Papa rented the partially furnished apartment above theirs and took us out of the *pension*. After being separated from our parents, it was wonderful to be with them again.

The yellow house

Since Maman had only come to visit us for a day, she was missing some essential kitchen utensils and some clothes, so she decided to make a quick daytime round trip to our apartment. She took the bus down the mountain to Grenoble; from there she boarded the next train north to Lyon. From the railway station the streetcar would take her to Caluire. It was a 20-minute ride. The Nazis were everywhere and therefore this trip was not without danger.

Maman went up the outside steps to our apartment and gathered the things she absolutely needed, that she could carry, and went downstairs. When Madame Giron opened the door she was surprised to see Maman.

"How courageous of you to come here under these circumstances," she said. "Come in and have a cup of tea. I buried your silver in the yard and I took your radio into my apartment. I am concerned that the Nazis might show up and search the house."

When Maman looked at the clock, she jumped up and frantically exclaimed, "My goodness! I cannot miss my train!"

She immediately grabbed her bundle, said a hasty thank you and good-bye, and raced down the road to catch the streetcar on the west side of the river Rhone which took her within walking distance of the train station. She ran across the bridge for cars and pedestrians and made it on the train just as it began to move. The train crossed the river again in the opposite direction. As she looked out the window, still catching her breath and taking off her hat, she saw that the Nazis had cordoned off the bridge she had just run across and were checking everybody's papers. She had miraculously escaped. If they had asked for her French I.D. card, her very Jewish last name Gutmann and her birthplace in Germany would have undoubtedly gotten her arrested and most certainly we would never have seen her again. Thankfully, Maman returned safely to us in Autrans.

My brothers and me in 1943

Concerned that the Nazis might show up in Autrans and check I.D. cards, she went to the local mayor's office to get new ones.

"I can only give you new identity cards if the current ones become illegible," the city clerk informed her.

As soon as she got back home, Maman dropped them into the wash "accidentally," then hung them up to dry. The next day she returned to the clerk's office and handed him the illegible cards. He smiled and issued new ones. It was June 6, 1943. Now Papa was Rodolphe Guilhaud, born in Besançon, France, and Maman was Charlotte Gallian, née Lepin, born in Brussels, Belgium. It was safer not to appear married in case one of them was captured. Now the date of issue was adjusted by the clerk to October 2, 1941.

To prepare, Maman would wake up in the middle of the night and shake Papa awake, to ask him, "Where were you born?"

He would reply, half asleep *"In Besançon."*

"Your last name is now Gallian," Maman told us children "Never say that your name is Gutmann or that you speak or understand German!" Despite what was going on in the rest of the country and the world, we children still felt relatively safe in Autrans.

I kept thinking about what the nurse had told us in *Clairfontaine* about sex.

"Maman, what does one do to have a baby?" I asked her out of the blue one day, as I was helping her in the garden.

Somewhat embarrassed, she answered, "You are too young to understand. I will tell you when you turn 13."

Once a week Madame Mégoz took the train to Grenoble to meet Papa near the train station with new files to work on and to pick up his completed files. Papa was very thankful that he could continue to work as an attorney and earn a decent living. He did all his work by hand, since he didn't even have a typewriter. Because of the war there was hardly enough to eat. Three times a week he rode his bike to the nearby farms, hoping to trade his alcohol and cigarette stamps for half a pint of milk straight from the cow, or two eggs or two potatoes. He paid with cash. Sometimes Papa brought back milk, and Maman let it sit until cream formed on the top. She showed me how to beat the cream until it turned into butter. Maman also taught gymnastics in the field behind the yellow house to earn a little extra money and she sewed our clothes and knitted sweaters.

Another day Papa came back with three eggs. It was enough to make a crepe for each of us. Raymond and I watched Maman pour some dough into the frying pan. A few minutes later she flipped the dough over. Then she moved the luscious, thin-as-cigarette-paper pancakes onto a plate. They smelled divine, so when Maman was not looking, I quickly snatched one and snuck out of the kitchen. I had barely made it to my room when I heard her yell, "Who took a crepe? I know I made three and now there are only two left! Raymond, you took that crepe!"

"No, Maman, I did not take a crepe!" I heard my four year-old brother say fearfully.

"Raymond, you are lying! You took a crepe. Go to your room. You won't get dessert."

I so feared that she would slap me hard if I confessed my crime, that I let my innocent little brother get punished. After the meal, I shared my crepe with him in our bedroom. Why didn't I give him the whole crepe? To this day I have not forgiven myself for having been so scared and selfish to let him be punished in my place. I have apologized to him many times.

Five minutes from the yellow house was a boys' school that accepted girls and other refugee children because it was wartime. Maman enrolled me. I was 11. Monsieur Bourdon became my French and Latin teacher. After school I did my homework, played hopscotch with Colette from downstairs or helped Maman with chores. For us children life seemed fairly normal. We did not know any better. As I reflect on what it must have been like to parent three young children during the war, I am amazed at how hard Papa and Maman worked to successfully protect us from fear. I did understand, though, that our lives were in danger.

Papa managed to get a radio again. Every day he listened to the BBC news with the pillow over it, intently following the advancement of the Germans who kept moving steadily south, and were now getting very close to Grenoble.

Serge, Claire and their daughters Maggy and Michèle, her husband Henri and their baby girl Cathy followed us from Lyon to Autrans where they stayed in a nearby motel.

Every now and then, Maman got together for a cup of an awful brew of chicory with two refugee ladies from Paris. When Maman returned home she told us that Madame Babonneau said, "When the war is over I will take a bath in coffee!" And the other lady said, "And I will buy a new girdle!"

Madame Babonneau was very worried about her husband, who was fighting against the Nazis somewhere. She had not heard from him for a long time. She went to see a psychic.

"Hand me your wedding band!" the psychic said.

Madame Babonneau took off her ring. The psychic clasped it in her hand and concentrated.

"I see your husband," she began. "He is wearing a ring with the initials R.B. (his first name was Roger). I see him lying somewhere with something white around his head. It is very hot where he is. He is neither dead nor alive." (Years later, after the war, Madame Babonneau moved back to Paris. What the psychic had seen had been true. Her husband had returned and explained that after he suffered a head wound during the North African Campaign, he had been lying in a coma in a tent in the Sahara Desert).

By September 1943, the BBC radio transmitted the news that we had all feared. The Nazis had reached Grenoble and were looking for Jews and anyone who was helping or hiding them. It was just a matter of time before they would come up the mountain to Autrans, so Papa rode his bike to three farmers he knew and asked if they were willing to each take in one of us three children in case the Nazis showed up. They would say that we were their niece or nephew from Lyon, and that they took us in because food was scarce in the city. Thankfully they were willing to help. Then Papa scouted the surrounding hills, hoping to find a cave where he could hide important documents that he had placed in a box, some drinking water, a few hard-boiled eggs and some cash, in case we had to run for our lives. Maman also packed a small bag for each one of us with a few clothes so that we were always ready.

Communications were difficult. If the people of Autrans wanted to make a phone call or send a telegram, they had to go to the post office. No one had a telephone at home. On the other hand, we needed good communications, in case the Nazis attempted to come up the mountain to Autrans. Several times, they had failed because the roads were too narrow and winding for their trucks. However, each time they started up, the danger was real. The post offices had set up communication networks to warn everyone who needed to hide. The first post office on the way up would phone the second, which would phone the third and so on. As soon as each post office received the news, it would send two people running, for instance, to the bakery and the hotel to warn people as quickly as possible. From the bakery and the hotel, two people would run to warn two more, who it turn would run and warn two more and so on. Within five minutes of receiving the warning, the news spread like wildfire. Everyone needing to hide was warned, and had time to take off into the woods, rain or shine, day or night, even when there was snow on the ground.

Several times, Papa and Maman rushed us to the three farmers and then hid in the woods. "You smell terrible, Raymond. What did you do?" Papa asked when he picked him up the next day. "I slept in the stable," Raymond explained.

Thankfully there were many false alarms. Our landlords, the Ravauds, were not affected by these alerts.

Nazi alerts continued into the winter. It was minus 25 degrees Fahrenheit. Maman put on her fur coat and grabbed some blankets. That particular day, there was just enough time to take Ernest and me to the farmers, so they pulled Raymond with them on a sled into the woods where they waited for hours in the snow. We were never sure which of the eight roads the Nazis would take up the mountain. In winter Papa went to the farms on skis. Food became even more scarce and he had gotten very thin.

In April 1944, news spread that the militia had burned down several farms in the village of Vassieux. From the newborns to the centenarians, all the inhabitants were killed. The entire area around Grenoble was completely destroyed. The very word Vassieux conjures up destruction and devastation in my memory.

On June 5, 1944, General Charles de Gaulle, on the BBC, called upon the French underground fighters in the Vercors, the general region where we were, to take up arms against the Nazis. The French *Résistance* (*Le Maquis*) had concentrated in the Vercors, because it was an impregnable high plateau. Its operations reached their peak, with numerous attacks, considerably hampering the activity of German troops. Unfortunately, they were not well enough armed or organized, or numerous enough, and had been praying for the Americans to land in Normandy.

On the evening of June 6, 1944, Papa heard on the BBC: "The Allies have landed in Normandy! The Germans are fighting fiercely, but are forced to progressively retreat." We prayed for Allied success and were hopeful they would soon land also in the Midi (south of France) so that this nightmare of being hunted would come to an end. Eventually, when the Nazi armies were pushed back towards Germany by the Russian armies, Papa attached a map of Russia to the kitchen wall, and followed the Russians' daily gains over the Nazis with a red yarn and several pushpins.

In June the Vichy regime finally collapsed.

To celebrate Bastille Day on July 14, 1944 Papa planned a family picnic. It was a beautiful, sunny day. Happiness was in the air as everyone feverishly awaited liberation from the Nazis. We hiked to Bellecombe, a grassy mountaintop. From there we had a superb view of Autrans, the valley of Lans, and Villard-de-Lans on the other side of the mountain. Down below the houses were bedecked with flags. All of a sudden a humming interrupted the peaceful atmosphere and airplanes were coming towards us.

"Those must be Allied planes!" Papa said excitedly, hoping they would bring the promised reinforcement that the French Underground Forces of the Vercors (*Forces Françaises de l'Intérieur* or FFI) were waiting for.

We followed the planes with our eyes as they passed over our heads. Then we saw bombs dropping on our valley. All I remember is racing down the mountain in lightning speed looking for shelter in the forest.

"The net is tightening. I must join the FFI," Papa said to Maman. "If I am going to die, I will die with a weapon in my hand."

Fortunately in Autrans nothing was destroyed. The next day Papa, and our longtime friends, Serge Levier and his son-in-law Henri, joined the FFI underground forces. The women and children were left alone to fend for themselves. We were devastated.

A few days after the men left, and after one more alert, Maman and I were looking out of our second floor bedroom window at dusk when we spotted dark silhouettes coming over the hill. The Nazis had made it to Autrans! The next morning, when she opened the shutters, we saw farms burning in the distance and the smell of smoke permeated the air.

"The Germans were looking for Jews at the sawmill," I overheard Madame Ravaud say to Maman. "A 17-year-old boy got so frightened that he ran into the fields. The Nazis shot him on the spot." He was not Jewish. Just a frightened kid. The next morning we saw a horse-drawn cart pass by with a covered body, legs dangling. Then we heard loud banging on the entrance door downstairs.

"Children, go to your bedroom immediately and close the door!" Maman ordered.

From our hiding place we heard the door being opened, and a male voice speaking German. Maman heard Mr. Ravaud call her "Madame

Charlotte" asking her to come down. Terror-stricken and with legs made of jelly, Maman walked down the stairs, knowing very well that not only her life and her childrens' were at stake, but those of the Ravauds as well. If these men found out they were lodging Jews it would mean death for all of us. At the door stood two men in Nazi uniforms, an officer and his orderly.

"Madame Charlotte, you speak a little German," Mr. Ravaud said in French. "Please translate what these men want."

Maman faced the men.

"*Wir brauchen ein Zimmer zum schlafen,*" one of them said in German.

"What... you say? Me ...not understand good," Maman said, pretending to speak broken German with a strong French accent. They explained it again.

"They need a room to sleep," Maman translated for Mr. Ravaud.

"Would you mind giving them your bedroom since your husband is away?" Mr. Ravaud asked Maman in French. "I have an extra bed that I can set up in the attic for you."

Feigning a search for words, she told the two Nazi officers, "Yes, have beds...you sleep... upstairs."

She had no choice. She had just told the enemy they could stay.

"How come you speak such good German?" one investigated skeptically.

"Learn German ... school...one year," she replied.

The answer seemed to satisfy them. They left, saying they would be back shortly, never suspecting she spoke German as well as they did — and unaware that she and her children were Jewish.

Mr. Ravaud and Maman had just finished setting up the bed in the attic when the Nazis returned. They followed Maman upstairs and deposited their bags in her bedroom. Now my brothers and I were going to sleep next to the enemy. We knew enough to keep quiet and remain invisible. What a miracle that my father had left just in time not to get caught! If they had seen him, they would have most likely shot him on the spot. He looked very Jewish, even though he had blue eyes. We would have all been killed. My mother and we children were blue-eyed, my brothers and I had blond hair. I remain convinced that this saved our lives.

Night after night Maman sat at the attic window, her eyes fixed on the road. Sometimes she fell asleep only to wake up exhausted with the same anguish. Papa had been gone for three weeks and we had no news from him. We heard that there were battles all around our area, and we did not know if he was still alive. She also feared that Papa might show up, under cover of darkness, and throw a pebble to her bedroom window to wake her up so she would unlock the front door for him downstairs.

Every day Madame Ravaud had to feed our undesirable guests and then, at night, they slept next to us three children. During the day the two men were not around. A week later these Nazis still did not seem to be in any hurry to leave. Maman was a good-looking woman in her early thirties. It was obvious that the orderly found her attractive. He came into our kitchen to bake a cake. He placed flour and other hard-to-get ingredients on the kitchen table.

"I would like to bake a *Schokoladen-Marmorkuchen* for my boss," he said, standing there in his shorts.

"*Schokoladenkuchen*? I....not...understand," Maman replied.

"Cake with chocolate inside," he said.

"Yes," she replied.

While she watched him make the dough, she involved him in small talk, designed to pretend that she had nothing to fear.

"Where ...you from?" she asked, pretending to search for German words.

"I am from Leipzig," he replied.

"What...you do... before war?"

"I am a baker," he said.

"And ...wife ... alone... Germany?"

"No, a French soldier helps her in the bakery."

"French soldier...with ...wife??" Maman asked.

The Nazi became very serious. It was obvious that he did not like to hear that.

Soon the scent of freshly baked cake permeated the house.

"*Allemagne kaputt. Hitler kaputt*," Maman continued defiantly.

"No," he replied. "The war will be over in 1945."

"How... you know?" Maman asked.

"I know," he said.

"Why not... you go home?" Maman investigated further.

"Officers won't go."

"Why?"

"Money!" he replied. "In the occupied zone we get a higher pay."

Finally he took the chocolate cake out of the oven. It smelled so good.

Maman was hoping he would give her a tiny piece for her children, but he just walked by her, with the cake in hand, and out the door.

One day I overheard Mr. Ravaud say to Maman, "Yesterday I was sitting on the bench in the yard and enjoying the August sunshine when the Nazi officer sat down next to me. Your son Raymond was on the swing. He observed the child intently for quite some time, and then he said in very poor French, "This blond and blue-eyed boy reminds me of our beautiful German children." Little did he know...

Every other day Maman sent me to two spinster ladies, who lived on a nearby farm, to get a little milk. As I was walking down the narrow village road with my milk jug, a group of young Nazi soldiers came toward me.

"*Halo, blondes Mädchen!*" (Hello, little blondie). Of course I understood, but said nothing. I continued walking fast, scared to death, my eyes fixed on my shoes.

On August 15, word got around that the Allied Forces had landed in the south. Now the tables were turning. When the two Nazis heard this, they finally left. I can only imagine Maman's and the Ravauds' relief! On August 23, the Nazis started to leave Grenoble. For the Vercors the war was over. But where were Papa, Serge and Henri?

On August 30, my mother went up to the village to run an errand. When she came back, Ernest and I said to her: "Maman, the priest came to see you!"

Now I will let my mother tell what happened next, in her own words:

August 31, 1944
Un jour pas comme les autres (a day unlike others)

> *To understand the 31ˢᵗ of August 1944, a brief introduction is necessary. In November 1942, the Germans occupied the majority of France, leaving occupation of the Midi (Southern France) to their Italian Allies. We had taken refuge in Autrans, a village in the heart of the Vercors, at an altitude of three thousand feet above Grenoble. For a year, we lived there relatively undisturbed, and especially, better fed. In September 1943, Italy made a separate armistice with the Allies, and the Italian troops retreated from the Midi. The Germans replaced them and imposed their harsh regime. During the winter 1943-1944, they made dreaded incursions into the Vercors, a high*

mountainous plateau whose abrupt slopes could be reached by eight different roads. It is a true natural fortress. At the time, it was being held by the Forces Françaises de l'Intérieur, a small resistance army that opposed the enemy and the Vichy government. It was much talked about and the Germans themselves thought the army was much larger and better armed than it in fact was. On June 6, 1944, the Allies landed in Normandy and we prayed for their success from the bottom of our hearts. The Germans fought desperately, but were forced to progressively retreat. In Russia as well, their situation was becoming catastrophic, and we were filled with a wild hope that the moment would arrive when the Allies, coming from North Africa, would land in the Midi.

The day after our July picnic, my husband, Serge and his son-in-law Henri left to enlist in the Resistance. My husband did not leave to become a hero, nor did he presume to help victory along. Later, he never claimed the title of "résistant" (a resister), although he had fully participated in the battle of the Vercors, at once the first and last combat of the small army. The Germans had landed their gliders in the vast area of Vassieux and unloaded their troops among the dismayed members of the Résistance ready to salute the Allies. The Germans massacred all ninety inhabitants of Vassieux, from the youngest to the oldest; they discovered the cave of the Luire, and slaughtered all the wounded, their doctors and their nurses; they destroyed scores of farms, savagely killing the farmers as "FFI accomplices"; they fought violently against the Résistance in Herbouilly, Valchevrières, and the Barraques. The casualties were heavy: 500 soldiers, 200 civilians.

The headquarters of the FFI then ordered the dispersion of the troops into the dense and wild forest of Lente, which rendered all combat impossible, and the Germans left the Vercors. If the Vercors army, some two thousand to four thousand men, did not achieve victory, they had nevertheless, at a crucial moment, detained two German divisions—which were thus missing in the south. My husband and his friend Serge, trading their alpine soldier uniforms for civilian clothing found in the camp, decided to leave the mountainous Vercors in the direction of St. Martin d'Août in the Drôme where Serge had a friend. They felt that the Vercors was still dangerous. Henri was in a hurry to rejoin his young wife and one year old daughter, and first joined a group going towards Autrans, but, in Rencurel, he decided to go directly to Autrans across the mountain, alone. It was to be a shortcut. He fell into the hands of a German patrol, which executed him on July 24, along with three "suspects" found in the surrounding area. The group he had left followed their more careful route, and arrived safely in Autrans. On August 12, I had a terrible foreboding, and sure enough, was informed of Henri's fate. I went to Rencurel with one of Eva's schoolteachers to exhume his body, and place it in a coffin, while Maggy Levier was on the look-out to warn us, should a German patrol arrive. I could only recognize Henri's body by his perfect teeth! To this day, I cannot say all that I experienced and felt at that moment. Perhaps just as I am doing this horrifying task for my friend, someone else may be doing this for my husband. One spoke much in Autrans of the savagery of the battles, the atrocious agony of some, the uncertain fate of others left to die of hunger and thirst, the skirmishes everywhere. Grenoble was liberated on the 23rd of August 1944. For the Vercors the war was over. But I still had no news of my husband.

On August 30, my children were playing in front of the house. When I returned from my shopping, they greeted me. "Maman, the priest was here, he wanted to speak to you. He left a message upstairs."

I climbed the stairs with legs suddenly made of jelly. On the kitchen table lay a piece of paper, quickly torn out of a pad, without a date, no doubt written by the priest. It said:

"M. Gutmann and Cdr. Levier are in St. Martin d'Août, in the Drôme lacking money and civilian clothing. Asking that one of their wives, preferably Mme. G. bring them money and clothing…"

To this day, I cannot understand why I did not dash out to see the priest to find out how he happened to possess that piece of paper, or that information, how old the message could be, and to thank him. Instead, I ran to Claire Levier's house to tell her the good news, tempering my joy because Michelle was grieving:

"Our husbands are safe, they need money and clothes. I must go immediately by bicycle towards St. Martin d'Août to bring them those items." Her daughter Maggy, 17, insisted on coming with me. We quickly found two bicycles, and I did, however, go to ask the advice of Dr. Chauve, and the butcher, Mr.Barnier, who had both been of invaluable help to the FFI. How can we reach St. Martin? Through Grenoble? A road map? Was the Grenoble area already safe? "Careful," they said. "There are still skirmishes here and there! Go towards Grenoble to the Red Cross. If they tell you that you can continue, fine! If not, entrust your package and the money to them, with name and address, and they will deliver it as soon as possible."

While feverishly preparing the clothing and a snack, I packed the children off to Clairfontaine. For a long time the Menthonnex had told us: "In case of hardship or difficulty, send the children to us, simply with their suitcase." Roland and Geneviève Menthonnex — we called them Parrain and Marraine, may they rest in peace — had a few papers in their safekeeping and the name and address of our friend in Paris, Mr. Plasseraud. He would have done what was necessary to send our children to my parents in Palestine, after the war, if anything happened to us.

My mind at rest on that score, I leave with Maggy on the road to Grenoble. As we start climbing to the Croix Perrin pass, we push our heavily laden bicycles to the top. We eat our sandwich and begin the descent towards Lans. After the first few hundred meters…

"Oh my God, my brakes don't work! How will I arrive safely at the foot of the mountain? In case I fall, should I keep to the left, the rock, or to the right, the precipice?"

I brake furiously with my bulky hiking boots. I release the brake, and here we go again. Bend after bend, and once more, no brake. Then, at top speed, on the road, a little wider before the oncoming very narrow hairpin curve, the fall. Dragged dozens of meters on my stomach, my right hand clinging to the useless brakes of the handlebar which pulls me with it, I remain sprawled out in the middle of the road, the left side of my face skinned and bleeding, my blouse ripped, my left hand, elbow and knee encrusted with pebbles. My left ankle is broken, my right thumb completely dislocated, the flexor tendon torn, the first joint hanging on by skin. Maggy falls at the same time, with a big part of the brake stuck in her forearm. Our expedition is over, and I can only lament incessantly:

"My husband…my husband…how will I reach him now, my husband…my husband…"

Maggy cries.

People suddenly appear out of the forest, where they were picking berries and mushrooms.

"What can we do for you?" they ask.

"Please find us some kind of transportation in Lans, 2 or 3 kilometers away. You see my foot, and our bicycles." One man dashes towards Lans, others transport us as gently as possible into the hollow of the curve, and set us down on the embankment. One man even has brandy on him, and a sugar cube. I insist he give it to Maggy, who is in a state of shock. After some time, the man returns from Lans with a bottle of fresh water, and says that a vehicle will arrive shortly.

While they are carefully taking out the numerous pebbles embedded in my skin, and washing my wounds with some water, I let myself go and the tears roll down my cheeks.

Our two men had set out towards Romans and the Drôme. Relentlessly they walk, throwing themselves down in the fields at the approach of German patrols, sleeping in barns, receiving a piece of bread here, a glass of milk there, from compassionate farmers. From one such farmer they borrow a wheelbarrow filled with hay to hide their knapsacks, in order to pass under the noses of the German soldiers. Walking very slowly, they pushed their wheelbarrow like farmers returning from the fields. Our men are older than the average members of the Résistance; they slowly cross a well-guarded bridge at Romans without arousing suspicion, their eyes fixed on their mountain boots...Finally they reach St. Martin d'Août.

They are cared for, they rest, they chat at night with the mayor, the priest, with the inhabitants, thirsting for news of the Vercors up there. They are taken for officers of the Résistance, coming perhaps from England because of their accent. They tell the young priest, Father Petit, of their worry for their families in Autrans, where the Germans could have killed like everywhere else. Father Petit is full of initiative: "Listen," he says. "I will go to Grenoble, and from there to Autrans, to reassure your loved ones and to bring you news of them."

"Father," they respond. "We cannot accept this. The area is still infested with Germans. They will take you for a priest of the Résistance. You risk too much. And...we are Jews."

"That does not matter, I would even say on the contrary! Leave it

to me; I will plan my trip before going off to Grenoble. If the Germans stop me, what could I tell them?"

"There is a large sanatorium for 300 to 350 children in Autrans."

"Good! I'll tell them that my parishioners who have children there are anxious about them, and I would like to get news of them."

Father Petit takes his bicycle, and sets out for Grenoble. On the way, he sees horrors, the cruelty exercised by the Germans near Voiron on those they suspect... He goes to St. Joseph's church in Grenoble, and spends the night at his colleague's. The following morning, he begins the climb and arrives at the home of the priest of Sassenage. From there he continues his ascent towards St. Nizier. Suddenly he is surrounded by German soldiers who ask him threateningly where he is from, where he is going, is he part of the Résistance, and they take him to their officer who asks the same questions.

"I come from the Drôme," he says, "and exercise my ministry at St. Joseph's in Grenoble. Because it is so close, I would like to go to the sanatorium in Autrans to get news of the children of some of my parishioners who are very worried."

A phone call is made to St. Joseph's where the priest confirms that his colleague Petit said mass there, and wishes to go to the Autrans sanatorium. The officer becomes more accommodating and says to Father Petit:

"You do not need to go to Autrans. The sanatorium has been evacuated, and the children have been placed with the inhabitants. You can reassure your parishioners, their children are fine. I would even have you taken up there by car, but it is not necessary. Go back." (This was not true; the sanatorium had not been evacuated.) There was nothing left for Father Petit to do but to retrace his steps with a heavy heart. He passes once more by the church of the Sassenage priest where he eats something, and, before departing, writes a few words in his notebook and tears off the page. He gives it to his colleague and asks him to have it brought to his Autrans colleague as soon as possible. Father Petit returns without incident, and recounts his adventure immediately to our men.

They thank him for his good will and his great courage, but my husband says to him:

"The only thing that worries me is the message you left with the priest in Sassenage. Imagine that he succeeds in passing it to someone, and that it reaches my wife. If I know her, she will dash out immediately, and if ever she falls into the hands of the Nazis, on her bicycle laden with men's clothing, she will be accused of supplying the Résistance, and her fate will be sealed. I must get to Autrans at all costs, to prevent my wife's departure."

He leaves at dawn the following morning. Serge Levier cannot go with him. While helping to bring in the hay, he hurt his foot, the wound got infected, and he could not walk. At the price of a thousand difficulties, my husband walks relentlessly, rides a train part of the way, falls into the hands of a group of FFL (Forces Françaises Libres, communist rivals of the FFI); he is suspected of being a German in civilian clothes because of his accent, and threatened to be shot. But he can give details of the FFI, and is released, even provided with a pass. In another group, he is recognized by one of his former companions, who identifies him. He finally arrives in Sassenage, where he is told:

"You are lucky…the cable railway towards St. Nizier has been working again since this morning." He walks the last 5 or 6 kilometers that separate St. Nizier—totally in ruins by now—from Lans where he arrives in the afternoon, exhausted. He recognizes an inhabitant, standing on the threshold of her house, and asks her: "Is there any way I can get to Autrans before nightfall?"

"Here is Mr. X," she answers. "He is leaving with his cart towards the Croix Perrin. Apparently two women have had an accident! This will help you for part of the way anyway." He hoists himself up next to the driver.

As Maggy and I are waiting by the side of the road, I suddenly hear in the distance the trot of a horse approaching and finally a cart appears around the bend. In a few moments, which seem like an eternity, the wagon stops close to us and a man's voice startles me: "Charlotte!" It is my husband, perched on the cart, next to the farmer.

This is how we found each other. Without our accident, Maggy and I would have been far away already, close to Grenoble. My husband would have found an empty house and known terrible anguish. He took us to the Lans infirmary. A young surgeon, Dr. Fabre, who came from Marseille, took care of us. With his delicate hands, which fascinated me, he washed and disinfected, stitched and bandaged our various *wounds, sewed the tendon of my right thumb, immediately warning me that it might not hold. It did, in fact, tear a few weeks later, and to this day I have a stiff thumb. He put a cast on my left ankle and recommended that we go to Villard-de-Lans the following morning to have my swollen left elbow and knee X-rayed. Luckily, we found transportation that took us to Villard-de-Lans. When we got out of the carriage, a man passing by recognized us as residents of Autrans. Impressed by Maggy's large arm bandage, and my numerous ones, he returned quickly to Autrans, and the first person he met was Claire Levier: "I saw your daughter with another person, both seriously hurt, there was one man with them, not your husband." From this remark it took one step for Claire to believe that her husband was no longer alive, otherwise wouldn't he have wanted to return to Autrans too? The poor woman was in inexpressible anguish. But Serge joined us in Lans, where we were resting for a few days. Then, together, we returned to our loved ones in Autrans.*

This is how my mother retold those events. This miraculous accident saved my mother's and Maggy's lives. They would not only have missed my father, because they were going to take a different road, but they would most probably have fallen into German hands on that road and looked suspicious enough with men's clothing and money on their bikes to be executed on the spot. The area was still full of Nazis.

Isn't truth sometimes stranger than fiction?

CHAPTER 4

LIBERATION & MY TEEN YEARS

On October 10, 1944, Lyon was liberated. It was safe to return to Caluire, so Maman called the Girons to let them know that we were coming home. We said goodbye to the Ravauds and the yellow house, and left Autrans with the Leviers (Michèle, Maggy, their parents and little Cathy). Madame Giron had washed and rehung our curtains, and prepared spaghetti and meat sauce to welcome us back. I shall never forget this!

"Thank goodness I hid your silverware in the garden!" Madame Giron said. "Eventually the Nazis *did* show up. My heart was racing when I saw them walk up the stairs to your apartment in search of valuables. I knew you had left all your Jewish books and candlesticks behind and I was so worried that they might burn the house down. But as they reached the last few steps, they received the order to retreat immediately."

"What a miracle," Maman replied. "Somehow we were protected. Thank the Lord!"

Gutmavor envelope

Madame Giron handed Maman a formal-looking envelope with a stamp from Palestine. "To M. R. Gutmavor, 2 Chemin des petites Brosses, Caluire – Rhône," Maman read.

'Why Gutmavor and not Gutmann?' she wondered. Then she noticed that someone had changed Gutmann to Gutmavor. There was no return address, just an official stamp. The first word was hard to read but the second one said '*Apostolique – Vichy',* dated

19 May 1944. You could tell the envelope had been opened and resealed with thick tape.

Maman pulled out an official form. *Delegatio Apostolica* was written in the top left corner below a logo, and Jerusalem on the right. Some headings were in four languages, Name, Address, Nationality, Religion, Race and relationship to the sender. The form was handwritten: "We are doing fine. Wish to hear from you. Your parents Adolphe and Else Lewin. Date: Gedera, 9.11.1943, Palestina.

Gutmavor card

This card looked like a true denunciation, and someone somewhere must have realized that it was dangerous and changed our name to Gutmavor, so that Gutmann would not attract attention as a German Jewish name. My grandparents were terribly worried, not knowing if any of us were still alive.

It was wonderful to be home again. Even though the war was not officially over in the rest of the world, it had ended for us in Caluire/Lyon.

Papa started working again at the Lyon office on *Rue des Quatre Chapeaux*. There he found out what had happened to Monsieur Weissman, founder of the law firm, who had a superb, very valuable stamp collection. His stamp merchant betrayed him to the Nazis, who came to his apartment in the middle of the night to pick him up and deport him to Auschwitz where he was murdered. Papa was shocked and absolutely devastated. He had had the highest esteem for Mr. Weissman, who in turn had highly appreciated my father and welcomed him as an employee in 1933.

I finally started a more consistent and normal education at a high school in Lyon, and travelled by streetcar every day. My parents also sent me to have private lessons with a rabbi, and I started to learn the Hebrew prayers. This was the beginning of my formal Jewish education.

My brothers attended school in Caluire. Six year-old Raymond started elementary school. He was so infatuated with his teacher that he wanted to marry her. One day his teacher asked Maman to come to school to talk to her. She wanted to know if Raymond was a liar. "Madame," she said. "The other day, when we talked about the war, I noticed that he kept looking out of the window. He was fidgeting in his seat and seemed very uncomfortable. So I said, "Gutmann, what's the matter with you?" And he answered that his name was not Gutmann, but Gallian. Why did he say that?" Maman explained to her that she had pounded into him that his name was Gallian, while we were in hiding during the war. It was essential to his survival, if he was ever questioned by the Nazis. The teacher was moved to tears.

In October 1944, as published in the *Journal Officiel,* the decree of the Ministry of Justice of June 1941 was reversed. Those, who had lost their nationality because they acquired it by naturalization, were reinstated as French nationals with full rights. We were all French again! Finally the war was over with the signing of the Armistice on May 8, 1945.

All over France, movie theaters opened again. In the weekly newsreels that preceded every movie, American soldiers were reporting about concentration camps and the atrocities they encountered. Every day the headlines revealed more unbelievable truths about the war. The newspapers were filled with articles about what had taken place. Until then, no one had known the truth.

In Lyon, Maman noticed posters on the walls about the extermination camps. It was only then that she became aware of them and understood what terrible fate we had escaped. She told me that she cried when she learned about the concentration camps. Papa and Maman thought of Otto Freundlich and wrote to him. They soon received a letter from his partner. Her beloved Otto was taken by the Nazis; he had been betrayed by villagers where they were hiding. We learned later that he was gassed in the Majdanek extermination camp in March 1943. Madame Kosnick-Kloss had survived because she was not Jewish. Some French people were helping the Jews, some were informing on them. We were eternally grateful to our French friends, who helped us.

The war was over. Maman could finally get in touch with her parents in Palestine and tell them we were alive and well. For the last six years they had lived without knowing if we were alive or dead. We heard that Uncle Alfred and Aunt Tsilli were settled in kibbutz Kfar Szold in the northern area of Palestine.

Papa and Maman made arrangements to transfer Grossmutter's remains from Caluire to the plot Maman had purchased in Le Vésinet back in 1941, after Grossvater passed away.

Gutmann family after the War

The French government had printed new currency and Papa had to exchange the old.

"Papa, did you take your money to the bank in a wheelbarrow?" I asked when he returned.

"No," he said.

"But ...did you put it in a suitcase at least?"

"No," he replied again. "Why are you so concerned? I just took my wallet!"

"So we are poor!" I wailed.

"Eva, what's the matter with you? Do you want for anything?"

"If we are poor, how will I get a dowry?" I lamented.

Another time, I asked my father: "What does your friend Mr. B. do?" to which he replied: "He sells insurance." "What's insurance," I asked. "It's a policy we buy so that, for example, if our house were to burn down, the insurance company would give us the money to buy another one." I was baffled! "You mean that, if we lost our home, we would get lots of money for it?" "Yes," was my father's reply. "Great!" I exclaimed, "Let's burn the house down!" Clearly, I was obsessed with money, for my dowry I suppose, and to find my prince someday.

After a year and a half in Caluire, we said goodbye to the Girons and moved back to the Paris area in the summer of 1946. Papa rented an apartment on the upper floor of an apartment building in Maisons-Laffitte, another suburb of Paris, in the same general area as Le Vésinet. He closed the office in Lyon and started working in the Paris office again, this time as a partner. The company name was changed to Cabinet Plasseraud, Devant, Gutmann and Jacquelin.

While we lived in Maisons-Laffitte, I attended *Le Lycée de Jeunes Filles*, the girls' high school in St. Germain-en-Laye, a half-hour away by train. At school, I met Marie-Claire, a beautiful, slender girl with long blond hair, large brown eyes, and a dazzling smile of perfect teeth. She was a year younger than I and the oldest of eight children, extremely bright, and talented. She happened to live in Le Vésinet. She could read a book, knit a sweater and listen to music at the same time. We quickly became very close friends.

My brother Ernest and I washed the dishes one night to surprise our parents who had gone out for a stroll after dinner. They were so happy to see the dishes done, when they came back, that they gave us each a 100 francs bill as a reward (the equivalent of a dollar bill today). The next day, at dinner, my father asked my brother: "So, Ernest, what did you do with your 100 francs?" "Well," Ernest replied, "I bought a beautiful little toy motorcycle with a rider. I showed it to my friend Jeff, who lives downstairs, and he gave me his army of lead soldiers in exchange for my motorcycle." My father was not happy. "You exchanged your beautiful new motorcycle for a few used soldiers. That was a silly thing to do! How much did you pay for the motorcycle?" "99 cents," Ernest replied. "So, what did you do with the cent left over?" "Eva sold me a blotting paper for it." In those days, we wrote with pen and ink and our parents, of course, gave us all the materials we needed for school, including blotting papers. I cheated my brother out of his last cent!

After a year in Maisons-Laffitte, I was glad to hear that we were moving back to Le Vésinet. Papa was able to rent the same three-story villa we had lived in before the war. I even returned to the same bedroom. Now I could ride my bicycle to Marie-Claire's house and we could ride the train to school together.

Papa was doing well financially, so Maman hired a maid to help with cooking and cleaning.

"Raymond, this is Letitia, our new household help," Maman said. "We'll call her Leti for short."

"No, Maman," he replied. "I will call her Leticia. I have time."

Raymond fell in love at age eight. Michele's three-year old daughter Cathy, whose father Henri had been killed during the war, was very cute and became his "fiancée." One day he asked, "Maman, why do you have three wrinkles on your forehead?" Maman thought for a moment, then replied, "Well, I have three children and each child gave me one wrinkle."

"When I grow up and Cathy and I are married, I will ask her to only lay (from "laying an egg") one child. I don't want her to have more than one wrinkle."

Raymond was a keen observer. When Maman came home from the hairdresser with very short hair, Raymond looked at her, puzzled.

"Maman, are you as young as you look now or as old as you looked before?"

He loved to tour the neighborhood on his bicycle and look at everything in great detail. He dreamed of becoming a gardener. One day he came running into the kitchen, excited.

"Maman! Come! I want to show you something!"

"I am cooking, Raymond. Can I come in a little while?"

"No, Maman, you have to come *now*. PLEASE."

Maman took off her apron and followed her impatient little boy down the street, my brother pulling her by the hand. He stopped in front of a peach tree, laden with pink blossoms.

"Isn't this beautiful, Maman?" he said, in awe. She readily agreed, moved by his sensitivity and love of beauty.

Now that I was fifteen, I had lots of questions and was eager to find answers. I asked, "Maman, what do you do to have a baby?" She brushed me off again. After that I started to talk with my classmates about those things, and no longer asked my mother that specific question. But one day I surprised her:

"Maman, do people have to take advantage of kissing when they are young?"

"Why?" Maman said surprised, feeling uncomfortable to talk about sex.

"Well, we never see you and Papa kiss."

Maman grew increasingly fidgety and managed to say: "Maybe we kiss at night when you are not around?"

"What?" I exclaimed. "You get up in the middle of the night to kiss? Well, when I am married, my husband will leave me alone. Night time is for sleeping!" Maman was speechless. Proudly she told all her friends about my innocence. In her later years, it was difficult to even take her to a movie. A kiss that lasted more than two seconds made her squirm in her seat and she would blurt out, "Why do they have to maul each other?"

Most of my teachers remarked on my report cards *Jeune d'esprit, très jeune d'esprit, trop jeune d'esprit* (immature, very immature, too immature). Maman was proud. "Immaturity is a good disease. It always gets cured," was her response.

Marie-Claire and I walked arm in arm as friends do. We spent a lot of time at each other's homes doing homework together, playing cards and word games. She lived in a mansion that was surrounded by a beautiful garden. Her parents, Mr. and Mrs. Ferlet, intimidated me. They were devout Catholics and lived like French aristocrats. Marie-Claire could play the piano with great feeling and sensitivity. "Please play Chopin's *Fantasie-Impromptu* again!" I begged. I so loved that piece that I asked her to play it again and again. Seventy years later, I cannot hear this piano piece without thinking of Marie-Claire...with whom I still have lunch every time I am in Paris.

Marie-Claire and I were inseparable, and continued our teenage adventures together. By the time I was sixteen, I always had a crush on someone or other, or fancied myself in love.

Every weekend, Marie-Claire and I went to the tennis club around the corner from her house to watch the games. That is when my passion for tennis began. My first crush was a tennis player. He was a very athletic-looking twenty-six year old young man, ten years my senior. His white shorts showed off his strong muscular suntanned legs. He always rode his bike to the tennis club. I haunted the streets on my bicycle on weekdays, hoping to run into him. Then, one day, I did. We said hello and got off our bicycles, but when he put his hand on my shoulder, just to be nice I am sure, I fled, terrified that he was going to take advantage of me. My infatuation was killed in an instant and I rode home elated, free of that crush.

On the train ride to the girls' high school in St. Germain-en-Laye I noticed this tall, dark and handsome young man with a little distinguished-looking moustache. He was always surrounded by a group of male friends and went to the boys' high school. We exchanged furtive glances, but we never spoke with each other. Yet, the world looked bleak on days when I did not catch a glimpse of him. As soon as I got out of the house in the morning I put on lipstick and carefully licked it off before I got back home. One day I didn't do such a good job and Maman noticed, so she slapped me hard. Sometimes I had to lie or do things on the sly, even once feigning an epileptic seizure when she slapped me, but she did not buy it.

Then I had a crush on Michel, another boy from the boys' high school, perhaps because he was the first boy who ever really paid attention to me. I was very attracted to his dark hair and his piercing blue eyes. Soon we became friends. After school we took long walks on the esplanade of St. Germain-en-Laye, a beautiful park with a wonderful view overlooking Paris. One day we sat down on a bench. He put his arm around me and suddenly I felt his tongue invade my mouth. I saw fireworks. After a while he wanted to make love, but I was adamant about remaining a virgin until marriage. Eventually we both graduated, and I never saw him again. Papa and Maman never knew. They were content to see me "go to the library" twice a week. This sums up my involvement with the opposite sex until I met THE ONE.

I began to immerse myself in other peoples' stories and live their joys and miseries vicariously. It was easier! I started going to movies without my parents' knowledge because I did not think they would approve. If they went out, it was theater, opera, or a concert. Fearing that our parents would not allow us to go, Marie-Claire and I told them we were going "to the library" or "to each other's house." In September 1948, the British feature film *The Red Shoes* came out, based on a fairytale by Hans Christian Andersen. A young ballerina is torn between the man she loves and the pursuit of her career. We went to see it one afternoon and it was a beautiful and very sad movie. Our parents never found out. I started to develop a passion for movies.

Another time, on my way home from the *Lycée* in St. Germain, a poster advertising the movie *"La Symphonie Pastorale"* with Pierre Blanchar, Michèle Morgan and Jean Desailly caught my attention. It was based on a small book with the same title by Andrè Gide, a great French writer. Unbeknownst to my parents, I went to see the movie and was very moved by the story. In a Swiss alpine village a middle-aged pastor comes to administer last rites to a deaf grandmother and finds a young, blind orphan in the barn. The girl is dirty and in rags. He feels sorry for her and takes her home, where his wife Amelia cleans her up. Gertrude, who has never heard a human voice, has to learn to speak. The pastor raises her with fatherly love, neglecting his own family, teaching her about music, the beauty of nature and the goodness of love. As the orphan develops into a beautiful young woman, he falls in love with her. When the pastor's handsome son, Jacques, comes home from college and sees Gertrude, he falls in love with her also. An operation restores Gertrude's eyesight. When Jacques visits her in the hospital, she thinks that he is the pastor and falls in love with him; but then, when she comes home, she realizes that the pastor is actually an old man and the world is not quite as beautiful as the pastor taught her. It is Jacques she loves. When Jacques asks his father if he can marry Gertrude, the jealous pastor refuses and sends his son away. Jacques, devastated, enters the priesthood, and Gertrude drowns herself in a nearby stream. The last image is harrowing, the pastor carrying the lifeless body of Gertrude. I left the movie theater devastated, and, of course, in love with Jean Desailly, the actor playing Jacques. I bought his photograph and carried it with me for months, until I discovered Laurence Olivier in Hamlet!

"Eva, I think you will like it," Maman said as she handed me a book entitled *Le Juif aux Psaumes* (The Psalms' Jew) by Sholem Asch, a Polish-Jewish novelist. A young orthodox boy grows up to become a rabbi and creates a terrible dilemma for himself in adulthood. I could not put it down, it was so gripping that I lent the book to Marie-Claire. I just meant to share it with her.

The next morning, Marie-Claire said: "You know, Eva, I was reading your book in bed last night, and my mother suddenly burst into my bedroom without knocking. I quickly shoved the book under my blanket, but she saw my gesture, and asked sternly: "What are you hiding, Marie-Claire?" I had to show her the book, and she was angry. "Where did you get this book?" "Eva lent it to me." The next day, Madame Ferlet stormed over to see my mother while we were in school. She was still angry and mostly fearful that I was trying to convert her daughter. They met for the first time. My mother sat Madame Ferlet down, offered her a cup of tea, and reassured her. The two ladies got acquainted, and had a long conversation about Judaism, Christianity and the Bible. They both acquired a healthy respect and admiration for each other, and became friends. Marie-Claire was allowed to finish the book. It was the beginning of a long-time friendship, not only between her and me, but between our mothers. For years afterwards they would meet annually for tea in Le Vésinet, before going together to visit the graves of their respective husbands in the cemetery.

Maman had not seen her parents since we had left Berlin and moved to France in December 1933, fourteen years earlier, so she really wanted to go see them. She had never been to Palestine or seen their grocery store. They had never seen Raymond who was now 8 years old. Since Palestine was still under British rule, it was not easy to get a permit to enter the country. They feared that families would stay for good and would not give visas to all of us.

"You go with Raymond, Charlotte, and I will take Ernest and Eva to the Hot Springs in southern France," Papa suggested.

So, in the summer of 1947, Maman and Raymond boarded a ship in Marseille for Palestine and we left for southern France. When Maman and Raymond returned, they had much to share with us.

"How are Grossmama and Grosspapa?" we asked.

"They have aged, of course, but they seem healthy otherwise." After years apart, we finally heard the full story of their very difficult voyage to Palestine. Maman spoke:

"We talked much about the war and how they ended up in Palestine instead of China. Grossmama said that they left with two sheets, two backpacks, a wash bowl, soap, groceries for fourteen days, coffee, sugar and a big sausage. When Grosspapa saw that shaggy little boat that was supposed to take in 560 passengers, he was alarmed. Nevertheless, they boarded. Grossmama climbed up the ladder wearing layers of clothes on top of each other.

Instead of ten to twelve days as promised, they were on the ship for forty days under terrible conditions. They slept on straw beds. They traded all their money, furs and jewelry for food and water. Grosspapa got very sick because there was not enough drinking water and he was already suffering from diabetes. Every two days the boat stopped somewhere to buy coal, potatoes and vegetables. By the evening of the ninth day they saw the lights of the beautiful bay of Haifa, but the next morning they were on the open sea again. The British had not allowed the boat to dock to let the passengers come ashore, so they kept traveling around various islands for three more weeks.

Finally seamen were willing to row them to the land, of course for more payment. The passengers gave them everything, even their wedding rings. They boarded many boats, 28 persons per boat. Half dead, they made it to the shore and fell into the sand with nothing other than the clothes on their bodies. They were taken to a camp. In the afternoon, a few cars arrived from Gedera. Dr. Ben Geffen had found out that refugees had arrived and were kept captive. He explained to the officer that he was a doctor and that he needed to examine them because they might carry infectious diseases. He ended up bringing about 200 refugees to Gedera. But Grossmama and Grosspapa were not picked up. In the evening they were transported to Jaffa in Jewish and Arab buses. On the way to the night camp, many people lined the street with sacks filled with oranges and sandwiches. The refugees were very hungry. Around 11 p.m. the authorities disinfected their coats. They were immunized, fed and then transported to a British Army camp in Sarafand. Here beautiful, bright rooms and fresh drinking water awaited them. Afterwards the Jewish community of Tel Aviv sent them food and clothes.

In the meantime, Alfred had found out where they were, and showed up, disguised as a policeman, so that the guards would let him in. They were ecstatic to be reunited. Alfred knew a widow who owned a store with attached living quarters in Gedera, who wanted to sell the store. Alfred helped his parents buy it and on July 1, 1940, they had a grand opening."

"This is incredible," Papa said. "Did you also find out how they came to write that note to us that would have surely endangered us?"

Grossmama explained that she read in the paper *Representative of Vatican in Jerusalem transmits messages to families in Europe*, so she took the first bus to Jerusalem. She filled out an official form with an official stamp and addressed it to M. Rodolphe Gutmann. During the war, it was the only way to get in touch with anyone abroad, Grossmama said."

We wondered what really happened. Maman still had the postcard and took it to the Center of Jewish Studies in Paris. They said they had never seen such a form. To this day, we wonder why people in Palestine seeking their Jewish relatives in Europe had to indicate race and religion. Nevertheless, we are eternally grateful to the smart and kind individual who protected us. He understood that the name Gutmann would have immediately attracted attention, if the Nazis had been looking.

Thank goodness my mother was able to visit her parents that summer of 1947. The country was about to become a war zone, with the war of independence ending the British Mandate in May 1948. Violence continued in the new country, Israel, into 1949.

Although I enjoyed these relatively sheltered teenage years, I faced challenges — some similar to typical teenagers, and some as a result of the war. Together they produced in me a severe lack of self-worth and a great inferiority complex, mainly because I was Jewish and born in Germany.

I had a difficult relationship with Maman. She was still a strict German mother, criticizing me all the time. I always tried to please her to gain her love and acceptance, but I never did. I argued with my mother when she said something I did not agree with. I just could not help it. Papa was unhappy about the tension in the house. "Eva, please, you don't always have to have the last word," he said.

I suffered some post-war impact as well. For example, I did not like the basement where we lived after the war. It was very dark and, some-how, reminded me of hiding or of being pursued. Whenever Maman sent me downstairs to get her some flour or sugar, which she kept in a small room adjacent to the coal cellar, I was scared to death. As I walked down the stairs, I commanded myself, "Eva, go slowly! There is nothing to be afraid of." Once I reached the bottom, I turned left, past the coal cellar, and slowly walked into the storage room. I opened the chest, grabbed the flour or sugar, slammed the chest shut, and raced back upstairs, in a panic. Although this clearly did not constitute a major impact on me in the grand scheme of life, it affected me then and still does. To this day, I hate basements. I also, to this day, fear being in a forest by myself. I remember how people found corpses in the woods after the Nazis had passed through there.

More importantly, I developed a huge inferiority complex. Born in Germany, yet living in France, I felt inferior, even though I was a French citizen, and spoke French fluently. It didn't matter. The war could not erase my feeling of being a second-class citizen. That was the first strike against me. The second was being Jewish in a mostly Catholic environment. Maybe this also caused me to be extremely shy, well into my fifties.

My Jewish education felt obligatory, not joyful. I continued to learn Hebrew, I attended Torah commentary classes, and we sometimes went to Shabbat services. Not so far from Le Vésinet, we went to the conservative *Grande Synagogue de Paris,* also called *La Victoire*, for Rosh Hashanah and Yom Kippur. Papa and my brothers sat downstairs with the men and Maman and I climbed up the stairs to sit with the women. While the ladies showed off their latest fur coats and seemed more interested in chatting with each other, or passing around photos of their grandchildren, Maman followed every word of the sermon and I was bored.

On May 18, 1950, I turned 18. Maman made me my favorite food — sauerkraut, a knackwurst sausage and boiled white potatoes. I graduated from *Le Lycée de Jeunes Filles* of Saint Germain-en-Laye. As a reward for graduating, Papa and Maman took me with them for the first time on their annual summer vacation to Switzerland and Italy. Papa took his camera everywhere and captured breathtaking landscapes. I was so taken with the majestic Matterhorn, the landmark of the Swiss Alps, that I went to every gift shop, hoping to find a picture that captured its beauty, but I could not find one I really liked.

From Switzerland we continued on to Milan where I saw my very first opera, *Pêcheurs de Perles* (The Pearl Fishers) by Bizet at the world-renowned opera house, La Scala. It was an impressive auditorium with plush red velvet seats and gold decorations. Rows of seats in the balcony were arranged in an oval shape. A majestic central crystal chandelier illuminated the golden interior. While the orchestra fine-tuned their instruments in the pit, I read up on the first act. Then the noise died down and the red velvet curtain opened. A village appeared. Pearl fishers walked around with their nets, singing in Italian. On the island of Ceylon two men, a tenor and a baritone, vow to each other eternal friendship in an unforgettable duet, but they are both in love with a virgin priestess. The duet was so extraordinarily beautiful that I could not hold back my tears. Maria Callas, a wonderful soprano, sang the role of the priestess. She was dramatic and electric, and for me unforgettable.

That music seemed to come directly from God. At intermission, it took me a moment to get back to reality.

"Why are you crying? You don't like it?" Mama asked me. "I *loved* it," I answered as I wiped off my tears. "I am crying because I am so moved."

I was an incurable romantic. What can move a girl of 18 more than true love?

Our next stops were Rome, Naples and the island of Capri. In every restaurant the waiters were watching me fight with the spaghetti, until one of them kindly showed me how to twist them in a spoon. It was a wonderful trip and I was so thankful to my parents. The future should have seemed exciting then, but I nevertheless lacked self-confidence and direction for my life.

CHAPTER 5

MY YOUNG ADULTHOOD

Once the state of Israel had been established for two years, Maman became a volunteer, devoting all her free time to the Women's International Zionist Organization (WIZO, also known as Hadassah in the U.S.), raising funds for educational and healthcare programs that benefited children and women in Israel. The WIZO headquarters was only several subway stations away. Maman had found a new purpose, something worthwhile to dedicate her time to. The WIZO became her new passion. She taught the laws of *Kashrut* (eating kosher) to the North African Jewish women, who had come to live in Paris. Raymond, 9, and Ernest, 13, were in school, so she had the time to devote herself entirely.

Since she was teaching the laws of *Kashrut* to others, she felt that she too should live by those laws. So she started keeping kosher again at home. In restaurants she ate only fish, no meat.

When I graduated from high school. I had no idea what I wanted to study, so Maman, being an ardent Zionist, arranged for me to go to Israel for a year and live with their old friends from Berlin, Walter and Thea Jacobson. I would learn Hebrew, and get to know my grandparents, uncle, aunt and cousins better. The Jacobsons and my parents had known each other since they were newlyweds in Berlin. They, too, had left Germany on a ship to Palestine before the war. They now had a daughter, Ruth, who was just a little younger than I. "You will live with them and their daughter will come and live with us," Maman said.

I did not like the idea, but I did not know what else to do, so I found it easier to comply. All I knew about Israel was that the country was only two years old and Maman was never home because of the WIZO and I resented that.

I hardly knew Grossmama, Grosspapa and Uncle Alfred. Maman had forced me to write to them regularly in German. She said it was my duty as their granddaughter and niece. It was always a chore for me to write in German, but I did it.

"The WIZO has opened an all girls' home economics school in Nachlat Yitshak, a Tel Aviv suburb. You will learn Hebrew and you will learn to sew, cook, iron and clean," Maman said.

This did not sound exciting, but I tried to be open-minded.

At the end of that summer, I felt a little uneasy as I hugged my parents goodbye at the airport. To be away from home and my familiar surroundings for a whole year seemed like a long time. I did not really know my relatives in Israel nor did I know Hebrew or the Jacobsons and I had no idea what to expect. But Papa surprised me with a special gift — an excellent camera. I was delighted.

Hours later, the plane landed at the Lydda airport near Tel Aviv. It was just a small structure surrounded by sandy roads and hills. A couple, similar in age to my parents, was already waiting for me.

"Are you Eva?" the man asked me.

"Yes," I replied.

"Welcome to Israel! I am Walter and this is my wife Thea," he said.

He took my suitcase and I followed them to their car, noticing that Thea walked with a distinct lean to one side. In Tel Aviv, a few blocks from the beach, Walter stopped in front of a five-unit apartment complex, on Smolenskin Street.

"This is where we live. You will stay in Ruthi's room," Thea said.

We walked up to the third floor. Once I finished unpacking Thea explained the rules of the house to me. We spoke in German, as they did not know French and I did not know Hebrew. Since I was to replace their daughter, Thea expected me to do chores — change sheets every two weeks, wash the floors and sweep the balcony. This was new to me. Other than cleaning the guest bathroom sink at home, I was not used to helping with anything else. It had been our maid's job.

Thea enrolled me in the home economics school in Nachlat Yitshak, southeast of the city. Every day I rode the bus for 20 minutes and attended classes from 8 a.m. to 3 p.m. I was the only foreigner and understood nothing.

"*Tsiltselu c'var?*" the students asked me during recess.

It took me forever to understand that it meant *did they ring the bell yet?* I learned to sew, do laundry, iron shirts, wash floors, cook, and speak the language. At that time Israel faced many problems. Food was scarce so the Israelis had become quite creative in making food tasty and finding substitutes for ingredients not readily available. Since eggs were not plentiful, I learned that seven olives had the same nutritional value as one egg. I also learned to make apple pie by soaking zucchini slices in sweetened lemon juice overnight, and they tasted like apple slices by morning.

Every two or three weeks Thea exploded.

"You haven't done your chores, Eva! You were supposed to clean the fridge on Wednesday! Yesterday you forgot to sweep the balcony! Last week you were late changing your sheets!"

Every time Thea scolded me I felt bad about myself. Why did she not tell me right away when I forgot something or made a mistake? Why did she store up resentment for three weeks until she exploded? I felt little and miserable. Even though I wrote to Papa and Maman regularly, I never told them how unhappy I was. Fortunately, Walter was a kind and gentle man, and that helped a bit.

Thankfully Aunt Tsilli's younger sister Hilde, who was in her late twenties, lived with her husband in Ramat Gan, a beautiful residential community about twenty minutes from my school. Usually she was home at 3:00 p.m., waiting for her children Michael, 7, and Daniela, 5, to arrive home from school. Twice a week I took the bus there.

"Shalom *Evchen!*" she said, welcoming me with open arms. "I am so happy to see you. Come on in."

We communicated in German as my Hebrew was not yet good enough. "You look like you could use a friend. Have some cookies and hot chocolate!"

"Thea makes my life miserable," I told her. "I can't do anything right for her."

"Unfortunately we can't please everybody," Hilde consoled me, gushing with love.

"You are a wonderful young woman. She is probably not a happy person and she takes it out on you."

When the children came home, she greeted them with a cup of hot chocolate.

"Thank you so much for your hospitality and for listening to me, Hilde," I said before I left. "I feel so much better."

"You are always welcome, *Evchen*," Hilde replied. She became my angel, and I went to see her very often.

One day Hilde's best friend Tina Waxman, who lived in Jerusalem, dropped in. She was about Hilde's age, tall and thin, kind, generous and dynamic.

"Eva, come visit us in Jerusalem. My husband Eliezer works for the government. He can show you a few places that tourists don't get to see," Tina suggested.

The Israelis were very hospitable, even to people they hardly knew. A few weeks later I visited Tina, her husband and their baby boy. Their lovely apartment was in one of the best neighborhoods of Jerusalem. Their home was peaceful. They treated each other with so much love, kindness and respect. *This is the kind of relationship I want to have one day with my husband*, I thought to myself.

Eliezer took me to the top of the Tower of David near the Jaffa gate, the main entrance to the Old City. From there we had an amazing view over the hills.

Tina and I talked a lot about the war, and about Maman and Thea.

"My mother is a remarkable woman, but she is a very tough mother," I said. "She is controlling and does not show her love easily. In my heart I know she loves me but I wish she would tell me sometimes. In many ways, Thea is a lot like my mother, just as tough and cannot show affection. That's why I often go to Hilde's after school. She is so loving. She listens and she understands me." I told her I was hoping to get married one day and that I wanted a husband eight years older than me because my father was eight years older than my mother and they were happily married. "I need an older husband because I know that I am very immature," I confessed.

Tina listened attentively. I visited several times during the year. She was my other angel. On Friday nights, after services, she and her husband hosted a weekly *Oneg Shabbat* (refreshments and socializing) for foreign students. Every time I left Tina, I felt recharged and rejuvenated.

Once a month on Friday after school, I took the bus to Gedera to spend Shabbat with Grosspapa and Grossmama. It was such a small community that their address was only: Lewin, Gedera. The bus stopped on an unpaved and sandy road around the corner from my grandparents' small grocery store, with living quarters in the back. I had to sleep on their enclosed balcony on the lumpiest, narrowest mattress ever. When I woke up in the morning I ached all over.

Grossmama and Grosspapa were happy to see me. Grossmama was a little taller than Grosspapa and almost gaunt. Her legs were bandaged up to her knees and little boots supported her ankles. Grosspapa had a moustache and wore glasses. His gold watch was hanging on a chain out of his pocket, probably the only jewelry they had been able to save from their jewelry stores in Driesen and Berlin. Grossmama now called him Yitshak and no longer Adolf (thank God!). We spoke German. Jewish immigrants from many foreign countries had sought refuge in Israel and most did not speak Hebrew. They all communicated in Yiddish. My grandparents spoke German with their Yiddish-speaking customers, and communicated very well.

Every day Grossmama got up at 4 a.m., took the bus to the beach, went for a quick swim in the ocean, and then returned refreshed. She was a hard worker. Grosspapa did not seem to work as hard. He spent much time chatting with his customers and keeping up with the news. He also was in charge of purchasing goods. I found him to be rather authoritarian and not very loving and affectionate, although I am sure that he loved Grossmama and me in his own way. He also got angry easily and did not take "no" for an answer. One day he went to Tel Aviv to buy merchandise and when he came back he told us, "Guess what happened to me today. Once I was done with the errands, I went to the central bus station to take the bus home. I did not know which bus to take.

"Excuse me. Which bus goes to Gedera?" I asked a young soldier in German. He was also waiting at the station.

"Ani lo meivin germanit" (I do not understand German), the soldier replied in Hebrew.

"I was annoyed and repeated my question in German, accentuating the words 'bus' and 'Gedera' which are practically the same in Hebrew. Again the young man repeated, *"Ani lo meivin germanit."*

This time I got angry and exclaimed, still in German, "OK, buster. I'll speak to you in Hebrew after you zip up your fly!"

The young man immediately looked down at his pants.

"Aha, you DO understand German! Now tell me, where is the bus for Gedera?"

Grossmama was always busy doing something, making dinner, cleaning, selling in the store. We never talked about the war, their life in Driesen or their escape. I later regretted this, as it would have been a fabulous opportunity, but, as I said before, I was immature. Grossmama gave me a long black skirt with pink roses and green leaves. I thought it was a strange present. She said she couldn't wear it anymore. It was to become useful years later.

Just around the corner lived the parents of Aunt Tsilli and Hilde. Every once in a while their younger brother, Werner, a dashing young man in his late twenties — tall, slender, clean-shaven and good looking — came to visit his parents. He looked impressive in his army uniform and I was infatuated. Every time I went to visit them, I was hoping to see him, but he barely noticed me.

One day Grossmama and Grosspapa showed me a photograph they had received in the mail. It showed my parents in elegant gala attire, Maman in a long, sumptuous black gown and diamond necklace, and Papa in a tuxedo. Not wanting to be outdone, my grandparents put on their best clothes, and asked me to take their picture, standing tall and proud, outside of their store, with dusty shoes on the dirt road.

Papa and Maman at ball in Paris   *Grosspapa and Grossmama--*
well dressed

I also often visited Maman's brother Uncle Alfred and his wife Aunt Tsilli with their two children, Judi and Gadi, in kibbutz Kfar Szold in northeastern Israel. It was a scary location, just below the Golan Heights border from where the Syrians could shoot straight into the kibbutz. Their community was a three-hour bus ride from Tel Aviv. Every couple shared one room. All children lived in the children's house and were supervised all day while their parents worked in the gardens growing vegetables, in the poultry farm tending to the chickens, in the barn feeding and caring for the cattle, and in the kitchen cooking for the whole community. All the women showered in the same shower room without walls or doors. I felt very embarrassed to shower at the same time.

One day, while Uncle Alfred and Aunt Tsilli were at work, a book on their shelf caught my attention: *Die vollkommene Ehe: Eine Studie über ihre Physiologie und Technik (Ideal Marriage: A Study of Its Physiology and Technique)*. I ploughed through that very scientifically-written book like there was no tomorrow, even though it was written in German. With every page I read, I became more knowledgeable about the facts of life. I learned a lot about physical love, and things my mother could never bring herself to talk to me about, while significantly improving my German at the same time.

"How do you feel about the war, Eva? How did it affect you?" people kept asking wherever I went. I told them what I remembered and wished that Maman would write down her memories. I also told them that I grew up with a terrible inferiority complex in France, because I was born in Germany — and I was Jewish.

It was an interesting year for me, but when it came to an end I was happy to sail back to Paris in June 1951. I had to adjust to living with my parents again. Papa was very proud of the quality of my pictures when I showed them to him.

"Maman, could you please consider writing down your war memories for me? In Israel our relatives asked me a lot of questions and I only knew some of the answers." My mother always evaded my request with the excuse that no one would be interested.

I still had no idea what I wanted to be or to study. Papa and Maman expected me to go to college or university. It never occurred to me to go to business school, which, in hindsight, would have been my best choice. But business was for boys. Girls were expected to become nurses or teachers. I felt only really gifted for languages, so it was decided that I would go to the world-renowned International Interpreters' School in Geneva, Switzerland. In addition to English, German and Spanish language classes, students had to take classes in another subject matter. I chose patent law, my father's field. It was so interesting that it briefly occurred to me to study this subject in more depth. Learning new things excited me.

In Geneva I shared an apartment with three girls. One of them was strikingly beautiful. She had black, short hair, large blue eyes and very red lips. These girls had been around the block. Even at the young age of 18 or 19, they were a lot more experienced than I was. They wore makeup and lipstick! I did not fit in, but I was happy to be away from home, and I enjoyed being on my own. Besides, life in Switzerland was not that different from life in France, especially since everyone in Geneva spoke French. I enjoyed the classes, but did not do much else.

Having observed that one seemed to get happier when drinking a little too much, I once had two glasses of wine with the other girls. However, I was not used to drinking wine, aside from a little sip with a good meal. It did not take long before I got sick to my stomach. The girls laughed and sent me to bed. I lay there in the dark, feeling sorry for myself, while they went out and had a good time. I vowed I would never drink again and I never have had more than half a glass of wine at a time.

In April 1952, Raymond turned 13. Papa and Maman decided to celebrate his bar mitzvah in my grandparents' synagogue in Gedera. So within a year of returning from Israel I was going back.

Once the plane landed on Israeli soil, an amazing feeling of joy overcame me. I felt like I had come home. These were my people. Regardless of where they came from — Germany, France, Russia, North Africa, etc., they were all Jews and it was our country. I had not expected to feel that way. Now I knew that I wanted to live in Israel one day. In Israel, I belonged!

"If you want to find work in Israel as a new immigrant you should become a nurse," someone well-intentioned advised me. "With the constant conflict between the Jews and the Arabs, nurses are in high demand here. Languages won't get you anywhere. Everyone in Israel speaks several languages." I was finally finding some direction, and was looking forward to exploring my options to go into nursing.

Paris had a School of Pediatric Nursing (*Ecole de Puériculture*) that specialized in caring for premature babies. When we got back from Israel, I immediately quit the Geneva school, packed up my few belongings and moved back in with my parents and brothers at the villa at *15 bis, avenue Maurice Berteaux* in Le Vésinet.

In September 1952, I started a three-year program at the *Ecole*. Every day I took the train to Paris and then got on the subway, which stopped within walking distance of the school. In the mornings I worked in various hospitals and branches of medicine and surgery as a nurse-in-training under the supervision of the more experienced nurses, and in the afternoons I attended classes. I also worked for several months with the premature babies.

It was nice to come home to a set dinner table and Maman's homemade food.

"What's for dinner tonight?" I asked.

"Einen jungen Hund mit Schoten" (young dog with green peas)! she would answer.

The new Nurse

Maman had many sayings — some were quite funny — and I still quote her often. When I asked what I should wear, she would say: *"Das gute verkehrt"* (the good one inside out). When we were sitting doing nothing, I asked what I should do now, and she would say: *"Hänge Dich an die Decke und trommel auf dem Bauch"* (Hang yourself on the ceiling and play drums on your belly)." When Maman insisted on accompanying a friend who was leaving after tea to the front entrance five floors below, the friend would say, "Charlotte, I can find my way. You don't need to come with me," Maman would tease, "I want to make sure you are leaving!"

Papa gave me money to buy a book of ten meals so I could eat in the school's cafeteria. After I had the ten meals, I asked him for the money to buy another ten meals, but instead of eating at the cafeteria, I often bought myself a pastry for less at the local bakery. The difference I put aside, keeping scrupulous records of the number of meals I was supposed to have consumed. I invested the three-year savings in what I researched to be the best radio/ record player and I still had enough money left to buy two exquisite art books with gold embossed letters on the cover, *Pour Une Renaissance de la Peinture Française* and *Sur l'Evolution de la Grande Peinture Etrangère* (history of French and foreign painting).

Claude, a Jewish medical student I had known for several years, invited me to the movies one day. *Maybe I could fall in love with him,* I thought. *He would make a good husband.* He was not tall and not particularly good-looking, but he was a nice young man about to become a doctor. Unfortunately he was six months younger than me and this bothered me since I still wanted somebody eight years older. Besides, I was not attracted to him. We attended Hebrew classes together, and he remained a good friend.

The parents of one of my nursing school friends owned a vacation home in the countryside. In 1953, this friend invited me and two other girls to spend the weekend there. I entertained them for two days with jokes that I had heard at my parents' table.

"A priest, a pastor and a rabbi are good friends. Over a glass of wine they commiserate about their lack of money for the church and for themselves," I began. "The pastor and the rabbi ask the priest, 'What do you do for money?' And the priest says, 'At mass we take the collection and after mass, when everybody is gone, I go outside in the yard. I draw a circle on the ground with chalk and I throw all the money up in the air. What falls into the circle is for my church and what falls outside of the circle I keep for myself. And you, Reverend, what do you do?' The pastor responds, 'I pretty much do the same thing. After mass I draw a circle on the ground and I throw all the collection money into the air. What falls into the circle, I keep for myself and what falls outside of the circle, I keep for my chapel.' 'And you, Rabbi, what do you do?' the other two ask. And the Rabbi answers, 'I do pretty much the same thing. I throw all the money into the air and what God grabs is his.'"

My friends were thoroughly amused, and I enjoyed making them laugh. We laughed all weekend. Most of my jokes were Jewish, as Jews have no problem making fun of themselves.

Every month I worked in a different department in a different hospital. I was not the best academic student, but my applied nursing was good. One month I was assigned to the Maternity Department of a large hospital and I was excited to attend the birth of a baby for the first time. When I walked into the room, the young woman's contractions were already very strong as she had been in labor for several hours. She was pushing so hard that her forehead was covered with beads of sweat. Finally I could see the baby's head come out, then its body followed. The doctor grabbed the blue, wet and limp newborn by its ankles, held it upside down and slapped it on its bottom. The baby immediately took a huge breath and started crying. Then the doctor placed the little creature in its mother's arms. The mother's face was filled with joy and every pain was forgotten in an instant. Witnessing the beginning of life with that first breath and that first cry was incredible. I was overwhelmed with emotion. Seeing the joy and serenity on the mother's face after hours of hard labor made it clear that it was all worthwhile. Instead of being scared of the pain I was looking forward to having children of my own one day. I could not wait to go home and tell my parents and Grossmama, who had come to visit from Israel, about the miracle I had experienced that day. And what a miracle it was! At the dinner table I described excitedly and freely what I had just experienced, in vivid detail, in the presence of my younger brothers, who listened attentively. Grossmama sat frozen on her chair, stunned that my parents did not stop me. To her this was a forbidden subject. How could I talk so freely of things she had hardly been allowed to think of when she was my age, and in front of my brothers! I remembered the story she had once told me and I understood why she was reacting that way.

When she was 18, in 1904, her mother Johanna took her to a neighbor's house where a woman was in labor. All the village women came to help the new life into the world. Even at 18, Grossmama was never left alone at home, so she was brought along and made to wait in the living room while the hustle and bustle went on upstairs. Finally, hours later, she heard a faint baby's cry. Her mother burst into the room, shouting excitedly,

"Else, Else, come to the window, quickly! Can you see the stork? Look, it is flying away. It just brought the baby." To that day she was still convinced that she had seen something fly away.

In the summer of 1953, I had completed my first year of studies at the *Ecole de Puériculture*. We were still living in le Vésinet and every day Papa and I had to walk 15 minutes to catch the train to Paris. Then it took another half hour before we reached the Gare St. Lazare. It was time to purchase an apartment in Paris to cut down on travel time. Every weekend my parents browsed through the real estate ads in *Le Figaro* and *Le Monde*.

One sunny Saturday morning an ad caught their attention. Everything seemed right — the location, *73 avenue Niel* in the 17th arrondissement; the size — it was close to 2,200 square feet — the number of rooms and the price. Paris was an exciting city and I loved the idea of living there. Papa made an appointment, and we immediately went to see it.

We got into Papa's Peugeot and 30 minutes later, we reached our destination, *73 avenue Niel*, a wide and busy street in an affluent, mostly residential part of town. The sidewalks were lined with tall trees. There were a few small luxury shops: a high-end dress store, an eclectic wine store and an antique store. Fine gold-rimmed porcelain cups were displayed in the window. We immediately fell in love with this location.

Papa opened the impressive, ornate wrought iron double gate of the seven-story early 20th century building and the three of us squeezed into a tiny elevator that brought us to the 5th floor. Maman rang the bell at the large double door. An older, elegantly dressed lady greeted us amiably and ushered us into a ten-foot wide hallway. There were three spacious rooms: a dining room, a library and a living room in a row. Floor-to-ceiling double door windows opened onto the balcony that ran along those three rooms, above the avenue. The living quarters had a bright and airy feel. We could see the *Arc de Triomphe* nearby. Papa already envisioned his library and desk in the middle room.

All our heavy, massive shiny German furniture, which had followed us all these years, could fit into this apartment. Papa made an offer immediately.

"I am sorry, Mr. Gutmann, but someone has already made an offer, he is supposed to get back to us" the owner replied. Very disappointed, we left. The next day the phone rang,

"Mr. Gutmann, the apartment is yours."

We were thrilled. The only drawback was that the pigeons also loved the trees on our street and enjoyed leaving their mark on cars that parked beneath them. But that was not going to deter us. We moved out of our rented Le Vésinet villa and became proud and happy Parisians.

Papa stored all his slides and camera equipment in large built-in cabinets in the wide entrance area. The painting with the Jews poring over the

Torah under a single light bulb and the portrait of an elderly Jew, which was a little dark for my taste and made me feel sad, now embellished the walls together with a reproduction of *l'homme à la chaîne*, a painting by Titian, of a handsome man with a silver chain, along with several Freundlich paintings around the apartment. In the middle room, my parents' German and French encyclopedias, literature and art books had found a home in the newly-purchased oak *bibliothèque* and a beautiful desk stood at the window, on a beige rug with green leaves.

The furniture my parents had brought from Germany — the large buffet, the round dining table with four expandable leaves, and china cabinet fit perfectly into the spacious dining room. Maman placed the bronze statues of an athlete and of a beautiful Venus on the buffet and hung up sheer curtains.

Maman enjoyed playing the piano again. I loved to listen to her play Brahm's Hungarian Rhapsody and Chopin's *Etude Révolutionnaire* while I read *The Count of Monte Cristo* by Alexandre Dumas.

On the radiator stood a light blue tin box with a slit on the top through which we would regularly put some money. It was imprinted with a Star of David and a map of Israel. Maman told me that these blue boxes were distributed to Jewish communities around the world for donations to make the Jewish dream of a Jewish country a reality. A man by the name of Theodor Herzl had created a national fund to help establish a Jewish homeland.

Usually Maman took care of the cooking, but when she did not have time, she gave Nini, our maid, a chubby woman from Spain, exact instructions on how to prepare the meal. Nini loved watching Maman "kasherize" the meat (making it kosher). After soaking it in cold water for half an hour she salted it with special kosher salt. Then she let it sit for an hour so that some blood could drain out. Finally she rinsed it briefly under cold water. Now the meat was beautifully red, and looked clean and appetizing. Nini loved Maman's meat so much that she also "kasherized" her pork at her house!

Every two years Maman made *Gefuellte Milz*— stuffed spleen — Papa's favorite dish. She did not make it often because it took a lot of work. The smell revolted me. Apart from that dish, her cooking was always simple, healthy, and delicious, German or French. Her chocolate mousse was to die for. I thought that I would take a few lessons from her when and if I ever got engaged.

On Fridays, when French Catholics always buy fish, Maman usually served fish, since it was always very fresh in the market. For dessert she made a vanilla custard that she served with strawberry or raspberry syrup. We all loved that dessert.

I was thrilled to live in Paris. Now I could commute to school by subway. I was in my second year at the *Ecole de Puériculture*. At the end of the school year, in June 1954, the finals came for the Diploma of Registered Nurse. I relied on my visual memory and always waited until the last minute to prepare for exams. Nonetheless I passed the written exam with flying colors. Now Maman helped me study for the oral exams. Having studied medicine herself, she was very interested in the subjects. When she asked me to explain a particular term that I repeated by rote, the meaning of which I did not know, she made me look it up in the dictionary.

During the oral exam the intimidating professor asked me to explain the meaning of that particular word. Confidently I quoted the definition from the dictionary: "In the shape of a kidney."

"Are you, by any chance, related to Professor Gutmann of the Faculty of Medicine of the *Sorbonne*?" he asked, impressed.

"No, sir," I responded.

"Well, you could be."

That was quite a compliment. I graduated 18th of 400 new nurses of the Paris region. Maman was pleased, but one of my teachers was not too happy about my success.

"It really is unfair, Eva, that you did so well, when other students, who worked much more diligently than you all year long, passed with lower grades."

Tough! I thought to myself.

I looked forward to the third year at the *Ecole* to become a registered pediatric nurse. I especially wanted to take care of premature babies. The hospital attached to my school was known for its advanced incubators and specialized pediatricians. The most difficult cases were flown in from every corner of France to be treated there. Every morning I had to weigh each baby as every ounce it gained was crucial to its development and survival. The incubator was a big transparent plastic box with two holes in the side. To feed the baby, to wash it, to change its diaper and to weigh it, I had to put my hands through those two holes. There was also a small hole on the top of the incubator; to weigh the baby, I placed a scale above that hole, with a spring attached to it that went through the hole, and I would gently transfer the baby into a little hammock and attach it to the spring. The scale then registered the weight. The smallest baby I took care of weighed about a pound and a half. To give him a shot in the upper outer quarter of the buttock was a challenge. It was so tiny that I could hardly find the buttock, let alone the upper outer quarter.

Babies that stayed with us for several weeks became "our" babies. On the subway ride home my nursing friends and I loved to talk about these babies. We referred to them as "my son" or "my daughter." I could see the confused looks on the other passengers' faces who happened to overhear our conversations. Obviously they could not figure out how we could have so many children at such a young age, and all of us wearing a uniform.

One day Maman came home with a beautifully prepared piece of sirloin.

"Oh no!" she exclaimed. "I forgot to ask the butcher for the exact weight in order to know how long to roast it!" "No problem, Maman," I said. "Hand it to me, please!"

I took the roast in both hands, closed my eyes and imagined that it was a premature baby that I was weighing.

"1,800 grams," I declared confidently.

Maman took out her scale. The roast weighed 1,850 grams. I was off by two ounces.

When Mr. and Mrs. Plasseraud heard that we had moved to Paris, they invited us to their lovely villa. Mr. Plasseraud, to whom we owed our livelihood during the war years, was a good-looking man, dressed in a suit and bow tie. His voice was soft, his manners aristocratic and his choice of words were those of a well-educated person. His wife was also very classy, but thin and rather fragile looking. It was obvious that she had learned good manners in her cradle. Their living room was decorated with exquisite furniture such as a coffee table with tiles depicting running gazelles reminiscent of the Paleolithic cave paintings found in Lascaux. We were treated to a catered lunch with hors d'oeuvres and drank the finest wines in crystal glasses.

At the end of the school year, in June 1955, I graduated as a registered pediatric nurse. It was a very sought-after diploma. Most of my friends found jobs in hospitals or as directors of daycare centers right away. I was not in a hurry to start working, so instead I spent a week in Milan, with Papa's cousin, Hans Mayer, his wife Vittorina and their two children.

My mother continued her volunteer work at the WIZO and kept very busy. Raymond loved to go out on the balcony and forecast the weather.

One morning Maman was getting ready to attend an important WIZO meeting and intended to wear her brand new wool suit. Well aware that my brother, 16 by now, loved to predict the weather from looking at the clouds, she asked, "Raymond, can you tell me what the weather will be like this afternoon?"

Raymond went out on the balcony and looked at the sky. There were just a few little white clouds, nothing to fret or be concerned about. The sun was shining. It was a glorious day.

"You know, Maman, it may not be the best day to wear your new suit. There will be a thunderstorm this afternoon," he reported.

"Thank you, Raymond," she replied, thinking *what does he know about the weather*? She left as the sun was still shining, without a raincoat or umbrella. While she was in the meeting, black clouds appeared and the sky grew darker, then the storm came, furious and destructive. For the next four hours torrents of rain battered the city. My poor mother came home soaked to the skin, in her wet wool suit, which she had to take to the cleaners the following day.

Madame Kosnick-Kloss reconnected with my parents and came to tea with her new boyfriend who rubbed us the wrong way. He was utterly disagreeable. My parents were still grieving for their friend Otto.

Kosnick-Kloss was organizing a posthumous exhibition of Otto Freundlich's works and asked Maman if she could borrow the paintings she had of Otto's, including the painting on wood that he had painted for Maman while he was hiding in the Pyrenees. Maman readily agreed. After the exhibition Madame Kosnick-Kloss refused to return that painting. My parents wrote to her, and she wrote back that they will get it back after her death. It was her way of getting revenge on my mother. She claimed that Maman had "stolen" her boyfriend, because her boyfriend had broken up with her. Nothing could have been further from the truth! Papa, being the gentleman that he was, loathed the idea of suing her.

Sometime later, at another gallery exhibition, my parents happened to see the painting on wood again, this time in a glass case under lock and key.

"Monsieur, this painting belongs to me," she said to the manager of the gallery. "If you look on the back, you will see, in the artist's handwriting: *To Charlotte Gutmann for her birthday September 22, 1941.* I demand that you not return this piece to Madame Kosnick-Kloss. It is mine. Here is my ID." That still did not work, so finally in 1955, a court order forced Kosnick-Kloss to return the painting to my parents.

On one of their trips to Israel, Papa and Maman visited Mrs. Dallman, the widow of one of Papa's college friends from Berlin. On the balcony, behind her fridge, Papa saw one of Freundlich's oil paintings, a gift from the artist to her husband. She never liked it and it was in very poor condition.

"Paula, would you entrust this piece to me?" Papa asked Mrs. Dallman. "I would like to have it restored, and donated to the Israel Museum in Jerusalem after my death."

Mrs. Dallman was only too happy to get rid of it. Papa had it restored and for many years it hung in his office. Like many of Freundlich's abstract paintings, it was composed of various colorful triangular shapes, with two straight sides and a rounded one. We called it *The Flame of the Revolution*.

In the fall of 1955, it was time to look for employment. I would have loved to become a midwife, but I was told that I would have to live in the country and drive to farms to deliver babies. That did not appeal to me. I wanted to stay in Paris where births took place in hospitals under a doctor's supervision. The Jewish Daycare Center of Paris (*Crèche Israélite de Paris*) in Montmartre was looking for an assistant director, preferably one who was Jewish and who had diplomas from my school. I applied and was invited for an interview at the home of the elderly chairperson of the board who had supervised the center for many years, a formidable lady, gaunt, with intimidating, piercing eagle eyes.

"Mademoiselle Gutmann, you are so young. Surely you will get married and leave us," the lady expressed her concern. I still looked like a teenager.

"Well," I replied, "first of all I do not know anyone at the present time who wants to marry me, or whom I want to marry. Secondly, if I got married, I would not necessarily stop working. Thirdly, even if I got married and left Paris, I would give you sufficient notice to find a replacement."

My answer seemed to satisfy her. She decided to hire me and told me that I would assist the present director to learn the ropes, and eventually replace her. I was to start work in January. When I did, the director spent about 30 minutes educating me about her responsibilities, and I was then told to go take care of the babies. I was delighted as I was in no hurry to replace her and be stuck in that job; she had been there for 30 years. All I was interested in was to meet my future husband and make *Aliyah* with him (i.e. emigrate to Israel).

Now that I was 23, I worried that I might never meet someone I could fall in love with or who would fall in love with me. For years I had dreamed of meeting my soulmate and sharing my life with him. Every time I met a nice, eligible young man, I immediately thought, *Will he be the one?* I felt that this thought jinxed my chances immediately. Being a proverbial wallflower, I feared that I would never meet THE ONE.

One day my parents offered to take me to a ball. Maggy lent me her long, pearl-gray shantung gown from Carven, and I was thrilled. "You look lovely, Eva," Maman said. That comment meant a lot to me since she complimented me very seldom.

At the ball, no one invited me to dance. I felt miserable and uncomfortable, sitting there with my parents. It was obvious that my parents felt sorry for me. I tried to sit by myself, but that did not work either. Everyone else was dancing with his or her partner and having a great time. Finally Papa got up and walked over. "Eva, may I have this dance?" he asked with his kind and gentle voice and a smile on his lips as he reached for my hand.

"Thank you, Papa," I whispered, relieved. Papa kept stepping on my feet — he was not a great dancer — but it did not matter. I felt his love and that made it alright. At least I danced once.

Another time, I went to a dance with a group of young people. We sat at a long table. The dance music started and once again every young man invited the girl next to him to dance, except the guy next to me. Disillusioned, he was looking across the empty table at the dancing crowd, then turned to me and said, "Phhh…there are no pretty women here tonight." I was crushed.

When I started working and earning my own money, I decided to increase my chances of meeting someone, and joined Madame Blumenthal's Jewish singles group. Its members met regularly for dinner at the luxurious *Hôtel George V* on the Champs-Elysées. Madame Blumenthal, a petite, elderly lady, prided herself in having facilitated numerous marriages. While a prisoner in Auschwitz she had sworn to herself that, if she ever made it out of that hellhole, she would help match up Jewish singles. At the meetings the young men usually talked politics. I couldn't care less about that and felt out of place. Besides, no one paid attention to me anyway. I sat there timidly and did not speak. Madame Blumenthal insisted on always introducing me as "the director" of the *Crèche Israélite de Paris*, even though I was only the assistant director at present. She wanted to make me look more important than I was but I did not like that! I found Mme Blumenthal to be quite intimidating. One day I was in her home and overheard her on the phone. A young man had called to tell her about the date he had the night before. Excitedly she asked, "Alors, how did it go last night?" She listened, clearly getting angry…and then shouted, "WHAT? Come on, Alain, be reasonable! Her father has millions!" I did not like hearing that either.

The following month I met a young man I kind of liked at one of those Blumenthal dinners. He was nice and good-looking, but we were not particularly attracted to each other. He asked me out once. Having witnessed the miracle of birth at the hospital, I really wanted to have at least one child in my lifetime. So, at some point, I dared to ask him if he would agree to father a child for me if I didn't find a husband.

"Okay," he said.

I never saw him again.

In April 1956, I started to take driving lessons and was very motivated to pass the test since Papa had promised Ernest and me that we could borrow his car to go on a vacation of our choice in the summer, and we had already made plans to go to Austria. Papa and Maman's 25th silver wedding anniversary was coming up on August 6th and, instead of their usual summer vacation, they had decided to visit the United States in September. Ten months earlier, they had reserved a cabin on a ship to New York.

"Happy birthday, Eva," Papa said on May 18. "I know how much you would like to meet a very special young man and get married. Now you are 24, and I wish that you will meet him this coming year."

On June 11, Maman left for Israel to visit her family again.

CHAPTER 6

MEL, THE LOVE OF MY LIFE

"In the blink of an eye, something happens by chance — when you least expect it — that sets you on a course that you never planned, into a future you never imagined."
Nicholas Sparks

When I got home from work on Friday, June 22, 1956, five weeks after my birthday, my 17-year old brother Raymond was fixing his bicycle in the courtyard of our apartment. "Eva," he said. "A young man from Israel came to see you. He left you a note in your room."

Who was this man? I was mystified. I did not know any "young man from Israel". I rushed upstairs and found the note:

June 22, 1956
"Dear Mlle Gutmann:

Your name was given to me by Mrs. Tina Waxman in Jerusalem. I just came from Israel where I have been studying at the Hebrew University for the past year and am now on my way back to the United States after a little trip of three weeks through Europe. I will be in Paris for four or five days and would like to get together with you if at all possible. Your brother said you would be home about 7:30 p.m. and I will try to call you at about that time, or stop by here again. If you will not be home this evening, I would appreciate it if you would call me to leave a message. I am staying at Hôtel de la Gare, 8 Rue de la Harpe, Tel. ODE 35-40.

Hoping to get in touch with you very soon,
Sincerely,
Mel Perlman

The note annoyed me. I did not particularly like or dislike Americans. The little I had heard about them, though, was not exciting. Besides, I had planned to do a few things the next day, *and* he was now returning to the States anyway.

I had planned to attend another one of Madame Blumenthal's singles' dinners that night and this stranger was messing up my plans. I picked up the phone and dialed the number of the *Hôtel de la Gare*. He was not there, so I left a message, asking him to call me the next day at noon. Then I went to the dinner. That night Madame Blumenthal invited me to a café for the next day, Saturday afternoon, to meet a few other young people.

"I'm sorry, Madame, I won't be able to come. I have to take some American sightseeing," I told her, frustrated. I felt an obligation to Tina, with whom I had stayed in touch since my year in Israel. The thought *Could he be THE ONE?* never crossed my mind.

That Saturday morning at 10 a.m. I went for my driving test and was appropriately nervous. Much to my surprise and delight, I passed and went home with wings at my feet. As a reward I purchased the lacy white blouse I had been eyeing for weeks in a store window on my way to and from the subway. By 11:45 a.m. I was back home, waiting for the American's phone call. Noon came and went. 12:30 came and went. I felt myself getting angry. After all I had given up the singles' meeting at the café for this stranger. Finally, at 1 p.m., the phone rang.

"Hello?" I said, upset.

"I am so sorry," I heard a pleasant voice say, in English. "I just woke up and only got your message now. I was out late last night."

"I see," I said. He continued, "I felt lonely, so I attended a Shabbat service at a synagogue where I met a girl. We went to a café and talked until three in the morning."

"I see," I repeated.

"I like your voice," he remarked after a moment of silence.

"Well, why don't you pick me up at 2 p.m., and I'll take you to see a few places," I suggested.

"Ok, that sounds good," he said.

Two o'clock came, 2:25 came. To be late for a date was considered very rude in France. Finally, at 2:35 p.m., I heard the doorbell. By then I was furious. I stomped to the door and opened it. *Oh, my goodness!* We stared at each other in total amazement. A gorgeous young man stood there, tall and slim, with short curly dark hair, dark eyes, a dimple in his chin, and clean-shaven. In one electrifying moment, my wrath evaporated. We just looked at each other, speechless. I could tell that he was taken with me as well.

"Please come in for a moment," I said, in English. Although I had a basic knowledge of English after seven years of studying in high school, I was not fluent. I introduced this handsome stranger to Papa. Nini, our maid, was off for the weekend and Maman was in Israel. Usually I had to cook for Papa and the boys when Maman was out of town, but this evening he was invited out to dinner, so I was free to go. Mel and I left right away.

Instead of taking the elevator, we walked down the five flights of stairs, barely watching the steps, still staring at each other. As good-looking as he was, his clothes were terrible. His navy blue pants were wrinkled and shiny from wear. The points of his off-white shirt collar were turning upward, and he wore a yellow knitted tie. His maroon corduroy jacket needed patches on the elbows, and his shoes were scruffy, but none of that mattered.

We walked along the beautiful Avenue Niel and up Avenue Mac Mahon to the *Arc de Triomphe*.

"Let's go to the top. From there we'll have a beautiful view of Paris," I suggested.

"I don't have change," Mel said.

"I'll pay for the two of us. You can reimburse me later," I said.

We hardly noticed the stunning view of Paris from the top with its star-shaped avenues that radiate out from the *Arc de Triomphe*. We just kept looking at each other. We spoke little yet understood each other perfectly. Since Mel did not speak French, we communicated in Hebrew and English.

As we strolled down the Champs-Elysées, we talked about our mutual friend, Tina.

"Tina had an *Oneg Shabbat* every Friday night for foreign students, so I went every week," he said. "I got to know her husband Eliezer and we all became friends. When Tina heard that I was planning to stop over in Paris for three or four days and then travel through Europe with friends, she gave me your phone number and the number of another girl in Rome. She said both girls speak English and it would be good to have some local contacts."

I enjoyed listening to Mel and I felt an immediate connection. For some reason I felt comfortable and safe in his presence.

"During my year in Israel it became clear to me that I wanted to become a social anthropologist so that I can help Jewish immigrants from various parts of the world integrate into Israeli society and culture. I also realized that I want to spend my life in Israel."

"You want to live in Israel?" I repeated, excitedly. "Me too!" 'My goodness! This IS the ONE!' I thought. "I also spent a year in Israel and want to live there."

Forty-five minutes after our meeting at my door, this short exchange did it! It felt like a miracle. Maybe it was Godsent. I found out that he was nine months younger than me, but this no longer mattered.

We continued walking to the *Jeu de Paume* Art Museum on the *Place de la Concorde,* near the Seine river, to see an exhibition of Impressionist paintings. Again I paid the entrance fee for both of us and again, instead of looking at the gorgeous art — the Van Goghs, Manets, Monets and Degas -—we sat down on a bench, talked and gazed into each other's eyes. I found out later that he had arrived in Marseille by ship, and traveled to Paris in a boxcar. He had just enough money for bare necessities. He arrived in Paris on Friday June 22, 1956, almost broke.

After the museum, we strolled along the Seine to the *Pont Neuf,* and from there to the *Ile de la Cité,* the island with the *Notre Dame* cathedral. There we settled on a bench in a little park.

Mel struck me as very mature. I could be totally myself with him. It was like we had always known each other. He was so humble and natural. He did not try to impress me and I did not feel that I had to impress him. I had known him less than two hours. I wished he would kiss me.

"Let's stop by my hotel for a moment," he suggested. "It's not far from here."

"Sure, why not?" I replied.

We crossed the *Pont Saint-Michel* and strolled down the *Boulevard St. Michel* to his hotel. Mel opened the door to his room.

"Excuse me, I have to go to the restroom down the hall. I'll be right back," he said as he rushed off.

The way he had excused himself was so natural. Until that moment, I had always felt terribly embarrassed when I was with other people and needed to excuse myself. Suddenly it became such a natural thing, as this guy thought nothing of it. This was a discovery for me; I never felt the same embarrassment again.

When Mel came back, he took me in his arms and we kissed.

"Please don't think that I kiss just any guy after I have known him for two hours!" I said apologetically. I was embarrassed.

"Eva, I would never think that," he replied with a smile. "If you had not responded to me the way you did, I would not have known that you feel about me the way I feel about you!"

We left the hotel hand in hand to meet my brother Ernest, whom I had previously arranged to meet for dinner. Ernest and Mel met and we had a lively conversation. Guess who paid for Mel? After dinner the three of us went to see *Gentlemen Marry Brunettes* with Jane Russell. By the time we got home, it was 11 p.m. Papa had not returned from his dinner yet. Ernest went to bed, and Mel and I settled on the green velvet couch in the living room.

"What are you doing tomorrow?" he asked with his pleasant, manly voice.

"We are invited to the wedding of a friend of mine in the countryside," I said.

"May I go with you?"

"I would love for you to come along, but I am not sure that Papa will agree to it."

Then I heard the key in the door and Papa walked in. He seemed surprised and somewhat puzzled to see that Mel was still there.

"Papa, could Mel come with us to the wedding tomorrow?" I asked.

"No, I am sorry," he said. "He is not invited, but if he is willing to take a walk while we attend the ceremony, he is welcome to join us for lunch at a restaurant afterwards and spend the rest of the day with us." *Dear, dear Papa!*

The ceremony was beautiful, but all I could think of was Mel. I could not wait for this to be over so I could see him again. We found him waiting for us nearby, and took him to the restaurant.

"I want to sit across from you so that I can look at you!" he whispered softly into my ear, as we waited to be seated. A tingling went through my entire body.

It was a pleasantly warm summer day. After lunch Papa drove us to the *Château de Fontainebleau*, about 35 miles southeast of Paris. We walked through this magnificent palace, and its manicured gardens and fountains. "Can I see you after dinner?" Mel asked me as I sat next to him in the back of Papa's Ford Vedette on the way back.

"Let's meet at the *Arc de Triomphe*."

I really wanted to invite Mel to join us for dinner as I had to cook for Papa and my brothers, but I did not dare. I cooked spaghetti and set the table quickly, ate and did the dishes in a hurry. How will I tell Papa that I was going out again? I had to see Mel at any cost.

"Eva, what is going on?" Papa asked concerned, obviously sensing that something was brewing. I was his only daughter and "the apple of his eye," so I understood his concern, but I was 24 now and no longer a child.

"Mel is waiting for me," I finally dared to say. Then I took my purse and rushed out the door.

It was a beautiful warm evening. From afar I spotted Mel, patiently waiting on a bench at the *Arc de Triomphe*. When he saw me, his face lit up.

"Eva," he said, "I am so glad to see you."

"So am I," I answered with a big smile. We sat down. We had known each other for exactly 30 hours.

"I am supposed to meet my three best friends from Yale, who will arrive tomorrow, and they will want to leave immediately on their three-week tour through Europe. I feel that there is a strong possibility that we might want to get married once we get to know each other better, so I would like to stay in Paris instead of going with them. What do you think?"

I was thrilled and, of course, wanted him to stay. At the same time, I was concerned that Mel would miss out on an amazing trip if nothing came of us. But the next day, I said "Yes, please stay!" and Mel informed his friends of his change of mind and heart.

We saw each other twice each day, on a bench near my Day Nursery for a sandwich lunch and at night at the *Arc de Triomphe*. Immediately, we started saying "If we get married, we'll do this…" and "If we get married we'll do that…" We spoke for hours, shared our life stories, our dreams and hopes. I learned over the next few days about Mel's background.

He was born Melvin Lee Perlman in Pampa, Texas, in 1933, the third son of Abe and Bertha Perlman. He was named after his maternal grandmother, Malcah Leah. His parents divorced when he was only eight years old, and his mother took him back to Kansas City where all her family lived. She eked out a living working in a hat factory, and raised Mel by herself. His older brother, Ralph, was already eighteen by then and soon to be on his own. Jonathan, his parents' second child, had died of peritonitis at the age of eleven, before antibiotics became readily available.

Mel went to Central High School in Kansas City, and excelled in his studies, on the swimming team, and in the drama department. He was able to win a four-year scholarship to Yale, to which his mother would never have been able to send him. There again, he was an excellent student, also active in Jewish affairs and president of *Hillel*—a Jewish Students' organization on campus. Upon graduation with a BA in Human Culture and Behavior in 1955, he got a small grant to study for a year at the Hebrew University in Jerusalem. For this purpose he luckily got a deferment from the Army, since in 1955 military service was still compulsory for young men in the United States. During the year in Israel, he decided he wanted to spend his life there, and become a social anthropologist. Every Friday night, Mel went to Tina Waxman's home. She noticed him very quickly, because he was tall and handsome, and he ate all her cookies! Mel's grant covered his tuition and lodging, but little else, and he often went hungry, living on fish and vegetables.

While at the Hebrew University, Mel became friendly with several of his professors, as he was one of very few foreign students who talked to them after class, asking questions, seeking explanations. He was a very serious and dedicated student, thirsty for knowledge, and wanting to get the most benefit from his year in Israel.

In the mid-1950s, many new immigrants arrived from Yemen and Ethiopia, and needed help adjusting to their new life. Mel met a doctor who ran a free weekly medical clinic for those immigrants; Mel asked if he could observe the clinic. The doctor replied that he could observe if he stayed quiet. He told me a funny story. He was present when these patients were shown a short, American-made, educational film, showing the importance of personal hygiene and the necessity to fight flies. The movie even enlarged a fly to show how dirt and germs were propagated by the feet of the fly. After viewing the film, one man exclaimed:

"No wonder you Americans have such huge problems with flies! Your flies are sooooo big!" and the man illustrated his words with a large gesture of both arms.

Towards the end of the academic year, Mel told his professors that he was interested in becoming a social anthropologist.

"In that case, you should go to England for your graduate studies, Mel. England is the cradle of social anthropology," they advised him. "Oxford, Cambridge, and London are the best schools."

On June 26, we had known each other for 3 days. Mel said, "I've applied to the Social Anthropology departments at Cambridge, London and Oxford, and hope that I still have a chance to get admitted for this coming academic year. Students usually apply a year before they start their studies." Two weeks later, London and Cambridge wrote back that they "were afraid" it was too late. "We are 'afraid' does not necessarily mean no," I said. Of course it meant no, but I didn't yet know the nuances of the English language.

Only Professor Edward Evan Evans-Pritchard from Oxford (later knighted 'Sir') replied that Mel might have a chance if he managed to become a member of a college first. "I will have to go to Oxford. If I apply in person I may have a better chance," Mel said.

Every time we met, we discussed other topics that were important to us. We realized that we both wanted at least three children. Somewhere I had heard that if two siblings give a presentation or play a skit, they still need one sibling for an audience.

"Life is a series of problems," Mel loved to say.

"Why do we need to have lots of problems in our lives? Can't we have a life without problems?" I asked, fighting his idea.

"Well, problems will come our way. That's life, but we'll just solve them, one at a time. Together we can do anything," Mel replied.

As much as I wanted to be close to Mel, I had made up my mind as a teenager that I would stay a virgin until marriage. Mel understood. On our fifth day, he gave me a paperback titled *Love Without Fear*.

On the eighth day I was ready to say "Yes!" But Mel waited.

On the thirteenth day we met again for a sandwich in the little park.

"OK, let's get married!" he said out of the blue, while munching on his sandwich.

"OK," I replied, without a second of doubt. He did not even ask me to marry him! It had been a *fait accompli* since day two.

"I'll talk to your father tonight."

That afternoon I floated back to work. I had great difficulty containing my happiness and concentrating on my work. How could I possibly tell the director that I was getting married and leaving — exactly six months after I started working there. And... what will Papa say?

That Friday evening July 7, Mel came over for dinner. We sat in my room with Papa.

"I love Eva and I am asking you for her hand in marriage," Mel said confidently.

Papa was the kindest, most understanding man, but in the absence of Maman he felt lost.

"Well, I did not expect things to happen that quickly," he said. "You've only known each other for less than two weeks! You seem to be a very nice young man, Mel, and I understand that you love my daughter, but I know nothing about you. Can you give me three character references from the United States, and the names of three of your professors in Jerusalem?"

"Yes, I will," Mel said.

"And how are you going to support Eva and yourself as a student?"

"I will cash in my $5,000 life insurance policy," Mel replied. "I have to return to the States to ask for a further deferment from the army so that I can study Anthropology in England. While I am there, I am hoping to get a scholarship or a grant. I know several rabbis and I have many Jewish friends who may be able to help."

Papa seemed satisfied with Mel's answers. As difficult as it was for him, he took it with equanimity, and rejoiced for me.

Before he left that evening, Mel jotted down three references: Chet Lieb, professor of philosophy at Yale; Rabbi Gumbiner, the Director of *Hillel* at Yale, and Jo Solomon, the director of the Jewish Community Center in Kansas City, which Mel had attended regularly while in high school. Mel helped Papa write the letters and mailed them the next day. He also gave Papa the name of three professors in Jerusalem. With that information at hand, Papa called Maman immediately.

"Charlotte, I am so glad you are in Israel! I need your help! Eva met a young American just two weeks ago. His name is Melvin Lee Perlman. He is very nice, and they seem very much in love. They want to get married! Oh, how I wish you were here! He just came back from Israel where he spent this past year at the Hebrew University. He gave me three references. Go immediately to Jerusalem and see if you can meet those professors to find out what they think of this young man!"

"OK, I'll go next week. *La maison ne brûle pas!* (The house isn't burning!) Maman replied calmly.

"Yes it is!" Papa exclaimed "It is of the utmost importance, and it is urgent!"

"Fine," she gave in.

"You can also go see Tina Waxman when you are in Jerusalem. She knows this young man and suggested he meet Eva."

Maman shared the news with Grosspapa. He advised her to go see Dr. Roetler, the director of a nearby retirement home and a good customer and friend of the family. He would most certainly be able to help locate these people. Maman had met him a number of times at her parents' grocery store. When she told him her story and Mel's name, Dr. Roetler exclaimed, "I know him! Mazel Tov! Very nice young man! He came to my clinic in the immigrants' camp."

Dr. Roetler gave Maman the name and address of a Mr. Katz who worked in a jewelry store in Jerusalem. He would certainly be able to help her locate the three professors as he was involved with *Hillel* and the student union on campus, and especially with foreign students. The next day Maman went to Jerusalem and found Mr. Katz in his jewelry store.

"What is this young man's name?" he asked while pulling out a heavy register from under the counter.

"Melvin Lee Perlman," Maman responded. He flipped through the pages and searched for his name.

"Mel Perlman!" he finally exclaimed. "Mazel Tov! I know him! He is a fine young man!"

Mr. Katz then accompanied Maman to the home of the first of the three professors and gave her directions to the second one. The third one was out of town. Both professors reacted the same way.

"Mazel Tov! Mel Perlman is a very nice young man, indeed! A good student with an inquisitive mind and a serious disposition for learning. Your daughter is a lucky young lady!"

The next day, Papa received Maman's telegram: *Good references. Coming home on the 19th* (of July). The reference letters from the U.S. arrived fairly quickly, outlining Mel's many great qualities and some of his minor short-comings. Mel was said to be a serious, caring and hardworking young man, and if he was serious about marriage, he could be trusted for the depth of his commitment.

On July 11, I told Madame Hanoune that I was not going to come back to work after August, during which time the day nursery would be closed for the summer vacation. She was not pleased but, hopefully she would have time to find a replacement for me. They would now be looking for a middle-aged woman, with diplomas from my school, unattached and unlikely to get married. (Actually poor Madame Hanoune, already in her seventies, had to work for another 5 years before she retired).

On Tuesday July 19, Maman landed in Paris at 9 a.m. That same evening, Mel came for dinner and met her. I feared Maman's reaction because she could be quite judgmental and critical of me. But things went well. I was twenty-four years old, after all. I wanted to get married and she understood there wasn't much she could do. Besides, I did not exactly have a line of suitors at my door, vying for my affections, and Mel was Jewish, and a very likeable young man.

"How was your trip, Maman?" I asked.

"It was wonderful. I met Tina. What a wonderful lady! When I told her you were planning to marry Mel, she got concerned because you told her that you were looking to marry a man eight years older than you. Now she feels responsible, especially if things were not going to work out."

"Mel is definitely more mature than I am," I said.

The very next morning after Maman's return, Mel and I went to the City Hall of the 17th *arrondissement*. For ten days, our names had to be posted outside the City Hall, so that anyone who might have an objection to our marriage could intervene. Mel and I wanted to get married quickly so I could sail to the U.S. with him. If I was married to an American, perhaps I might get a visa more quickly. Time was of the essence.

What a miracle that Papa and Maman already had tickets to board a ship for the United States since the preceding September, a gift to themselves to celebrate their 25th wedding anniversary. It seemed preordained. So it made sense to celebrate our religious wedding in Kansas City, where Mel's mother Bertha and her family lived. This way Mel's numerous relatives and friends could also attend our wedding.

Mel was on a very tight budget. He had barely enough money to pay his rent and return to the United States, so while I was at work, Maman took Mel shopping. She bought a cubic zirconia engagement ring and two wedding bands. She also bought him a navy blue suit, black leather shoes, and pajamas because I had told her that he told me he usually slept in the nude or in an old t-shirt.

When I got back from work that evening, I found Maman and Mel in the living room, surrounded by boxes.

"This is for you, Eva," Maman said, handing me a box.

Nicely wrapped in paper was a beautiful white, flowing, sheer nightgown. I was very touched that she thought of that. Later that night, Mel went back to his room with two big bags of new clothes.

When Mel came over the next day, he took me to my room and said with a warm smile, "Eva, I have a present for you."

Then he handed me a little box. In it was the ring. I was deeply moved, and absolutely delighted.

July 27 was my last day at the Crèche. I was glad to leave it.

Mel did not understand or speak much French and I was concerned that he might not understand the mayor when asked the important question.

I prompted him in French, "When the mayor asks you, 'Mr. Perlman, will you take Miss Gutmann for your lawfully wedded wife?' All you have to say is 'Oui,'" I kept reminding Mel. The night before the wedding, I rehearsed the words of the wedding ceremony with him.

Monday, July 30, 1956, was the day of our civil wedding. That morning Maman walked into my room.

"Eva, I wish you much happiness, but let me give you a word of advice. Do not get pregnant the first year! A young husband in love with his wife does not want to put up with headaches, or 'not tonight, sweetheart' nor does he want to see his lovely wife get fat."

Then she added, "You are older than your husband, so you must take good care of yourself. When a man turns forty, if his wife doesn't look good, he might look elsewhere."

I was shocked, but did not say a word. Mel was only nine months younger than me!

It was a beautiful warm summer day and I was the happiest of brides, feeling elegant in my white lacy blouse, the one I had bought after passing the driver's test, and attractive navy blue suit with white couture buttons. Papa drove Maman, my brothers and me to City Hall. A few of our friends and relatives, such as Papa's cousin Hans and his wife Vittorina from Milan, Mr. and Mrs. Plasseraud and Madame Ferlet were waiting for us. Mel was among them, looking handsome in his brand-new suit, a white carnation in his lapel and his precious camera in his left hand. I would have loved to fly into his arms. Marie-Claire, my wonderful best friend could not come; she was a student in Göttingen, Germany, at the time. We filed into a beautiful room. I took a seat on Mel's right in front of the mayor and Maman sat on his left. After a two-minute speech the mayor asked the crucial question.

"Mr. Perlman, will you take Miss Gutmann as your lawfully wedded wife?"

Even though we had practiced, Mel had a blank look on his face and did not react. He seemed totally unaware of the seriousness of the moment. For a few seconds the silence was unbearable. Although Maman and I had not rehearsed this, we both poked him in the ribs with our elbows at the same time. Startled, he exclaimed "Oui" with a jolt. The mayor turned to me and asked me the same question.

"Oui!" I said and he declared us husband and wife.

Wedding Day

We were married! No hesitation, no jitters, no doubts.

Papa and Maman had a lovely luncheon catered to Avenue Niel. I was forever looking at my finger. I couldn't believe that *I was a married woman!* The generous gift from Papa and Maman was a one-week honeymoon in Gerardmer in the Vosges mountains in eastern France after Mel returned from England.

On the evening of our civil wedding we brought Mel to the airport and the rest of us, including some of our wedding guests, went to see Charlie Chaplin's *Gold Rush* at the movie theater near our apartment.

While Mel was gone, I reflected on our whirlwind romance. It reminded me of the French movie *Happenstance* where thirty small events had to happen for this couple to find each other at the end. I would not have met my husband …

If I had known for sure what path in life I wanted to take when I graduated from high school, then Maman would not have thought of sending me to Israel;

If I had been happy in my substitute family in Tel Aviv, I wouldn't have gone so often to see Hilde;

If Hilde had not welcomed me with open arms any time I dropped in, I may never have met Tina...

I had no control over these events. Yet they shaped my life. Thank goodness Mel came to Paris first. Otherwise, he might have married that Italian girl!

When I received our wedding picture album, I was struck by how handsome Mel looked. I could not believe that I had such a good looking husband, and so wonderful inside and out. My true prince had arrived. I would go to the ends of the earth with him.

With our marriage certificate I went to the American Embassy to apply for a visa to the U.S.

A certificate from the Paris WIZO arrived in the mail. Three trees had been planted in Israel in honor of our marriage. We were very moved and grateful. To transform Israel's desert, lots of trees needed to be planted and every time a family celebrated a birth, marriage, an anniversary or any other special event, friends and relatives bought one or more trees. It was a way of showing that they cared, and at the same time it helped to develop Israel. Over the last 100 years the Jewish National Fund, which was established in 1901, has planted over 250 million trees in Israel.

Five days later, on August 4, 1956, Mel returned from Oxford. I waited anxiously for the train to arrive. As soon as he saw me, he exclaimed, "Eva, I have good news. I am now an official student of the Institute of Social Anthropology at Oxford!"

"Congratulations!" I replied.

We hugged and kissed as if we had been separated for ages! On the bus ride back to my parents' apartment, I stayed very close to him. It felt so good to have him back! At home Maman served dinner. Mel shared with us how he got admitted to Oxford.

"I visited a good thirty colleges and the response was always the same. 'Sorry, sir. The college is full for the coming academic year.' I was growing desperate. On the last day before I had to return to Paris, I decided to try my last college. On campus a carpenter was working by the back gate. 'What college is this?' I asked the man. 'Trinity College, sir,' he replied. The front door was open, so I went inside. I heard laughter coming from upstairs, so I climbed the stairs to the second floor and stuck my head through a door that was slightly ajar. I saw a man sitting at tea with several women. When he noticed me, he jumped up, rushed over to me and pushed me back into the hallway, closing the door behind him. 'May I help you?' he asked. 'I apologize for my intrusion, sir, but I am seeking admission to Trinity for this coming academic year.' 'Come see me at my office tomorrow morning at 9 a.m. and we'll talk. I am busy now,' the man replied. 'Ask to see Mr. Norrington. I am the President of Trinity College.' This was my first glimpse of hope. At 9 a.m. sharp the next day, I was in the President's office. 'First of all,' he started, 'it is too late to apply for residence in the college, but should you be lucky enough to find accommodation in town, would you be able to support yourself financially?' 'Yes,' I replied confidently. 'I just got married and my wife and I have to look for an apartment. I am on my way back to the United States. I know several people there who may give me a scholarship or a grant.' After two more questions which I answered satisfactorily, he finally said 'Alright, Mr. Perlman, I am happy to admit you to Trinity College.'"

Mel and I were overjoyed. Papa seemed relieved.

On August 6, we celebrated my parents' 25th wedding anniversary with a trip on a *bateau-mouche*, a tourist boat that goes up and down the Seine River, filled with dining tourists.

On the bateau-mouche

It was a beautiful day. I was in heaven! That night Papa took us to the train station, and we left for our one-week honeymoon in Gerardmer. I had always dreamt of being lulled by the monotonous sound of the wheels on the rails, going with my husband on our honeymoon. Now my dream had come true. Finally we were by ourselves, just the two of us.

The next morning I noticed that Mel was watching me wash his socks in the sink. Half-jokingly and half-seriously, he exclaimed, "Oh, how wonderful! Now that I am married, I have someone to wash my socks for me!"

I thought nothing of it. It was what I expected to do for my husband! How times have changed since then!

We went on a boat ride on the local lake and Mel took pictures of me. "I love photography," he said. "I got this camera for my *Bar Mitzvah*. One day I am going to show you a picture I took in Nazareth. A cobbler was working on a shoe in his workshop. The mood and the light were just perfect. I worried that the man might object or even run after me and take my camera, so I hid in a doorway to set the exposure and the aperture, and I managed to quickly point and shoot." That photograph would earn many ribbons, and even 'best of show' in international salons many years later.

The week went by too fast. After we returned, Papa and Maman surprised us with a gala reception in a beautiful Paris hotel. We were showered with love and good wishes. Mel and I also visited Madame Blumenthal. I was so happy and proud to introduce my new husband to her, and expected her to be happy for me. Instead she said with a shrug of disdain, "Oh! If that's what you were looking for, a handsome guy like him… I did not have one like that to offer you!" Her reaction shocked me. Why wasn't she just happy for me?

Mel wrote a long letter to his mother telling her all about me, and she simply replied, "I knew, son, that you would bring a bride home." I was disappointed by her reaction, showing no surprise or joy.

About a month later, Mel and I sailed to America on the steamship Maasdam. We were on the water for eight days. The Atlantic was rough. So Mel and I sat outside in the fresh, cold air and never got seasick. One day when Mel and I were enjoying our lunch, the sea got so rough that the ship leaned far on its side. Chairs rolled away from the tables and the tablecloths followed with everything on them. On September 14, just before Yom Kippur, we arrived in New York harbor. I had never seen skyscrapers! After eight days on the water it was wonderful to set foot on solid ground. I was excited beyond measure to be in America with my husband!

We arrived in Kansas City and a short, somewhat overweight lady with gray hair and kind eyes, was standing at the train station, waving from a distance. It was Mel's mother Bertha. She was so happy to see her son after an entire year.

"Mom, this is Eva, my wife," Mel said proudly.

Bertha welcomed me warmly. She was very proud of her son! I looked around. Everything was huge and beautiful — the avenues, the cars, the supermarkets, the stores, the homes. The cars in the parking lots looked like a candy dish of blue, red, white, yellow, and green cars. By contrast, in Europe most cars were black. As opposed to the small neighborhood grocery stores, I was blown away by the size of the supermarkets. Three cans of pineapple juice for a dollar! Everything could be bought in volume at a discount. WOW! I only knew of French housewives, doing their shopping multiple times per week for only what they could carry. Here every one had a car!

Mel's high-school teachers who had followed Mel's career with much pride, had a lovely reception for us in one of their homes. His French teacher attempted to speak French with me, but she had such a heavy American accent that I could hardly make out what she was saying. No wonder Mel did not know any French, though he had studied it for two years!

A few days later Mel and I went to the draft board in Kansas City. I stayed in the waiting room, but they called me in.

"Congratulations for marrying one of our boys," one of the officers said to me. "Do you know how to fix a hamburger?"

"I do," I replied with confidence, smiling warmly. I passed the test.

They laughed, then one of them said to Mel, "Sir, you can return to England. You will receive your deferment letter in a few days."

We left, excited. Out on the sidewalk I asked him, "What's a hamburger, Mel?"

He laughed and explained.

"I thought Hamburger was the Jewish last name of someone who lived in Hamburg," I replied.

Next we visited several influential people in Kansas City, Yale and New York — rabbis, former teachers and directors of educational programs, who knew Mel well, hoping to get a scholarship or grant to finance his studies at Oxford. Unfortunately we were unsuccessful and had to cash in his $5,000 life insurance policy.

A few days before the religious wedding Papa and Maman arrived, and met Mel's family.

On September 30, 1956, two months after our civil wedding in Paris, my parents walked me down the aisle of Mel's former synagogue in the white dress Maman had bought me in Paris. My face was hidden behind a veil. Mel wished to have both his parents walk him down the aisle, but they had an angry divorce years earlier, and could not agree. I felt so sad for him. Only Bertha, his mother, walked him to the *chuppah*. The synagogue was packed with people I did not know, friends and family of Mel's, his father Abe, a good looking man in his sixties, with his second wife Marie, a shy and reserved woman. His numerous uncles, aunts and cousins brought many beautiful gifts. It was going to take me years to figure out who was who.

Maman sat in the front row next to Mel's parents. The rabbi knew Mel well because he had gone to Sunday school here. His words moved me to tears. Mel's father hosted the luncheon for his family, Mel's mother hosted the dinner for hers. Everyone thought we got married so quickly because I was pregnant! We completely forgot to hire a photographer; each side of the family thought the other side would provide the photography. All we came away with was Papa's three-minute 8mm movie. In this little movie, everyone was kissing everyone. That was all. We never had any other photographs of our religious wedding.

Two days later, Mel and I flew to Colorado Springs to visit his dad and Marie. Having lived by herself most of her life, she was your typical old maid and had her little idiosyncrasies. She did not go out without white gloves. Before she married Mel's dad, she had dated his younger brother for 18 years and wanted to marry him, but for some reason that never happened. He died and she married Dad when she was already in her 50s. The two welcomed us warmly in their lovely little house. Behind it was an enormous orchard and Dad showed us his fruit trees with great pride. He was a jack-of-all trades. At one point he owned stamp machines. Another time he sold Bibles door-to-door, or travelled with a circus. Dad was always busy fixing things. He had been a contractor as well. Whatever Marie asked him to do, he did right away. They seemed to get along well, without interfering much with each other.

Dad and Marie took us to the top of Pikes Peak, a tall, snow-covered mountain towering over Colorado Springs. We also strolled through the Garden of the Gods, a natural landmark of stunning red rock formations. I was so thrilled to see all those sites with my husband. Despite my strong desire to be affectionate, even in public, I behaved like my mother would have wanted me to behave.

On October 13, we flew to New York to sail back to Europe.

CHAPTER 7

OXFORD: A STUDENT'S WIFE

Exhausted from the long voyage, Mel and I arrived in Southampton and from there we traveled to London. When we finally arrived in Oxford it was freezing cold. We stayed with Mel's friend Dick Kulka while we looked for a place to rent.

The next day Mel and Dick went to Trinity College together and Dick helped Mel find his way around. While they were attending the seminars, they expected me to cook. I had planned to take cooking lessons with Maman once I got engaged, but my engagement had only lasted three weeks, and there was no time! We arrived with just a couple of suitcases, so I went to the store and bought an ironing board, and a cheap frying pan. I also bought a lovely cauliflower. Back at Dick's place, I put it on the table and stared at it for a while. How was I supposed to cook this stranger? Eventually I managed somehow. We did not starve that day, but it was close.

Oxford was a lovely college town. Soon we found a furnished three-story, narrow row house on Woodstock Road for fifty pounds a month. It was located across the street from the local hospital, the Radcliffe Infirmary, and walking distance from the Institute of Social Anthropology, where Mel went for all his classes. There were two small rooms on the ground floor, and a bedroom and bathroom on each of the other two floors. The toilet was outside in a 10 square foot yard. To make ends meet, we rented out the best room in the house, on the top floor, to a student for 25 pounds.

Beginning life together as a married couple in Oxford was tough. We had no central heating, and the bathtub was in the kitchen. When winter came, the kitchen floor was so cold my feet froze. To warm up the kitchen, I opened the door of the gas oven and switched on the gas. The fireplace in the tiny living room burned our legs while our backs froze! That's where Mel had his desk, and we spent most of our time there. An hour or so before bedtime, I put on my winter coat, scarf, and gloves to go upstairs to the bedroom to switch on the small gas heater. I also placed hot water bottles in our bed. It was so cold in the house that, by morning, ice had formed on the inside of our windows and even Mel's ink froze in the inkpot.

Mel was a serious student, and completely dedicated to his studies. He spent all his time at the Institute, but was able to come home for lunch and dinner. Then he studied again at his desk until late every night. Even during meals, we talked about his work or I tested him for a quiz or exam.

To get to know the new students, President Norrington hosted a tea party at Trinity. Mrs. Norrington was particularly welcoming to me, perhaps because I was a foreigner, and few students were married.

"How are you coping with life in Oxford, Mrs. Perlman?" she asked. "Can I be of any assistance to you?"

"Thank you, Mrs. Norrington," I replied. "I *do* have a little problem that you might be able to help me with. I am looking for a special product to thicken soups, sauces and custards. I don't know what it's called and therefore I cannot ask for it in the store or find it on the shelf. In France we call it maizena. It is made from maize."

"You mean *cornflour?*" (in the United States we call it cornstarch).

"That's it. Thank you, Mrs. Norrington." I was very happy; this solved a big problem for me.

Mel and I ate frugally. I bought the cheapest food I could find – brussel sprouts, apples for compote and hot dogs. On the way to the market, I always passed by Marks and Spencers. Displayed in the window were beautiful sweaters, purses and shoes that I could not afford.

My parents started supporting us, but it was barely enough. To supplement our income, I found two jobs cleaning houses. I was desperately waiting for my period. Before we got married, I had gone to see a gynecologist. He told me my uterus was somewhat turned to the side and it would be difficult for us to conceive. He then prescribed some spermicidal cream that he said would be sufficient. We certainly could not afford to have a child, especially after my mother's warning.

As I arrived home from cleaning a house, Mel told me that a policeman came looking for me. "If we catch your wife working without a work permit, we will have to expel both of you from the country," the policeman warned us.

I tried another avenue — perhaps the Radcliffe infirmary across the street could apply for a work permit for me. I applied for a nursing position there. Even though I was a registered nurse in France, here in England I only qualified for a nurse's aide position. The matron who interviewed me seemed ready to hire me, but my honesty got the better of me. I informed her that I thought I was pregnant (our birth control efforts had obviously not worked). When she heard this, she immediately changed her mind and said, "Well, in this case, Mrs. Perlman, I am afraid we cannot employ you at this time. We already have too many nurses with family problems."

That was the end of my attempts to earn some extra income for us.

It was a challenging first year. Mel was always studying and I had hardly anybody to talk to. The house was cold and bare, so I was looking forward to having a baby after having taken care of other people's children. The thought of it brought me joy and inner peace. Mel suggested I learn to type. This was a good idea, it kept me occupied and would serve me for the rest of my life.

The 4-hour French movie *Les Enfants du Paradis* (Children of Paradise), came to Oxford in a little repertory theater. I had heard a lot about it, and since Mel was immersed in his studies, I went to see it by myself. The critics called it the French equivalent of *Gone with the Wind*. It had been filmed in Paris during the Nazi occupation. All movie theaters were closed because of the war, and so the greatest actors of the day were available for shooting. It had become the most beloved and esteemed movie in the history of French cinema. The movie was about four men, renowned French personalities of the 1820s and 1830s — a talented mime, an ambitious actor, a villain who took advantage of people and a snobbish aristocrat, who all fall in love with a beautiful woman, Garance. Each man experiences love in a different way. There is the idealistic and romantic love of Baptiste, the carefree profane love of Frederic, the possessive and jealous love of the Count, the carnal and selfish love of Lacenaire. I had also read that the scriptwriter was Jacques Prévert, a wonderful French poet.

The lights went out. On the screen appeared a bustling Paris Boulevard with its many theaters and cafes. A young woman is accused of stealing a watch. A mime witnesses everything. The woman throws him a rose in gratitude.

Four hours later the lights went back on. My mind had been transported to another epoch. It took me a moment to get back to reality. What a heartbreaking love story! Passion, jealousy, deception, even murder! The writing was wonderful: our hero describes the feeling of sipping a glass of red wine, *"C'est comme le bon Dieu qui vous descend dans la gorge en culotte de velours rouge"* (It is like the good Lord going down your throat in red velvet pants). The last scene is excruciatingly painful.

I came home shaken. Mel was still sitting at his desk. I sat on the couch with a lump in my throat. I could not speak for two hours for fear of breaking into tears. Those love stories spoke to my heart. Even if I had been able to speak, and share my feelings with Mel, he was so immersed in his work that I could not interrupt him. I was to see this movie over 30 times in my life.

Mel wrote all his notes and papers by hand. My parents asked him what he wanted for Chanukah. After speaking with me, he wrote that, if they could combine three Chanukas and three birthdays, he would love to have a typewriter.

When my parents came to visit for the holiday, they presented Mel with his first typewriter, a manual Olivetti Lettera 22.

"Thank you. Thank you. Now I no longer have to write my papers by hand," he said jubilantly. I had never heard him this exuberant. He was usually very calm, cool and collected. "It will save me so much time!" he exclaimed.

We gave them our bedroom, and Mel and I shared the little couch in our tiny living room. Not to fall off, I placed a chair next to the bed. I did not sleep well, but Mel did, and that was most important. I put myself in the background. Anything for Mel to do his work — not only because I loved him, but also because our future depended on him.

When I tried to cook for everyone with my rudimentary skills, Maman took one look at my newly purchased low quality frying pan and said, "Let's go and get you a good pan."

Remembering Maman's warning the morning of my wedding, I was afraid to tell her that I was expecting. Besides, we could hardly afford a child. Over Chanukah dinner I finally dared to say, "Maman, we have some news! We are pregnant."

She was surprised. She had obviously not expected this news so quickly. Papa, on the other hand, gave me the biggest hug.

"I will be happy to be a grandfather soon," he said with a smile.

After Maman had digested the news, she too was happy for us, and rejoiced with Papa over their upcoming first grandchild.

Every week Mel had to write an essay for his tutor. For the longest time, Dr. Pocock found his essays totally unacceptable, and Mel came home dejected and disappointed. By March, Dr. Pocock said, "Hmm, it is not too bad this time." From then on, Mel's papers improved, because he finally understood what British professors required. The undergraduate studies at Yale had not prepared him for the volume and the rigor of the work at Oxford. Finally Mel's hard work was paying off.

Meanwhile, I shopped for my Brussel sprouts and apples, I tried to keep warm, I cooked and cleaned, and my new baby, growing inside me, filled my thoughts and my heart. That was my life.

In the spring of 1957, there was a letter in the mail. Grosspapa Yitzhak had died of diabetes. He was just 72. I was very sad, and decided that, if we had a son, we would name him after Grosspapa.

At the end of the first year, Mel earned a Distinction in his Diploma in Social Anthropology. It was a first step towards a PhD, with the second step being a B.Litt, a Bachelor of Literature. No American student had ever received this distinction before. As a result he was awarded a scholarship for the next academic year. We rejoiced. What a relief!

In Oxford Mel happened to run into the curator of the Pitt Rivers Museum, Thomas Penniman. He asked Mel, "How did you get admitted to Trinity College as an American, and so late?" Mel explained and the curator said, "I don't know how you did it. Even God Almighty would not have been accepted to Trinity at such a late date!" It had been a miracle!

Shortly thereafter Mel and I flew to Paris to be with Papa and Maman for the birth of our first child. Mel tried hard to learn French since we had agreed to raise our baby bilingually. Papa took Mel and my brother Ernest on a short vacation to the Swiss Alps. Raymond was in Israel for two weeks. I stayed in Paris with Maman.

I did not show much at 8 ½ months and looked very young at 25. As Maman and I were leaving our apartment to run some errands, we ran into our concierge.

"How do you feel, madame? When are you expecting?" she asked, looking at my belly.

"I am due next week," I said excitedly.

"Oh la la! I *do* hope you will have an easier time than my daughter! She suffered terribly, with an unusually long labor!"

Maman and I just looked at each other and smiled.

"How thoughtless it is to tell a pregnant woman how difficult labor is going to be," I said to Maman.

The butcher's wife asked me, *"Alors, petite Madame, c'est pour quand, le grand évènement?"* (So, little lady, when are you expecting the big event?)

"I am due next week," I replied. I was wearing a loose raincoat.

"Really? You don't show much at all," she said, surprised.

On August 16, 1957, I woke up around 4 a.m. The bed was wet. "Mel, my water broke!" I rushed into the bathroom to wash my feet in the bidet. Papa drove us to the private clinic, *Les Cigognes* (The Storks), in the Paris suburb of Neuilly-sur-Seine. Nothing was too good for his daughter, and, after all, their first grandchild! I was in easy labor for most of the day. Mel stayed by my side. I wanted to share the miracle of birth with him. Around 8 p.m labor became intense. And at 11:35 p.m., on Friday night, Shabbat, our baby was born.

"It's a girl!" the doctor announced. She weighed six pounds, nine ounces.

"Is she alright?" I asked the doctor immediately.

"Elle a tout ce qu'il faut (She has everything she needs)," the doctor replied. We had a daughter!

Maman and Papa, anxiously waiting downstairs, heard the baby cry and rejoiced.

Since Mel and I wanted to live in Israel eventually, we gave our baby girl two Hebrew names — Ilana, because we loved the name, and Yael in memory of Grosspapa Yitzhak.

Grossmama flew in immediately from Israel, excited to see her first great-grandchild. Now that Grosspapa had passed away, she was more flexible and had left the store in the capable hands of a friend. My grandfather had been very authoritarian, and she lived all her life under his thumb. Now she had much more freedom and looked happier. My eighteen-year old brother Raymond had returned home from his two-week trip. He brought a sterling silver egg cup with jagged edges like a broken egg out of which a chick had just hatched. He had never seen a baby this close, and was in awe. Ilana was just a wonder to him.

I spent several days in bed to avoid phlebitis, while Mel sat for hours next to the baby's crib, just staring at this little breathing wonder we had created. On the 9th day, Ilana and I were allowed to go home. Papa and Maman, Grossmama and my brothers attended Ilana's daily bath in the bathroom sink. She was so cute!!

The 4 generations Oxford 1957

Every day Mel and I proudly took our new daughter out for a walk in the brand new stroller that my parents bought us. When we took our walk, I always dutifully asked Grossmama if she would like to come with us. She always eagerly ran to put on her coat and hat. We were anxious, though, to go out just the three of us, that is, without Grossmama. One day Mel and I came home and found Nini, the maid, alone with the baby. We immediately picked up Ilana, got the bottle, the diaper bag and the baby carriage and quietly left the house. We went to the nearby Parc Monceau, where we enjoyed sitting on a bench, just the three of us, glowing in parental bliss.

By early September, it was time for us to return to Oxford. Mel's second year was about to begin and now he was going to work on his thesis in Social Anthropology to earn his Bachelor of Literature (B.Litt) degree. The British system required another Bachelor of Arts degree, but far more specialized in his chosen field. His study schedule was just as backbreaking as the previous year. Fortunately my little baby girl kept me busy and happy. She slept in a bassinet in our bedroom. Mel had very little time to devote to her. He was always in his books and at his typewriter.

Toward the end of 1957, Mel was in bed with the flu. By noon, I had severe shivers and a high fever. I remembered from nursing school that the onset of pneumonia happens with a single, severe and awesome shiver. I knew right away. The doctor came and walked me to the hospital across the street. Since Mel was also sick in bed, the doctor called the volunteer ladies of the Red Cross to help. They came and picked up Ilana with some clothes, her pram and her bottles. For the next two weeks, while I was in the hospital, the ladies took turns caring for her. What a wonderful feature of the socialized medical system. Their help cost us nothing, except a huge debt of gratitude. I wrote to them every Christmas until the last one of those wonderful ladies passed away some 30 years later.

One day in January 1958, Mel and I needed some time to ourselves, so we planned to spend a day in London, a short train ride away. A friend offered to take care of five-month-old Ilana. I was so happy to have a day to myself with Mel. When we came back that evening, Ilana was crying and her face was so swollen that she could not breathe through her nose or drink from her bottle.

"Your daughter cried all day and she is hot to the touch," our friend reported, very worried.

We took Ilana home and called the doctor immediately. He examined her and said, "I'm sorry to tell you that your daughter is deathly ill. She has to be admitted to the hospital right away." Ilana was diagnosed with osteomyelitis of the upper maxilla, an infection of the jaw bone.

"Your daughter has to stay here. I am going to put her on achromycin, a brand new antibiotic," the doctor informed us. "I hope it works. I don't know what else to do!"

Mel and I were very worried. Ilana's face was so swollen she had trouble breathing. Fortunately, the treatment worked; the fever and the swelling came down pretty quickly, but Ilana was kept in the hospital for another week. Finally we were able to take her home and she was her usual happy self again. Mel had been right when he told me life was a series of problems!

In June 1958, the deadline for getting the thesis bound was nearing. Mel typed and I proofread three days straight. The last night we did not go to bed at all, staying awake by drinking lots of coffee. At 8:30 the next morning, Mel ran to the bookstore in his slippers and with a three-day-old beard to deliver his thesis to the bookbinder. But the pressure was not over yet. A few weeks later he had to defend his thesis in front of several professors and he passed the oral exam with flying colors and got his B.Litt.

in Social Anthropology. I was so proud of him. He deserved his success. Mel was happy, but he never bragged. He was just delighted that he could finally relax after living under so much pressure for so long.

Mel, Eva and Ilana 1958

"Now I need to get a job or a grant, so I can do research to write my doctoral thesis," Mel said. "This thesis will be based on field research in a native tribe somewhere. I heard about the Shuwa Arabs of Nigeria at the Institute, and I may be able to get a grant to study their customs. It would mean moving to Nigeria and learning Arabic to be able to speak with the Shuwa Arabs."

"I will follow you wherever you go, Mel. As long as I am with you, I am happy," I said.

We both began to learn Arabic. It was much more difficult than Hebrew. We made a great effort to speak English on Tuesdays, French on Wednesdays, Arabic on Fridays and Hebrew on Saturdays but in the end this did not work, and Mel didn't get the grant either.

Mel's studies were completed for now at Oxford, so we returned to Paris to live with my parents until Mel found a research project somewhere.

Ernest had passed his exams brilliantly and was invited to join the Plasseraud patent law firm as a chemical engineer. Like many fathers who pray that one of their children will follow in their footsteps, Papa was extremely proud that Ernest came to work with him. Raymond had become a pediatrician and opened his own practice.

To help pay expenses, Mel took on a paid research assignment at the *Musée de l'Homme* in Paris. He had to prepare a bibliography of African women. I got a job as a nurse in the maternity department at the *Hôpital Américain* de Neuilly just outside of Paris, near where Ilana was born.

Unfortunately, at daycare, Ilana cried for five days straight and refused to eat. Just as I started to really love my job, I had to resign to be a full-time, stay-at-home mom. I was really disappointed, but my daughter was my priority. Papa and Maman were very happy to live for a while under one roof with their first grandchild.

One day in the late fall, Mel's mentor, Dr. John Beattie, told him that he had heard of a research position at the Institute of Social Anthropology in Kampala, Uganda. Mel applied immediately, highly recommended by his professors.

In January 1959, Mel went back to Oxford for an interview before a committee that would pick the right candidate for the Uganda research position. In March 1959, after eight months at my parents', Mel finally received a letter with the answer we had been waiting for:

...First you will do in-depth fieldwork in Toro district in the western part of Uganda, at the foot of the Mountains of the Moon (Ruwenzori Mountains). After that you will spend a few additional months doing comparative research in other parts of the country. You will work under the supervision of the Director of the Institute, Professor Southall, with whom you will map out the details of the research once you get there.

"Eva, we are going to Africa for two and a half years!" he joyfully exclaimed. He would be researching marriage and family life in Uganda as a Junior Research Fellow at the East African Institute of Social Research (EAISR) at Makerere University College in Kampala, Uganda, in the Buganda district.

During dinner that evening we shared the news with Papa and Maman.

Over the next three weeks we prepared for our trip. Uganda was still a British Protectorate. So we felt we would be safe there. Two weeks before we were to leave, we started taking quinine to prevent malaria. We looked forward to this great adventure. Mel was my rock. As long as we were together, I knew that we would weather anything.

CHAPTER 8

UGANDA:
AN ANTHROPOLOGIST'S WIFE

On April 5, 1959, Papa and Maman drove us to the Paris train station Gare de Lyon where we boarded the night train to Genoa, Italy. Mel placed our three suitcases together with all the other luggage at the end of our passenger car. Then he pulled down the bunk beds and we lay down, so we would arrive in Genoa well rested for the long sea voyage. Upon arrival, we looked for our luggage, but it was nowhere in sight. Anxious and worried, Mel stopped a railway employee. "Where is our luggage?"

"Your suitcases probably stayed on the platform in Modane!" said the man. "You were supposed to get off the train and pass customs at the Italian border."

"Oh my God! We slept through it all!" Mel said frantically. "Modane is 162 miles back and our ship to Mombasa is leaving tomorrow morning!"

Mel made multiple phone calls. The next morning the suitcases arrived, just in time to make it to the ship. Problems never cease!

On April 7, the three of us sailed on a multi-story cruise ship over the Mediterranean Sea through the Suez Canal, the Red Sea, the Gulf of Aden and along Africa's eastern coast to the port of Mombasa in southeast Kenya. We passed by the area where the Israelites had once crossed the Red Sea. It was impressive. The sea was calm. Ilana was twenty months old, cute and always happy. Everyone on the ship noticed her with her beautiful alabaster complexion and a mass of blonde curls. She wandered everywhere and became our icebreaker, introducing us to three couples — American, Anglo-French and Belgian. The Belgian couple was returning to the Congo from their vacation. They had lived there for eight years. Their 10 year-old daughter loved to take care of Ilana. When they heard that we were going to the "bush," they gave us some helpful advice, which was indeed valuable even though Mel had read many ethnology books by various researchers.

"Be sure to cook your meat well," the woman said. "Many times the meat is infested with tapeworm and other parasites that cause havoc in your intestines. A pressure cooker is essential."

"If locals stop by to sell you eggs, make sure you test them in cold water before you buy them," her husband added. "Fresh eggs fall to the bottom, but old eggs float on top."

"Always bargain before you buy anything. For white people prices are inflated," another passenger chimed in. "And by the way, for the Africans all white people are called Europeans."

We were also advised never to stop on a road if we caused an accident or else the villagers would attack us.

"In the bush there aren't any hotels or motels. There are only rest houses, simple cement shelters with beds and a latrine close by. The British government built them for their officials. They don't have running water either," someone else added. I was told to read *Return to Laughter* by Elenore Smith Bowen, which I found in the ship's library. It is a fascinating lay account by the wife of an anthropologist of her everyday life among the natives of an African tribal village.

On the ship, Mel did not go anywhere without his beloved Rolleiflex camera, which he had bought with the money he earned at the *Musée de l'Homme*. He used his old camera for slides, always prepared to capture both precious personal and anthropological moments.

After seven days at sea, the ship arrived in Mombasa, Kenya, East Africa's most important port. An Indian fellow, sent by the East African Institute of Social Research (EAISR), welcomed us and helped us with our luggage. He took us to the best hotel. The next day he made sure we got on the train to Kampala. Much to our surprise the train was brand new, modern and clean. Our compartment had all the latest comforts — a sink, a fan, towels, soap and drinking water. As the train rushed down the tracks, we watched the lush green landscapes with marvelous trees and huts made of dirt, bamboo and wood.

Two days later, we arrived in Kampala where we were greeted by a warm, tropical breeze.

"You must be the Perlmans," an African man said with a smile as we got off the train.

"Welcome to Kampala. The Institute sent me to pick you up and take you to your apartment at Makerere."

We followed him to the car. Many buildings were white and no more than three or four stories high. The streets were wide, paved, and lined with Indian souvenir shops. Kampala is twenty-five miles from Lake Victoria and built on seven hills. Makerere, the Kampala University campus, is built on one of them.

After a short drive up the hill, the driver stopped in front of a small, one-story apartment building that was situated in the midst of luscious green lawns and magnificent tall trees. The atmosphere was peaceful and serene. The driver unloaded our three suitcases. We were looking forward to a good night's rest in a real bed. Ilana had been such a good traveler, a true camper!

Mel met with Professor Aidan Southall to map out his research assignment. He would begin fieldwork in Toro District, some 25 miles east of Fort Portal in western Uganda at the foot of the Ruwenzori Mountains. His focus would be on marriage and family life. Many native African men and women were leaving the rural areas, hoping to find work in Kampala, and he would be studying the effect the big city had on rural customs. The Uganda government would support the research. British district officers were anxious to get information on labor migration.

Professor Southall invited us to lunch. He was an academic-looking man in his late thirties, with bushy eyebrows and a kind smile, dressed in khaki shorts and a white shirt. "Welcome to Uganda," he said with a strong British accent and smiling eyes. "Just call me Aidan."

Even though he was very nice, I felt slightly uncomfortable in his presence. After all, a lot was at stake and I was hoping that Mel's work would measure up to his expectations. His British manners reminded me of Mel's professors at Oxford. I was still shy and easily intimidated.

The Southalls had two children, a twelve-year old son who was at school in England, and a two-year old daughter. His older-looking wife seemed a bit cold at first, but once she warmed up, she was charming.

During lunch the two men continued to discuss Mel's research assignment.

"I suggest that you settle in Mwenge County. It is one of the two most important, populous and traditional counties in Toro district," Aidan began. "Many Toro kings come from there and relatively few foreigners have lived there so far. Toro is one of the few districts in Uganda that anthropologists have not researched yet. Rutoro, the language of the Toro people, the Batoro, is relatively easy to learn. The first few months I suggest you settle in the Toro village Butiiti and learn Rutoro, meet the locals and get familiar with their customs. It will help you gather information so you can formulate a more specific research objective."

"Are we going to stay in a government rest house?" Mel asked.

"That's not a good idea," Aidan replied, "because these rest houses were built for the British government officials who travel through the area. The natives don't trust them. They fear they come to take their land away. You must disassociate yourself from them. Just borrow a tent from the Institute. I am going to write you a letter of introduction for the British district commissioner of Toro. His office is in Fort Portal, the biggest town in Toro. It is past Butiiti. The King of Toro also resides there. It will help you get the permit you need to be allowed to carry out the research for the Institute," Aidan continued. "I also suggest that you hire an interpreter for the first two months. I know a young, well-educated African from Buganda who speaks very good English and understands Rutoro. He will be of great help to you. I will make sure that he gets in touch with you. You can also borrow a van from the Institute so you can buy whatever you need to take with you to the bush. And one more thing. Every two or three months all the researchers from all over East Africa gather in Kampala to attend a conference. Each one reads his research paper and we all critique one another, brainstorm and exchange ideas. You are expected to attend and give a paper on your research."

We thanked Aidan and his wife for lunch and all their advice and made our way to the market to get supplies — canned tuna, toilet paper, toothpaste, soap and other necessities and most importantly, a pressure cooker.

Back at the apartment, Mel and I had just finished unloading the groceries when someone knocked on the door.

"Hi. I am Jona, your interpreter," a tall, handsome native in khaki pants and a T-shirt, said with a smile. "I will stay with you in the bush for the next two months, introduce you to the locals, help you get settled and teach you Rutoro." Jona would become an invaluable help to us and a dear friend. He was from Buganda, one of the biggest counties of Uganda, also a kingdom, and Kampala is its capital.

Next we needed a car. The Institute lent us some money, which we would reimburse with Mel's first paycheck. Mel looked through the local paper and saw an ad for a dark blue, second-hand Peugeot station wagon. He went to buy it immediately. Our first car! The mechanic recommended that we buy a few parts just in case we might get stuck in the bush. Mel bought several, but to be honest, he had no idea what the parts were for. After polishing the Peugeot for several hours it looked almost new.

On the tenth day, we were ready to set out on the 190-mile trip to Fort Portal in Toro County. It was still early in the morning. While I placed Ilana securely in the back, Mel loaded up our shiny station wagon with our three suitcases, an inflatable plastic bathtub for Ilana and the equipment we had borrowed from the Institute — a tent, some tin pots and pans, a Primus stove, three camp beds and mosquito nets, a pressure lamp, a water filter, our groceries, our vital pressure cooker, Mel's precious Olivetti typewriter and his cameras. Armed with the appropriate letter of introduction for the British District commissioner, we headed down the Kampala-Fort Portal Road toward Butiiti. This was the only road from Kampala to Fort Portal. It was just wide enough for two cars to pass each other in opposite directions. A few miles outside of Kampala the paved road gave way to *murram* (red dirt). April was the month with the heaviest rainfall in the short rainy season that lasted from about March to June. The long rainy season was from August to December. Here and there the rain had gotten trapped in many potholes and Mel had to drive very slowly.

Ilana and I enjoyed looking at the landscape, feeling the tropical breeze in our faces and watching the rolling green hills dotted with homesteads. Each homestead was several hundred feet away from the next and surrounded by a banana plantation. The rectangular mud-and-wattle huts were within shouting distance from one another. Most huts had grass roofs. Only more affluent homeowners could afford tin. Every so often we passed a village with two or three little African shops.

After about ten hours of being bounced and jostled about, we finally arrived in Fort Portal, the capital of Toro district. It was getting dark and Ilana was fast asleep. There we spent the night in a motel.

The next morning Mel drove to the British district commissioner's office and handed him professor Southall's letter. It was an important document as it would hopefully help persuade the local African chiefs to let us stay in the area and more specifically in Butiiti, in Mwenge County.

When Mel came back to the motel he said happily, "I have a letter for the local African chief. His name is Mogabu. In the letter the district commissioner explains why we want to pitch our tent in Butiiti and stay for a while. He also suggested that we pay a visit to the Mukama, the king of Toro here in Fort Portal. He is the most powerful man in the area. The commissioner gave me directions to his palace."

"Really? How do we get in touch with him? Not everyone gets to meet a king just like that," I answered.

"We can just drive to the palace and ask to see him. He was educated in England and he will certainly be interested in meeting someone who wants to do research about his people," Mel said.

Around eleven in the morning we arrived at his residence. Exquisite carpets covered the living room floor. After a short wait we were admitted to see the king. Amidst beautiful African women stood a handsome man, tall and broad-shouldered, dressed in a colorful caftan, a glass of whiskey in his hand.

"Tell me, what is the reason for your visit?" he asked in excellent English.

"I have come to learn about your people and their customs," Mel replied.

"Where are you from?"

"I am from the United States." The king turned to me and asked the same question.

"I am from Paris," I replied.

"I am delighted to hear this," the Mukama continued. "I will be staying in the French capital myself for ten days sometime in August or September."

"In that case I will give you the phone number of my parents-in-law," offered Mel. Surely they would love to invite you for a cup of tea." It was a fascinating visit. How often do you get the chance to meet a real king in your lifetime?

We drove back to Butiiti. The district commissioner had also told Mel about two Canadian priests called the "White Fathers" who lived close by, in a mission. They could be a valuable source of information as they knew the Batoro well, having lived there for years, and could also help in an emergency.

Jona, our interpreter, was already waiting at the bus stop.

"We need to see your county chief," Jona said to a local African. The man nodded and rushed off while we waited patiently in our car by the roadside. About thirty minutes later, the county chief showed up. Mel handed him the letter. After he finished reading, the chief suggested that we go to Kaihura to see the local chief there. It was late, so we spent the night in a rest house.

The next day we drove to Kaihura, three miles up the road toward Fort Portal to ask the local parish chief Mogabu where we could pitch our tent. Kaihura consisted of not much more than a bus stop, a community clubhouse and a little African shop where the locals could buy a few necessities like tea, sugar, salt, cigarettes, tobacco, matches, some commercial drugs like aspirin, candy, canned goods and some fabrics. Next door was an African medical clinic. Once again Jona asked the locals where we could find their chief. Word got around quickly that the Europeans were in town looking for the chief of Kaihura, and before long Mogabu showed up, casually dressed in khaki shorts and a western suit jacket. He was short and had little hair. Unlike other men, women and children who walked barefoot, he wore sandals made from a car tire. Mogabu did not speak any English and we were grateful to have our interpreter with us.

"The chief has no objections to you staying in the area," Jona translated, "but first he wants you to talk to the other local chiefs."

Two or three villages made up a small political unit and were governed by a chief. Mogabu called a council meeting in the nearby "clubhouse," a plain mud and wattle structure with openings for windows and a dirt floor. While I waited with Ilana in the car, Mel and Jona attended the meeting. In addition to the Toro chiefs, local people also attended.

I was somewhat anxious, because we had already learned that most locals were suspicious of Europeans. They only knew two kinds of white people, the White Fathers in their mission, who were actively trying to convert the Toro natives to Catholicism, and the British government representatives. The natives feared that the British would take their land. We needed to explain to them that we were neither priests nor government officials.

After some time Mel and Jona walked out of the clubhouse with a smile.

"Eva, we got permission to stay!" Mel said right away. "The chiefs and the people welcomed us in their community. At first they thought I was a detective who wanted to deprive them of their land. One person wanted to know how I was planning to deal with the general suspicion. Another asked whether or not I had ever made a similar study of other tribes in the area. The chiefs are fairly well-educated. Once they understood that I came as a friend to learn their language and customs, so that I could write a book about them, they became friendly. The chiefs were proud to hear that someone was interested in their customs and history. One of the chiefs wanted to know if we would eat with them at the same table. Among the Toro, only friends eat together. I told them that we would feel honored and I wanted to show them we were working hard to learn their language. I recited the Rutoro proverb we learned. The chiefs laughed and taught me a new one."

Mogabu, Jona and Mel walked across the Kampala-Fort Portal road and Mogabu said to Jona that we could pitch our tent right here by the main dirt road on crown land (i.e. British land) that belonged to all the people. This way we did not have to pay rent to any land owner. He said about fifty families lived nearby.

"I don't think we will stay here for more than two months," Mel said. "After the first conference in Kampala, I want to move further into the village, where we will probably have to build a little house, but for the time being this location seems to meet all our needs. It is close to the clubhouse, where the council meetings are held. It is on the main Kampala-Fort Portal road. So hopefully many natives will stop by to go either to the medical dispensary, the little grocery store, the council house, or the bus stop. We will be in the middle of everything to establish a good rapport with the locals, which is essential to obtaining reliable data, and lastly — a well is nearby," Mel explained to me. The dispensary was especially important for us since we had a 21-month-old child with us.

Not having any experience living in the bush, we depended completely on our interpreter Jona. We immediately set up our large, khaki green tent with a pitched roof. Mel placed the canvas camp beds with their two-inch mattresses along the sides and hung up the brand new mosquito nets while Jona set up two tables and camping chairs. Fortunately there were few mosquitos. I placed the cooking equipment, the water filter and the kerosene lamp on one table and Mel's precious Olivetti on the other. The three suitcases fit under the camp beds. There was just enough room left for the cans and other food we had brought with us. Mel's papers and books we left in the boxes.

Mogabu suggested we needed three things right away: water, a latrine and kerosene for our primus stove and pressure lamp. Soon his fifteen-year old son Arali was our porter. The boy returned from the well, carrying water in an old kerosene container on his head. Jona explained to me that the water needed to be filtered and boiled to be safe to drink and that I would have to take out the filter and scrub it every two weeks as it would get covered in green slime. With the help of Jona, Mel hired a few locals to dig a latrine, a hole in the ground, surrounded by sticks covered with leaves for privacy. We bought kerosene in Butiiti, the neighboring village, three miles away.

We were just about done setting up when curious locals started showing up. Some were on their way to the little shop. Others came to catch the bus. Rumors were flying, "There are Europeans in a tent on the roadside by the bus stop." Keeping a safe distance, they looked at us with curious eyes. Ilana, with her curly blond hair, was a subject of awe and wonderment. Children came in droves and stared at her without moving. We were the first white family they had ever seen, let alone staying among them. Those who had not attended the clubhouse meeting still suspected that we were government officials in disguise or some sort of spies.

Among the locals who stopped by was a tall Toro woman wrapped in a colorful cloth wearing a kerchief around her head. In her hands she held a tin bowl with two dozen eggs.

"She wants to know if you would like to buy her eggs," Jona translated.

"Fresh eggs fall to the bottom, old eggs float," I remembered.

"Tell her to give me the eggs," I said to Jona.

She handed me the eggs. I quickly filled a bowl with cold water and carefully placed the first egg inside. Sure enough it floated. Then I tested the next egg and it floated on the water as well.

"Jona, please tell her that I am not buying those eggs. They are too old," I said.

The woman took her eggs back and left. Word got around quickly that the European would test the eggs. No one ever brought me an old egg again. News about us travelled in the area with the speed of light.

Another woman offered us a pint of fresh cow's milk. I bought what we could eat or drink within a day, as we had no electricity or refrigeration. She was only too happy to make some money rather than give the milk to her own children. The milk was so rich I had to scrape off the cream before we could drink it.

The next morning, when Mel opened the flap of our tent, there was a lot of activity. The locals had set up a little market by the bus stop across the street. Vendors were sitting cross-legged on an old cloth they had spread over the dirt. Some displayed neatly arranged dried tobacco leaves. Others were selling native herbal medicines, coffee beans, spearheads, bananas, papaya, bead jewelry and witchcraft paraphernalia. Mel, Ilana and I crossed the road and looked at everything. Everybody stared at us. Aside from the bananas and the papaya, there was nothing we needed. In a grassy area one of the vendors had just slaughtered a cow. We watched a native buy parts of the animal. The vendor wrapped the chosen parts neatly in a banana leaf that he had passed over the fire. The meat looked good, so I bought some too. Wanting a piece without fat or bones, I pointed to my buttock. The vendor passed another banana leaf over the fire to make it soft like fabric; then he wrapped up the piece of the cow's rear end in it and tightened the little package with string. I was impressed by how they made use of everything.

Back in the tent I cut the meat into small pieces and cooked it thoroughly in our pressure cooker. Ilana was old enough to eat whatever we ate. She had plenty of sunshine and fresh air. Soon we were all tanned, as we spent all day outside.

When Jona arrived the following morning he suggested that we hire someone to help with household chores, make fire so we had warm water, make our beds, sweep the tent and wash our clothes. Jona advised us to hire Akiki, a tall and slender African in his late thirties with a nice smile but hardly any teeth, unlike most Africans here who had beautiful teeth. He came barefoot, in khaki shorts and a t-shirt. Unfortunately, we could only communicate with him through our interpreter.

"Come back tomorrow morning early," Jona said, "so you can make a fire and warm up the water so the Europeans can wash themselves, and the baby can have a bath."

That evening, around 7:30 p.m., the four of us had our first meal in the tent. It tasted pretty good. While Jona put up the mosquito nets, I put Ilana to bed. Mel lit our kerosene lamp and listened to the Kampala news on the little radio he purchased. By 10 p.m. Mel and I were exhausted and lay down on our narrow camp beds, under our mosquito nets. Jona stayed with a resident nearby.

The next day when Mel opened our tent, Akiki had already started the fire.

It was not easy adjusting to life in the bush and a much slower pace. When I asked Jona to ask the new 'houseboy' (as the locals refer to that job and to themselves) to wash our clothes, Akiki said, "The Batoro do not wash their clothes. They just wear them until they fall apart. They don't have enough water!"

Locals stopped by with chickens. They were all very skinny. Akiki looked for the fattest among them.

"Jona, please tell Akiki that I would like him to build a chicken coop so we can buy several chickens and fatten them up with millet," I said. Millet was one of the local main staples.

With Ilana and chicken

A month had gone by and we were feeling more settled and comfortable in our new life. On May 18, I turned twenty-seven.

"Happy birthday, honey! I am so glad you and Ilana are here with me; not every woman would put up with these living conditions," Mel said. To which I replied "I would never have wanted to stay in Paris with Ilana, while you spent two and a half years in Africa. I would follow you to the end of the earth and so far it's been an adventure that I would not miss."

It had never even occurred to me to question how primitive our living conditions were going to be, or to worry about bringing a small child to the depth of the African bush. I just knew this is what Mel needed to do for his PhD. Naturally, dealing with the basic necessities of life was challenging — this was not my parents' Paris apartment! But I was happy to be a wife and mother. Having been trained as a pediatric nurse gave me some confidence that we could handle whatever came our way.

Every Mutoro had a regular name and an *empako,* or nickname. They chose their *empako* from the seven available possibilities. They were *Adyeri, Amoti, Akiki, Arali, Apuli, Abuoli* and *Bala.* Our neighbors had heard me call Mel *motek* (Hebrew for *sweetie*), so they gave him the nickname *Amoti.* I became *Adyeri* and Ilana *Akiki,* which I chose because it sounded young. Whenever we met someone for the first time, the proper way to greet that person was to ask, *"Empako yawe?"* (What's your nickname?) Then we called each other by our *empakos.*

Jona was only going to be around for another month, so we had to learn the language as quickly as possible. Since we both already spoke several languages, the Rutoro grammar was not difficult to learn. It consisted of mostly prefixes and suffixes. For example, Toro was the county, a Mutoro was a person from Toro, Batoro was the plural of Mutoro, and Rutoro was the language.

Jona taught us a well-known proverb. *"Mpora mpora ekahikia omu-niongorozi ha iziba"* ("Little by little the worm gets to the well"). In other words, perseverance pays off. When we said it to the locals, they laughed. This showed we were sincerely interested in them. Eventually most of them accepted us in their midst and knew that we were not a threat.

Mogabu, the African parish chief, stopped by every so often to see how we were doing. He was pleasant and amiable and always smiled when he saw us, which made us feel welcome. African women with large wraps over long, flowery, colorful dresses with short puffy sleeves, soon became a normal sight. In one hand they held their wrap, with the other they held a basket on their heads.

"Let me introduce you," Mogabu suggested. "They are on their way to the clubhouse where they meet once a month to make pots and jewelry."

Together we walked to the clubhouse. Inside, several women were sitting on the dirt floor, rolling a sticky dough-like material into long, smooth coils. Others were stringing tiny colorful beads into necklaces or covering gourds with beads. "What is this?" I asked Mogabu, pointing to the coils. One of the African women told him that I should stop by her hut the next day and she would show me. I nodded.

She lived a half mile away in a simple square structure of mud and wattle with a thick grass roof. She gestured for me to come in. I had to bend to get inside. Short and tall black pots were displayed on the floor, like those that I had seen at the market and the bus stop. They were beautiful and she tried to explain what they were made of, but I did not understand, so she gestured to follow her. After a while we came to a river. She went up to her calves into the water, put her hand in the water and picked up a handful of mud from the bottom. With gestures she explained to me that this was the material she used to make the coils that would become a pot. I finally understood that it was clay.

Back at her hut, she sat down on the floor, took some of the clay she had brought back and shaped it into a flat bottom piece. Then she rolled another piece of clay into a long coil and placed it on top of the bottom, and kept curling it around in circular motion. Soon it looked like a clay pot. With a small stone she smoothed out the ridges between the coils inside and outside. Then she pointed to the fire in front of her house, and to another polished pot inside. I understood that the pot she had just made before my eyes had to be fired and polished before it could be used.

"By the way," Jona said, "the next time you go to the local market, buy some raw, green coffee beans. It is a Toro custom to offer them to visitors. They are pretty hard on your teeth. When you are a guest, be careful. It is very impolite to refuse them. If you don't want to damage your teeth, the only thing you can say that does not offend the locals is that the beans give you a stomach ache."

We soon started to feel fairly comfortable in our surroundings. Every Friday we went to Butiiti to buy some things we could not get in Kaihura and to mail our letters, Mel's slides and movies. The slides and movies we sent to Kodak to be developed with my parents' return address in Paris. Papa and Maman got to see the movies long before we did. It was a wonderful way to share our life in Africa with them regularly. I was looking forward to buying some fabric as I wanted to sew myself a top and a skirt by hand; I had never sewn anything wearable before. We also bought a manual meat grinder so I could make my favorite meat patties. Back at the tent I showed Akiki how to use it. The meat patties were delicious. For dessert we enjoyed fresh pineapple and oranges.

"I'm going to hang around the African shop for a while. Maybe I can strike up a conversation with the owner or some customers and gain their trust. I can offer them a cigarette or a ride to Fort Portal if needed. I can even pick up their children from school or give them a ride to the medical dispensary. It is very important that we participate in the community life in every way possible and that the locals feel that we are genuinely interested in their customs," Mel explained.

Jona knew that the African men met regularly at the local bar. It was within walking distance from our tent and turned out to be another good place to make contacts, mingle with the local men and hear the gossip of the day.

"I had banana beer today. It tastes awful," Mel reported when he came back. "When you ferment banana juice with millet it becomes beer. I don't care for beer, but to refuse a glass would be impolite and arouse suspicion. Some locals get quite drunk with that beer and then they talk freely."

Every two or three weeks we drove to Fort Portal to buy canned food, tea, sugar and cereal from the Indian grocery stores. There the merchandise was more plentiful than in Butiiti. We also bought a container of kerosene to operate our primus stove and our pressure lamp. The Africans had neither of those; they followed the rhythm of nature, and made wood fires outside their huts for cooking.

One day we went to visit the two missionaries who lived up on the hill. After a twenty-minute drive, a few simple, white-washed buildings with good roofs surrounded by flowers and a vegetable garden appeared in the distance. The mission was beautiful. Mel knocked on the front door. A corpulent and jovial man, with a large cross on his chest, opened and welcomed us with a smile.

"Good morning, Father. I'm Mel Perlman and this is my wife Eva and our daughter Ilana," Mel said. "I am here to study local marriage customs."

"Please come in. I'm Father Chaput. It doesn't happen very often that Caucasian visitors stop by."

Behind him stood another Father in his 60s with short hair and a cap. He was tall and thin. The two of them reminded me of Laurel and Hardy!

"This is Father McCauley. Make yourselves at home," Father Chaput said, as he pointed to comfortable-looking armchairs. "Would you like a cup of good English breakfast tea?"

"That would be lovely," Mel replied.

Mel had lots of questions, especially about the life of the Batoro.

"I have lived here for over fifty years and know the Batoro well," Father Chaput replied. "You are welcome to read through some of the written documents I have gathered over the years. Let me tell you a little about us. We are here to teach Catholicism, to convert and baptize, to marry and to bury. On Sundays we hold mass in our little church. Not too many locals attend. Many convert, but very few are ready to abandon their pagan religion completely. They continue to practice their pagan rituals on the side."

We had so much to talk about that it was soon lunchtime. Father Chaput invited us to stay and enjoy a simple meal and ice cream for dessert. The two Fathers had electricity, hot water, a refrigerator, and even a freezer. Compared to the Africans and the way we lived, this was decadent luxury!

"Please come back anytime you feel like taking a warm bath in a real bathtub," Father Chaput offered. We thanked them profusely.

When we returned to our tent, I saw something move.

"Mel!" I screamed. "A snake!" Mel immediately grabbed a stick and carefully pushed the snake outside and let Akiki dispose of it. I was so relieved that Ilana was not yet in the tent! Thankfully no other dangerous animals lived in the area. They were only in game parks like Queen Elizabeth National Park in southwestern Uganda. Mel added dealing with snakes to his fieldwork skills.

After a month in the tent, Mel wanted to move to a village to observe Toro community life more closely. The rainy season was starting soon and he was anxious to build a hut to protect us from the elements. The next time he saw the parish chief, he shared his thoughts with him.

"I suggest you move to Bwenzi which has three times more inhabitants than Kaihura and is located just one mile north of the main road," Mogabu suggested. "Come to the next council meeting and present your request. If the locals don't object, you can move."

The locals listened attentively to what Mel had to say. They liked him, but some still feared that he had a hidden agenda. "We will make a decision at the next council meeting," Mogabu said.

While we waited to hear back from Mogabu, Mel was preparing in earnest for the first East African Institute of Social Research (EAISR) conference in July in Kampala. Anthropologists from all over Uganda were returning from their fieldwork to attend, share their research and get feedback from the Institute's director and colleagues. All the researchers and their families would stay on campus in apartments. Mel spent the long summer nights at the camping table with the kerosene pressure lamp, organizing his detailed notes of what he had observed and the people he had met. He recorded everything he had done, heard and seen. Then he typed up his first research results on his trusted Olivetti, still unsure of how the fieldwork would progress.

Just before we were ready to leave for the conference, Mogabu stopped by to share some good news with us. "The locals have agreed to allow you to settle in Bwenzi, about one mile from the road, near my homestead," he said with a big smile. "I suggest you build two huts, a big one to live and sleep in, and a smaller one for the kitchen."

Jona, our invaluable interpreter, decided to return to Kampala so he accompanied us. Mel and I had learned enough Rutoro to make small talk with the locals and we were confident we could manage on our own when we settled in Bwenzi.

It was a beautiful summer morning. In addition to Jona, Akiki and our 15-year-old porter, Arali, who doubled as our babysitter, Ilana, Mel and I squeezed into our car. Mel also took his many rolls of precious black and white film to develop and print in the Institute's dark room. Hours later we arrived in Kampala where we stayed for the next two weeks. After two months in the bush living out of suitcases and cardboard boxes, it felt great to have hot and cold running water, electricity, a real bathtub and a toilet. What marvels we took for granted! Even opening a drawer felt wonderful!

The conference took place at Aidan's house. It was so helpful for Mel to meet the other six researchers and to exchange experiences and ideas. Three had come from Kenya and Tanganyika (now Tanzania). One of them studied a group of 500 natives who lived entirely on wild berries, roots and from hunting with poisonous arrows. Axel and Kirsten Sommerfeld, a couple from Norway, studied the Bwamba tribe on the other side of the Ruwenzori Mountains (Mountains of the Moon), west of Fort Portal. They had a little girl and another baby on the way. Axel had almost completed his research and was a great resource. He shared a lot of useful information with Mel. One of the researchers, who was about to leave Uganda and return to England, gave us his tall black dog, Sam, which we would take back to the field with us.

Between conference meetings, Mel spent every spare moment in the Institute's darkroom as he wanted to incorporate his photos and films in his presentation. Ilana kept him company. While Mel attended the conference, Arali took care of Ilana and I canned fruits, ran errands and made apple jelly. Friends gave me a little oven that fit on my Primus stove. Now I could bake in the bush. Arali was in awe. He had never been to the big city nor had he ever stayed in a house equipped with electricity. Ilana amused us to no end as she said *no* all day long.

"Aidan gave me very good feedback today," Mel reported when he came back from the conference late one afternoon. "He said I am very methodical and a perfectionist, but that I need to speed up my research."

We got invited to various dinner parties and I wondered how I would ever be able to reciprocate. My cooking skill was just good enough for us not to starve!

The two weeks went by fast. By early August, we were anxious to return to Kaihura to start building our mud and wattle huts. The rainy season was going to start soon and it was getting cooler. With the new bicycle we had purchased, attached to the back of our car, we returned to the bush. Now Mel would get to the various homesteads faster and I could ride to the local market.

On our way back it began to rain heavily and it was so windy we were worried about our tent. Sure enough it had collapsed. Fortunately our mosquito nets were not torn. We had just enough time to set up our smaller tent and move everything in before nightfall. The next day we packed up our few belongings, our tent and our chicken coop and set up in Bwenzi right next to where we were planning to build our huts. Most of our clothes we kept in the two suitcases. What an enchanting and peaceful place. To watch the sun set behind the green rolling hills was a spectacle. This time our tent stood in the middle of trees. The homesteads were well spread out, and surrounded by banana plantations. Mogabu was our closest neighbor and quite a character. His first wife was from his mother's clan. With the second "wife" he had two children, but they were not legally married. In addition, he had several other illegitimate children. He was very nice and helpful to Mel. He also loved to drink beer. Instead of purchasing sugar for his family, he spent it on alcohol. Although he had very little money, he was planning to buy our huts when we left. His son, Arali, was still our porter for well water.

Mel carrying water with our porter

Sam, our new dog, was a good companion for Ilana. Compared to all the other dogs that we had seen around, which looked skinny and malnourished, Sam was healthy and we fed him bananas, like the locals did. Akiki made him some kind of porridge with cassava flour, a staple among the

Batoro. Sam became part of the family and a good guard for our unlocked tent. It felt good to have him around, and Ilana loved to play with him. Unfortunately, his stay with us was short-lived. Because the natives were afraid of him, they stopped visiting us, so we had to give him away to people in Fort Portal.

By the end of August 1959, Mel understood and spoke enough Rutoro to have simple conversations with the locals. He managed to hire a few of the local men to help build our two permanent huts. However, the helpers were used to a much slower pace of life and were taking their time. Mel was concerned that the rainy season might start before the huts were completed, so he helped nail on the tin roof. Finally the workers stuck two sticks of different heights into the ground under the edge of the roof, then placed a banana stem on the sticks to serve as a gutter and lead the rainwater from the roof into the gutter, and then right from the gutter into a big container. We were ready for the rain.

Mel nailing the roof on   *Ilana playing in the sand*

We had hardly any toys for Ilana, so we bought some sand for her to play in.

Fresh vegetables were a rarity in the bush even though the soil was very fertile. I asked Akiki to help me plant a vegetable garden next to the kitchen, so the next time Mel and I went to Fort Portal, I bought some seeds, including tomato seeds. When I handed them to Akiki, he burst out laughing.

"Just give me the biggest tomato you have, Adyeri," he said.

Then he cleared a small area and turned the soil over. In one half he squeezed the fresh tomato.

"Adyeri, sow your seeds in the other half," he said.

Then he covered both sides lightly with soil.

A week later little seedlings were coming out on his side, but nothing ever happened on my side. Akiki smiled.

"Fresh seeds are wet and ready to germinate," he explained proudly.

He was right. This was the way to plant tomatoes. It was his turn to teach me.

We also planted radishes, carrots, lettuce, peas, green beans, turnips, parsley, and potatoes. The radish seedlings came out four days later. Every morning Ilana and I tended to our fragile-looking plants. Akiki also planted a banana tree and flowers.

Mel spent the evenings at his camping table, redefining the objective of his study, based on the feedback he received at the conference. He was focusing on marital histories of men and women who lived in the 180-odd homesteads in the village. He was investigating polygyny (a man having more than one wife), the payment of bridewealth, divorce and separation and what affected the stability of marriage. Mel was also interested in several legal systems that governed marriage and divorce here: the law of the Uganda Protectorate, the law of the Christian missions and native law.

On August 16, Ilana turned two. I gave her the teddy bear I had made and we enjoyed a delicious cake I managed to bake in my little oven, without a recipe. Ilana was happy and Mel was satisfied with my culinary efforts.

Surprisingly, the conditions were perfect to have a second child in Africa. Our daughter was healthy and growing. The climate was beautiful. The British hospital in Kampala was excellent and domestic help was cheap. We wanted three or four children without too big a gap between them.

It was October when we were able to finally move into our hut. As soon as the floors were dry, we moved the beds, the tables and chairs into the bigger hut and the kitchen utensils into the smaller one. Mel stacked up wooden boxes and placed them against the walls for his books and my tin pots. When I went to the tent to pick up the groceries, ants had found their way into the strawberry jam. When I opened one of our suitcases, our clothes were covered in a huge spider web.

One day, shortly after moving out of our tent, I was watching Ilana play with the chicken when heavy clouds began moving in. I quickly took down the laundry I had hung up. Mel had gone to the African store by the roadside to hang out with the locals. By the time the first drops fell, he was back.

The vegetables loved the rain. The lettuces were beautiful and one of our radishes was as big as a potato. The grass turned into a lush green and the nasturtiums I had planted in little boxes in front of the porch had come out. We appreciated the rain for our water, our vegetable garden, our lawn and our tea.

The next day Ilana helped me pick and peel a few vegetables for soup. Mel said it was the best vegetable soup he had ever eaten.

By now the locals were used to us. They stopped by to sell us things. One woman came with a rooster under her arm. Hoping that we might get chicks, I bought it from her. The next morning at five, we were woken up by a loud *cocorico*. The rooster's crow became our early alarm clock.

On Mondays I rode our bicycle to the roadside market to buy fresh meat. The locals followed me intently with their eyes. They had never seen a woman on a bike. And no white woman had ever bought meat from them. Usually I bought liver and tongue, which were very tender. When I got there, the cow was already lying on the grass with its belly cut wide open. While I was waiting for my turn I watched the locals. They only bought a small piece because that was all they could afford. As an extra bonus the vendor reached into the belly and pulled out a generous handful of entrails. *How disgusting,* I thought. When it was my turn, I pointed to the tongue and liver of the animal. This time the vendor looked disgusted as he bent down to cut off the tongue and pull out the liver. We were both experiencing culture shock!

Back at the hut, I cut the liver into slices right away and fried it with onions. We enjoyed it with canned applesauce for lunch. I also cooked the tongue in the pressure cooker with a few of our own vegetables. This way it would keep for the next two days.

Mogabu knew the villagers well and he was highly respected, so he offered to accompany Mel on his daily visits. His presence would help the locals feel more at ease and hopefully the interviewee would be more likely to talk and tell the truth. Mogabu drew a map of all the homesteads in the village, and Mel assigned a number to every homestead. Mel thought of questions to ask:

What is your name, your age, your religion?

Are you married?

How many times have you been married?

Do you have more than one wife?

Did you pay bridewealth for each, and if so, how did you pay, with money or with cows?

How many children do you have? Were any out of wedlock?

Have you ever been to Kampala or worked in Kampala?

A few hours later the two were back. "Erinisiti told you he was married only once. That's not true," Mogabu began. "I know for a fact that the woman you saw is his third wife."

"In that case we will have to go back tomorrow and confront him," Mel replied.

In some cases they went back five times before Mel felt that the information was accurate. When Mel started without Mogabu, it was more difficult to remember all the details. Therefore, after each visit, he quickly jotted down some notes, sometimes even in the latrine so no one would see him. In the evening, Mel typed up his notes in the dim light of our pressure lamp. I sat next to him, reading or knitting, and Ilana was already fast asleep. Overall Mel was quite satisfied with the results.

Soon we were drowning in Mel's notes. It was time to create some sort of filing system to find information more easily. After dinner, every evening, Mel began to type up the notes with two carbon copies, one I used to classify his notes and the other copy he sent to Professor Southall to keep him informed about his progress. When Mel went to the post office in Butiiti to pick up our mail, he ran into a woman he knew. They chatted for a moment and Mel, as usual, took this opportunity to steer the conversation. He was very interested in the native women's attitude towards bridewealth, polygyny, the birth of children out of wedlock and Christian marriage. Some of those questions were:

"Did you go to school? How long?"

"Are you married?" "Were you married in church or according to native customs?"

"Do you live with a man in common law marriage?

"Are you separated or divorced?

"How many times have you been divorced or widowed?

When Mel asked her if her husband had a second wife she responded, "Yes."

"How do you feel about that?" he asked.

"I don't like it, but I don't want to return to my father's home so I have to accept it."

One of the answers Mel got several times to his questions was quite puzzling. The first time he heard that strange answer was when he asked a woman how many children she had. She answered that she had two children and one "went into the back." Then, two years later, the baby came back to the front and she had the baby. In order to understand what she meant, Mel asked one of the local nurses at the infirmary. He explained it this way:

"There are several possibilities. The woman may think she is pregnant, because her periods are irregular and late, or she may have amenorrhea (absence of menstrual periods), which could be due to a lack of essential nutrients in her diet. Or she may really have been pregnant, but she miscarried in the latrine without being aware of it, and she believes that the baby went off somewhere, i.e. into the back, since she is no longer pregnant. Then, in the future, sometimes years later, when she is pregnant again, she believes that it is the same baby that disappeared earlier "into the back" and came back to the front so that the pregnancy could continue. The strange thing is that this is recognized in the native courts.

In November we heard a high pitched whirring and something that sounded like the flapping of wings.

"*Ensenene!*" the men shouted excitedly. They immediately stopped everything they were doing and rushed into the dry, grassy area toward what seemed to be a dark cloud. Mel and I were curious and followed them. As we got closer we saw swarms of grasshoppers. After a while Akiki came with a plastic bag in his hands.

"Adyeri, these are for you," he said and handed me a bag with a few grasshoppers. "I have already plucked their wings, feet and heads. Now you can fry them with onions in a little oil, then add one or two little tomatoes and a pinch of salt. This is a delicacy only for men. African women do not eat grasshoppers. The *ensenene* come only in the rainy season, and rarely.

That's why everyone is out there catching them. They even get some time off work to run into the fields to catch what they can!"

I put the cleaned grasshoppers into the frying pan, then watched them turn from green to gold. Soon the aroma of onions and tomato permeated the air. Mel and I looked at each other in disgust. To be polite we dared each other to eat one. To our surprise they were crisp and crunchy, and had no particular taste. Ilana ate one and then asked for four more, as she had no preconceived ideas. I got a kick out of her innocence.

Thanks to the rain our green beans had come out and our cauliflower looked promising. The carrots were almost ready to be harvested and the peas were flowering. Ilana helped me replant dozens of little lettuces. We were looking forward to having lots of salads.

We started to have itchy toes and found out that we got jiggers in them, little critters that live in the dust and bore into the skin of humans, who walk without shoes, to lay their eggs. The only way to get rid of them is to pry them out with a needle. The natives also get jiggers since they walk barefoot or with sandals. We found out that the only way to avoid them was to always wear socks and only closed shoes, sprinkled inside with insecticide powder. We never had jiggers after that.

Before we left for Kampala for our second conference, Mel asked our porter Arali to sleep in our hut while we were gone so that no one would attempt to steal our tin roof, wooden doors or windows. We took Akiki with us. We were looking forward to a break from fieldwork. Once again we stayed in one of the apartments of the Institute. A package from Grossmama was waiting for us. It was a pretty apron. Her other gift, the awful, long black skirt with pink roses and green leaves that she had given me back in 1950 in Israel, I wore often. Here, in the bush, I got many compliments from the native women — it was a conversation piece!

Once again in Kampala, critical comments from colleagues helped put Mel's research into a new perspective. While he met with his fellow researchers, I was thrilled to have a stove. I spent my time canning peas, tomatoes, apples and plums to take back to Toro, and Akiki looked after Ilana.

Around five in the afternoon, all the researchers and their families gathered in someone's apartment for tea or dinner. We enjoyed living in a community of like-minded people from various parts of the world. It was a pleasure to see the Sommerfelds again.

"You are not that far from our village. Come visit us in April before we return to Europe!" Axel suggested.

"We would love to," Mel replied and Axel gave us detailed directions.

In our complex Mel and I met a young psychology researcher.

"Would you be willing to do some research about optical illusions for me?" he asked me. "Sure, why not?" I replied. "It sounds like an interesting research project." He showed me a booklet with various pages of optical illusions.

"Africans do not grow up with books and therefore seem to only recognize three dimensional realities. When they see a picture or a photo in two dimensions on a flat page, they have a hard time identifying what they see," he said. They can recognize a cow in the field, but if I show them a picture of a cow on paper, they don't see that it is a cow." I remembered seeing a calendar in a local hut with a picture of the British Queen hanging upside down.

He showed me a page with two vertical lines that were converging toward the top. They were crossed by two horizontal lines.

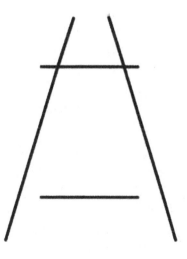

Optical illusion

"Which of the horizontal lines is longer?" he asked me.

I pointed to the top one.

"Incorrect. Both lines are the same length. Your brain is tricked. It is an optical illusion."

"My theory is that Africans who grow up in the bush do not have optical illusions. They see right away that both lines are of the same length. Moreover, when I show them a photograph or a painting of a landscape or a person, they don't recognize what it is. Westerners see two-dimensional pictures from the time they are babies, when they are shown books, but the Africans in the bush only know the world in three dimensions.

"Would you be willing, Eva, to show this booklet to, say, twenty-five African men, twenty-five women, twenty-five boys and twenty-five girls? A sample of a hundred should be enough to prove my point."

"I will be happy to do this research for you." I did, and it would corroborate our friend's theory.

Aidan was interested in the various herbs the natives used to treat health problems such as constipation, fever (malaria), headaches etc.

"Eva, you are a nurse. Could you do some research for me on native herbal medicine?" Southall asked. I agreed. "I can ask the women in our village and I'll find out."

At one of the gatherings at Makerere College, we met the Greenbergs. Mr. Greenberg had been a chef in an Italian restaurant, and was now retired in Kampala. Both he and his wife were Jewish, amiable, and a little on the heavy side.

"We would like to invite you to our Chanukah party," Mr. Greenberg said. "We have all the amenities of the West." Mr. Greenberg turned out to be a marvelous cook. He made a glorious dinner and topped it off with whipped cream-filled brandy snaps. How could I possibly reciprocate? At their party we met almost the entire Jewish community of Kampala, which consisted of about fifty people.

While in Kampala, I went to consult a gynecologist at the hospital, and she assured me that I should be able to have another child.

We also met another couple, Professor Derrick Jelliffe and his wife. Jelliffe was an internationally recognized expert on health education, especially in underdeveloped countries. He created East Africa's first pediatric health department at Makerere. I was impressed and intimidated by his stature and his importance. He looked very British and very distinguished. I conversed mostly with Mrs. Jelliffe, whose dark green nail polish intrigued me!

Based on what he had learned at the conference, Mel needed to stay two additional months in Bwenzi to expand his radius to include more households in order to have sufficient statistical data. We returned to Bwenzi without Akiki, who decided he wanted to stay in the big city. Our lettuces had grown two feet tall and gone to seed. So much for our salads! Now that Akiki was no longer with us, we needed a new houseboy. Fulensi, a nice young man in his early thirties, did not live far from our compound. Mel knew that he had worked in Kampala and that he was more experienced than Akiki, so Mel asked him if he wanted to work for us. He accepted.

"My wife is expecting her first child," Fulensi said.

"I would really like to attend the birth," I told him.

"I will let you know when the baby is coming," he promised.

Whenever I had a little spare time, I worked on sewing for myself a top and a skirt by hand and without a pattern. When it was done it looked quite nice and I was excited that it fit. I had never sewn before. In my new dress I went to the clubhouse with some wool and my knitting needles.

"What a beautiful dress!" one of the women complimented me.

"I made it," I acknowledged proudly.

I sat down next to the woman in charge, took out my wool and knitting needles and taught her how to knit a scarf. The next few times I showed her how to knit the various parts of a sweater and sew them together. Soon she could knit so fast that she produced more sweaters than she needed. When she ran out of yarn, she simply finished the sweater with a yarn of a different color. What mattered most was that it kept the wearer warm. The next time I went to the roadside market to buy meat I saw her there selling her colorful sweaters. In exchange she taught me to bead Toro necklaces.

Whenever I had a moment, I visited nearby homesteads to do my research for Aidan. I learned about twenty-nine herbs, three roots and two tree barks that were used to cure cough, constipation, intestinal worms and malaria. Now I, too, spent the evenings writing down what I had learned during the day — names, indications and usage. I gave my own paper eventually at the next conference, and it was well received.

Sometime in February, Mel, Ilana and I woke up with high fever. Concerned that it might be malaria, lessened by the preventative pills we took every day, Mel picked up quinine from the dispensary. Twenty-four hours later we were well again, thank God!

Occasionally, Ilana and I accompanied Mel on his visits. One day, as we approached a homestead, we saw an African dressed in a shirt and khaki shorts, standing in a pit lined with banana leaves. With his naked feet he was stomping on yellow and green bananas while family members added unfiltered water from the nearby well. We watched for a while.

"Have you ever worked in Kampala?" Mel asked at an appropriate moment, hoping to strike up a conversation. The man in the pit looked up and said proudly, "Yes, I have." He climbed out of the pit and ran through the dirt to his house, which was some 50 yards away. Soon he returned, triumphantly holding up a picture.

"This is me in Kampala," he commented, pointing at the person in the picture, before he jumped right back into the pit with his dirty feet. While we looked at the photograph he scooped some juice out of the pit with a tumbler and handed it to Mel. Talk about sanitation!

"Would you like some banana juice?" he offered.

Mel and I looked at each other hesitantly for a moment, but then accepted. Even though it was made with well water and his soiled feet, it tasted pretty good.

While we sipped the sweet banana juice, the man took the top half of a gourd and funneled banana juice through dried grass. Slowly the filtered liquid dripped into a larger gourd. Once all the liquid was filtered, he carried the gourd to a long tree trunk that had been hollowed, and poured the banana juice into the trunk, added millet and covered the whole trunk with lots of banana leaves.

"Now the banana juice needs to ferment," he explained. "In about a month I will have delicious banana beer. In two to three weeks I will start tasting it with a straw through a little opening between two leaves. When the taste is right, I will strain it again into the big gourd to eliminate the millet and then I will sell it at the local bar."

I did not like beer of any kind, but after riding my bike to the market and back in the heat one day I was so thirsty that I gulped down a glass without stopping to breathe. Fortunately the beer did not affect me.

Our hens were leaving poop everywhere and we were getting tired of getting woken up by the rooster every morning at 5 a.m., so we ate him.

By March, three months had gone by since I had seen the gynecologist in Kampala and I was still not pregnant, so when we went back for the third conference, I went to see the doctor again. She advised me to have a D & C (dilation and curettage) to rule out any obstruction. I checked myself into the hospital and had the procedure done, thinking of it as spring-cleaning.

"I can't find anything wrong with you, Mrs. Perlman," the doctor reported. "You can go home tomorrow."

The next day I left the hospital, feeling hopeful.

Two weeks later we were back in Bwenzi. While I was working in the kitchen I spilled a little milk on the mud floor. I did not think much of it, until I noticed an army of red ants, a foot wide, running across the kitchen floor. Ilana started scratching her legs and screaming. I took off her pants. Ants were crawling all over her legs and biting her. Thankfully Mogabu's wife lived next door and I ran to her for help.

"Hand me a container and some kerosene!" she requested.

In a panic, I could not find a container that quickly, so I gave her Ilana's potty. With a banana leaf she sprinkled the kerosene all over the floor and within two hours, the ants were gone. Ilana had scars for weeks. That night, when Mel took a book off the shelf, he noticed that ants had eaten whole sections of one or two of his precious books.

I was working in the garden when a village woman stopped by with a little girl. Her dress was so dirty it was almost black. In her arms she was holding a violet cone, the end of a bunch of bananas, wrapped in fabric. It was her doll.

"Can you help me, Adyeri?" the woman asked "I have fever."

By then I knew that she meant malaria. Knowing that I was a European, she figured that I might have some helpful drugs, but all I could give her was aspirin. In Kampala we had been advised not to give anything else to the natives. If someone were to get seriously ill or die, we would certainly be blamed for it. I never told anyone that I was a nurse.

"I have a pill that I can give you, but if it does not make you feel better, you need to go to the dispensary." She gladly took the pill, and thanked me. She trusted me more than the local infirmary.

One morning at 5 a.m. we were awakened by loud wailing from a neighboring homestead. Mel went to investigate. Half an hour later he was back.

"What happened?" I asked.

"A woman just lost the youngest of her four children. The child was only two years old. Sadly she had already lost three children. The day before, on her way to the infirmary to get free antibiotics, she ran into a well-meaning friend. The friend took one look at the child and said, 'Your child is going to die. There is no need to go see the nurse.' So the woman returned home with her child, and it died. The Batoro do not trust free drugs. They think a drug from the dispensary that doesn't cost anything can't be good." *How sad,* I thought. Antibiotics might have saved her child.

In March, word got around that the British governor of Uganda was coming to our area for a community lunch. All the notables of Toro, the Katikiro (prime minister of Toro), the county, sub-county and parish chiefs would attend. When Mogabu invited us we felt honored. It was a sign that we had become part of their community. Near the road was a large, empty field. The locals set up simple wooden tables in a long row. On each table were tin plates and cups, bottles of beer and Fanta, bowls with cooked yellowish plantains and brown millet, which had the consistency of a thick dough, and meat sauce. The notables had very short hair, were well-shaven and dressed in European style clothes — white shirts, ties, pants and jackets. Some wore hats, others had some sort of medal around their neck. I was the only woman and Ilana the only child in their midst. The British governor spoke from a platform.

Among the Toro people

140

Mogabu asked us to have a seat at the long table. We watched the locals take a small amount of millet out of a bowl, roll it between their hands into a ball, then dip it into meat sauce and eat it. The plantain tasted like potato and the millet did not have much flavor. It was the meat sauce that gave the flavor. For the locals, this was a special meal they could afford only once a month. I rolled a ball in my hands and gave it to Ilana. "Here we eat like the locals," I explained to Ilana, "but at home we use a spoon or a fork."

By the end of the meal we had become almost as adept as everyone else. Dessert was papaya and pineapple, and tea. After the meal we all posed for a picture.

One ordinary April day turned into the day I had been waiting for. An excited Fulensi showed up.

"Adyeri, Adyeri, the baby is coming!"

Ilana holding Fulensi's baby

I quickly made sure that Mel had time to look after Ilana and I left with Fulensi. After a fifteen-minute walk through the brush, we reached the entrance to his hut. It was so low that we had to bend to get inside. I heard moaning and groaning. There was little light. All I could see was a very tired-looking young woman in a half standing, half crouching position, who was being held up under her arms by two male relatives. Her whole family had gathered around her. I asked Fulensi if it would not be better for his wife to lie down.

"This is the way we do things here," he said firmly. I felt silenced in no uncertain terms.

"Where are you going to put the baby once it is born?" I dared to ask, as nothing seemed prepared. "To prepare for the baby before it is born brings bad luck," he explained.

A couple of hours later a baby boy was born. Fulensi held out his old dirty suit jacket. One of the women deposited the crying, wet baby on top of the lining and then wrapped him up in it. I congratulated the new parents and left, amazed by the lack of hygiene, and yet the baby was just fine. I was moved and grateful that I had been allowed to be present. A month later Fulensi brought his baby boy over and allowed Ilana to hold him. She was delighted.

Ilana and Fulensi

We had promised the Sommerfelds that we would visit them before they left Uganda. From Fort Portal we drove up a dirt road into the Ruwenzori Mountains. For quite a while there was not a soul in sight. Then we saw three young skinny boys, standing on the side of the desolate road, without shoes, wearing tattered, dirty clothes. One of them was holding a scrawny little dog in his arms. Mel stopped the car. He grabbed his Rolleiflex, got out of the car and indicated that he wanted to take their picture. The boys giggled. Then the tallest of them pointed at his dog and extended his hand. Mel pulled out a few coins and gave them to the boy. They posed for the picture and continued happily on their way.

Finally we arrived in the village where the Sommerfelds lived. Their mud and wattle house looked similar to ours. His wife Kirsten came out with a baby on her arm.

"You have a new baby?" I said surprised.

"Yes, his name is Muhindo."

"How lucky you are," I replied. (I briefly reflected that it was the end of April, and I was still not pregnant.)

She offered us a cup of hot black tea. It was nice to be with friends who had the same cultural background. Mel and Axel started to talk shop immediately.

"How do you do your research?" Mel asked. "Are your assistants helpful? Do the villagers accept you?"

"I have a wonderfully cooperative assistant, a revered elder in the village and a medicine man," Axel said. "He specializes in treating women and their problems — miscarriages, infertility, stillbirths etc."

"Would he be willing to treat me?" I exclaimed immediately. "I have been trying to get pregnant for several months. I am ready to try anything."

"The medicine man predicted that we would have a son here in Africa and here he is," Axel said. He called his assistant, who soon arrived, an elderly man with a grey beard and curly grey hair. When Axel asked him if he would be willing to treat me, the man laughed with embarrassment.

"He has never treated a white woman," Axel explained, "but he agrees to treat you. He will return after we have lunch."

After our meal, the medicine man returned with a basket. He told us that he had spoken with his spirits who informed him that we would have four children. Then he proceeded to ask us a few questions and Axel translated.

"He wants to know if your parents and siblings are still alive and well, and if you have ever committed adultery. Some native tribes believe that sterility is punishment for adultery," Axel added for our information.

We answered his questions. Satisfied, the medicine man pulled out of his basket little pouches of various powders. He rubbed a yellow powder into my hair. It was a hot day, and I was wearing a décolleté blouse so he put a black powder into my cleavage. He said something to Kirsten that I did not understand. She walked to the stove and came back with a cup of hot instant coffee to which he added various powders. I drank the odd mixture without hesitation. It still tasted like coffee. The medicine man took a hollow bamboo stick, into which he poured various additional powders, plugged it up, and handed it to me.

"When you get home tonight, sew yourself a belt, transfer these powders into it and wear it around your waist for at least three days."

"How much do we owe him?" Mel asked.

"Ten shillings," Axel translated. This was equivalent to about seven pounds of meat in the village market, a fair payment for his treatment, I thought.

Two hours later, we thanked our hosts and were back on the road. Back in our hut that night, I sewed a piece of fabric into a belt, with an opening on one end so I could pour the powders into it. I wore it around my waist for a week to make sure that it would work its magic. Before I went to bed I sat down and wrote to my parents about the unusual treatment I received.

A month after our visit to the Sommerfelds, in June 1960, Mel suggested we go on a little vacation to southeastern Uganda.

"Let's go to Muko in Kigezi District on the shore of Lake Bunyonyi. I have heard that it is a nice place to relax, and it's only a six-hour drive from Fort Portal, north of the Rwanda border and close to the Belgian Congo." I agreed with him.

A friend from Kampala suggested we stop by the Spiropoulos' home, a Greek miner and his wife, who lived on a mountaintop on the way to Muko. "They would be delighted to have visitors with whom they can speak English," our friend said. Unfortunately he could only give us rough directions. We would have to ask the locals for help once we got close, "but everyone knows the Europeans," our friend added.

We had traveled for hours through a wide, dry and flat expanse, when I noticed that Mel was getting nervous.

"Eva," he said, "I can no longer shift into gear!"

"*What?*" I said.

There was not a single dwelling or human being in sight. Mel got out of the car and lifted the hood. "Eva, get behind the wheel and move the gearshift!" he instructed me.

All of a sudden our car was surrounded by a dozen curious African children who had appeared out of nowhere. They enjoyed the distraction and kept watching us. As I moved the gearshift, Mel saw that one part seemed to be broken. It looked similar to one the mechanic had sold to him for a spare part. So my darling husband, who had never to my knowledge worked on a car, managed to fix our Peugeot thanks to the foresight of that mechanic! And we were back on our way!

Since we had only a vague idea of where the Spiropoulos' lived, Mel stopped at a parish. A kind priest gave us directions, but we still could not find it. So Mel asked a couple of Africans who were passing by.

"The Europeans?" they said. "Drive that way!"

After some more searching we finally found the road that led to their house. Unlike our mud and wattle house, their house was built of plaster and stone. It was a *real* house with a large, flat parking area in the front. Mr. and Mrs. Spiropoulos immediately welcomed us into their home.

"Please come in! We are delighted to meet you."

Their large living room was furnished simply, but very comfortably. Mrs. Spiropoulos offered us tea and cookies. She was delightful, with kind eyes and short dark hair. Though a little overweight, she was beautiful. Her husband was a stocky man in his fifties. He looked us straight in the eyes when he spoke, exuding strength and confidence.

"I miss my friends from the old country," Mrs. Spiropoulos said. We chatted for a while. Ilana sat next to us patiently and enjoyed the cookies.

"Would you like me to show you the mine?" Mr. Spiropoulos then asked Mel, who agreed immediately.

By the time they came back, it was already getting dark. Mel and I thanked them for their hospitality and continued on to Muko.

"Motek, you won't believe what Mr. Spiropoulos told me," Mel began as soon as he started driving. "God really *does* work in unexpected ways. His father was Greek, but he was born in Abyssinia. When the Italians invaded in 1938, he emigrated to Uganda hoping to find gold. He always felt that his true destiny was to be a miner. He did find some gold and made a little money, but not nearly as much as he hoped for. He was heavily indebted to the bank since he had borrowed money to build his road and his house, and to buy a car. Then one day, out of the blue, he discovered a large formation of pure bismuth, which he mined and sold to the Uganda government for 12,000 English pounds. With that profit he repaid his debt. Then, a few years later, he found wolfram, the ore from which tungsten is made to make weapons. Europe was at war and tungsten was in great demand. Business was booming again. He had about forty miners working for him and he had been warned by the British Government two or three times not to leave the mine for more than six consecutive days. If there was an accident and someone got killed while he was away, he would be accused of manslaughter. Many years ago, despite these warnings, he left the country for thirty days. On his way home he stopped in Kampala for his monthly grocery shopping and banking. Even though he was very tired, he decided to take a few extra minutes to fill up his gas tank. Then he went to bed early. In the middle of the night his long-deceased mother appeared to him in a dream, dressed in black. She repeated three times with great urgency, "*Go back, go back, go back!*" Mr. Spiropoulos woke up in a sweat. It was two in the morning. His mother's command frightened him to death. He started off immediately, feeling fortunate that he had filled his tank the day before. By 6 a.m. he arrived in Mbarara. He stopped to refill. Usually no gas pump was open at that time. That morning, however, a truck had just finished refueling the pump and was leaving as he arrived. Miraculously he was able to get gas. By 9 a.m. he arrived in Kabale, where he usually went to various Indian shopkeepers to get cash to pay his workers. Since there was no bank nearby, these shopkeepers were happy to exchange their cash for a check, which they could then mail to the bank. It was an arrangement he had made with them. Sometimes Mr. Spiropoulos had to go to several shopkeepers before he got all the cash he needed which could take up to an hour. This time he needed 10,000 shillings. Fortunately the first shopkeeper had the exact amount, and he did not have to go anywhere else. It was as if everything was happening to facilitate his speedy return home. With the cash in hand, he drove to the White Horse Inn, at the bottom of his mountain. As the road to his house was not yet built, he usually found two porters to help him bring his luggage and the cash box up the mountain. It was not always easy, and took time. On that day, as if by divine ordinance, the local African chief was just dismissing two prisoners. Mr. Spiropoulos immediately hired them as his porters and, because he was in such a hurry, the climb up the mountain took them an hour and 10 minutes, whereas it usually took well over two hours."

"As soon as he arrived at his house, hot, tired and thirsty, he tore off his raincoat, did not even greet his wife, and ran down to the mine. Inside were several tunnels, and why he chose to enter this particular one, he will never know. He immediately saw a crack in the tunnel wall above the entrance. Noticing that one section of the dirt had moved down six inches, he commanded the men to drop their tools and get out on the double. As soon as the last man was out, the tunnel collapsed!"

"Wow! What a series of miracles!" I exclaimed. I had been clinging on Mel's every word. "It proves to me again that Divine Providence is real."

"I have no reason to doubt what he told me. He felt that the tunnel caved in because his men had dug 120 feet without putting in a single support. I am quite taken by the man's story and view of life. He said that he had always felt that he was destined to be a miner. Whenever he tried to do something else, something happened that would always bring him back to mining. His philosophy was to accept life as it came, seeing where life led him — always back to mining." Mel, who lived mostly in books and research and intellectual endeavors, was captivated by this open and down-to-earth fellow.

That night we drove another two hours and finally arrived at the Muko rest house, which we had reserved ahead of time, on the shore of a peaceful lake. The moon was shining. We saw several small islands with one or two pine trees on each. While I got Ilana ready for bed, Mel took out pen and paper and wrote the Spiropoulos' story down. The next morning I felt nauseous. Had the medicine man and the belt worked their magic? Could I be pregnant? Never in my life had I been so happy to feel so lousy. We were very excited.

"How do you feel about taking a day trip to Goma on the banks of Lake Kivu in the Belgian Congo?" Mel asked. "In two weeks the country is going to become the independent Democratic Republic of the Congo. Independence has not gone smoothly for some African countries. This might be our last chance to go there. How do you feel?"

"I would enjoy that," I replied.

So the next day, all three of us drove further southwest over the mountain on a very rocky road. I held my belly, worried that something might happen to what I was hoping was a budding pregnancy.

In Goma the streets were lined with small European-style shops.

"Delikatessen," I read above one of the stores. "Let's go inside."

Mel parked the car. In the store, all kinds of cheeses — Gouda, Edam and Swiss — were piled high on the counters. Salamis, bolognas and sausages hung from the ceiling. The aroma was fabulous. We bought some cold cuts and cheese.

It was so wonderful to find some European products that we had not seen for a long time. I felt like a bush girl who had lost touch with Western civilization. We chatted in French with the Belgian couple behind the counter. They told us they had lived here for years and were worried about national independence.

"*Au revoir, Messieurs-Dames,*" I said upon leaving.

"*Au revoir, Madame!*" I heard a soft, high-pitched voice echo mine. Ilana had just spoken her first words at almost three. We were overjoyed, although we had not been terribly concerned. I knew that hearing several languages could delay speaking for a young child. All Ilana had ever said to this point was "no!"

Delighted with our memorable excursion and our cheese and salami sandwiches, we returned that night to Muko, where we stayed for another three days. When I opened the shutters on the morning of our departure, one of the bigger islands had moved out of sight and the other two islands had changed position. Floating islands! Imagine that!

Shortly after we returned from our vacation in Kigezi, the Congo became an independent Democratic Republic on June 30, 1960, and was no longer a Belgian colony. We were about 100 km from the nearest Congo border, far enough in the event there was trouble.

Soon it was time to pack up and move again. Kikonda was only four miles south of Fort Portal. Now Mel was going to focus specifically on employment opportunities, missionary centers and court archives. It had been a year since we set foot on African soil.

Mel made it known that we would leave soon. Locals asked him if they could buy our tin roof, the roof poles, the wooden doors and windows. He immediately agreed. It was a clear sign to them that we had no intention of claiming any of their land. Mel also thanked Mogabu personally for everything he had done for us as we said goodbye. We hoped that Mel's proper conduct would make it possible for other researchers to return to the area and be welcomed at some later date.

It was great to be in Kikonda and closer to the town. By now I knew I was pregnant! The medicine man's magical powders had worked! We were beyond delighted. Arriving in July 1960, we rented a small cement house with one big room and a tin roof. The cement floor was quite a step up from our hut in Bwenzi. A latrine was close to the house. We still had a well and no electricity. Clothes and shoes we kept in boxes. In the backyard were lots of trees. The avocado tree was gigantic and laden with avocados. I did not like avocados, but now I was going to try to adapt them in different recipes. We had no immediate neighbors. Again we had to find a porter to fetch water for us.

Akiki had returned from Kampala and became our houseboy again. One of his jobs was to cut the grass around the house so we could spot snakes easily. He planted flowers in front of the house and vegetables in the back.

"Adyeri, I was cutting the grass around the house, complaining that I was hungry," he said to me. "Ilana was watching me intently and then she said in Rutoro, 'Why don't you eat the grass?'" I was flabbergasted. I had no idea she understood Rutoro!

Mel returned from the Fort Portal post office with a letter from Maman.

Dear Eva,

Although the medicine man's story is lovely, especially coming from an anthropologist's wife, don't give it too much credence. Otherwise you might be terribly disappointed if it doesn't work.

I immediately shared the good news with her. Papa and Maman were thrilled. They even asked if I could send my belt to the children of friends of theirs who had been trying to get pregnant for fifteen years. I refused because I felt that the medicine man had custom-made that belt for me and I was concerned that it would not work for someone else. Besides, maybe I would have to use it again.

It was my second month of pregnancy. I felt nauseous all the time and had to lie down on my camp bed a lot. Each time I got up to prepare a meal, I felt dizzy. I read many books, which I borrowed from the Fort Portal library: *Anna Karenina, War and Peace*, and *The Quiet American*.

Mel wanted to grow a beard and I had to get used to it. Fortunately it started itching his skin, and, to my delight, he soon shaved it off.

Mel had studied ninety homesteads in Bwenzi, and chose an equal number in Kikonda. But this time he could not concentrate on the geographical area around our house because the sample would be too heavily weighted in favor of the wealthy landowners and would exclude most of the poor workers. So he randomly selected ninety homesteads, keeping it balanced for householders in regard to age, sex, religion, land situation and income. Mel was confident that he would get good data more quickly this time, as he spoke Rutoro fluently and knew exactly what he was looking for. It helped that his questions always revolved around the same subject with a few hundred words. Moreover, twice as many people lived in Kikonda as in Bwenzi, so he could get faster from homestead to homestead.

Compared to Bwenzi, this was an upscale Toro neighborhood. More mud and wattle houses had tin roofs, and some were even built of cement like the one we were renting. Mel created a file for every adult in every household, which included name, place of birth, age, sex, religion, marital status, number of children and whether he/she had ever been to Kampala.

On August 16, Ilana turned three. The next time I accompanied Mel to Fort Portal, I bought her another little doll and made a bed for it in an empty shoebox. I also baked a pound cake in my Primus oven. It was delicious. Native children always passed by our house in their soiled brown shorts or dresses. One day, when I walked into the backyard, about twelve of them were sitting on the dirt in a circle and Ilana was in the middle, prancing around, dancing happily. Her long, blond curls were shining in the sun. They were watching her intently, enjoying her performance. She was some kind of wonder to them.

Every once in a while I continued to accompany Mel on his visits. This particular family lived in a typical wattle house with a grass roof. They invited us in and offered us green coffee beans from a shiny, black clay bowl. Inside the house were two little wooden stools, a few gourds and some tin pots. The man of the house proudly pointed to a calendar with a photo of Queen Elizabeth hanging upside down.

An old European who was raising cows and pigs lived nearby. He sold us milk regularly. On his way back from Fort Portal one day he stopped by. "I just killed a pig. Would you like to come over later today and buy some cutlets?" I looked at Mel and said, "Wouldn't that be a nice change from our regular fare of fried liver, stewed beef and cooked tongue? Of course we shouldn't eat pork, I know, but once in a blue moon... do you think that God will forgive us?" "I think so," Mel said. He was always so understanding.

The cutlets we brought back were thick and juicy. I fried them with some onions. We enjoyed every morsel. It was the best meal we ever had in Africa!

Starting in November, Mel spent a lot of time at the courthouse in Fort Portal where he attended court sessions that were open to the public. One day when he returned he said, "Guess what, honey? A woman came to court today with a baby on her hip. She wanted the father to pay child support and claimed that they had a sexual relationship ten years ago. As proof she showed her baby to the judge and said, 'I got pregnant then, but the baby went into the back. Last year it came back to the front. See? Here it is.' The judge ordered the affluent man to pay child support. The man agreed immediately, happy to have one more child. Here the woman decides whom she designates as the father and, of course, always picks a man who can afford to pay. A Toro man wants as many children as possible, so that he has lots of people to take care of him when he is old." There is no stigma attached to illegitimacy in Toro.

The next conference was in a month and Mel was writing his next paper. Just before Christmas, Mel's work in Kikonda was complete and we prepared to move back to Kampala. We sold what we no longer needed — our two benches, our stools, etc. Even our old clothes sold like hotcakes. Since I was 7 months pregnant, I was afraid to go to Kampala by car because of the many potholes, so Ilana and I took the train, and I was glad to return to an easier and more civilized lifestyle. Thus, Mel had more room to transport our belongings and Akiki could drive with him. Before leaving though, we bought some authentic African clothes as souvenirs in Fort Portal.

Tuesday morning, December 22, 1960, our train arrived in Kampala. Our apartment was bright and sunny, and furnished with locally-made wooden furniture. What luxury to have again electricity, a bathtub, an indoor toilet, a refrigerator and a stove! Not that I ever complained, but it felt good to know I would not have to go back to the bush, especially with a baby on the way. Mel was getting great feedback for his research and his hard work was paying off. We were settled and happy to be in Kampala.

Now that we were staying there for good, we invited the Greenbergs to dinner. For months I had mulled over in my mind what I could possibly cook for them, since Mr. Greenberg was a gourmet chef. I only knew how to make very ordinary meals. Vegetable soup was easy to make and I felt confident that I could get it right. I had cooked it in the bush many times and it had always been good. I looked through my cookbook and came across *Pommes Duchesse*, swirly mounds of potato puree held together with egg. To get everything ready on time, I started cooking the day before. To make sure that the soup would not be too watery, I added an extra three little potatoes. Then I boiled the beef tongue with celery, carrots and leeks. Once it was soft, I took it out of the boiling broth, waited for it to cool, then peeled and refrigerated it so that it could be cut easily into perfect slices the next day.

In the morning I prepared a green salad, sliced the tongue and put it in a smaller saucepan with some of its cooking juices. I arranged my delicious-looking swirly potato mounds on a baking sheet. Just before the Greenbergs arrived, I placed my *Pommes Duchesse* into the oven and turned on the stove to warm up the soup and the meat.

The doorbell rang. Mel welcomed the well-dressed couple into our living/dining room and offered them some port. While he entertained them, I was sweating with worry in the kitchen, hoping that everything would go smoothly. I stirred the soup with my ladle. Shocked, I realized just how much it had thickened overnight. Then I opened the oven door to take out the *Pommes Duchesse*. Oh no, this could not be true! They had been too runny and with the heat had now turned into a flat mess. I scraped the puree off the baking sheet and put it into a bowl. So much for my fancy side dish! There was no way out. Embarrassed, I called Mel and our guests to the table. The soup smelled delicious.

"Unfortunately, the soup turned out a bit too thick," I said apologetically.

"Oh, don't worry, Eva. It will be alright," Mrs. Greenberg comforted me.

Yet I felt her husband's critical eyes on me. They ate the soup without saying a word. Next I served the beef tongue and the ill-fated *Pommes Duchesse*, now a mess in a bowl. When I tasted the tongue, I realized that it was really bland. Mel acted like the gentleman he always was and just smiled encouragingly.

"By the way," Mr. Greenberg then said. "Last week a young woman invited us to dinner on a weeknight, although she works full time. She dared to serve us frozen peas."

I wanted to disappear into the ground and could not wait for this party to be over. To add insult to injury, I served store-bought spumoni ice cream for dessert. For Mr. Greenberg this must have been a crime. At the end of the evening, our guests thanked us kindly. It certainly was an unforgettable evening for all of us. I tried to put that bad memory behind me. Yet I was not planning to invite anyone over again anytime soon, especially not a gourmet cook.

We never saw the Greenbergs again.

Aidan Southall asked Mel if he would be interested in doing an extra 6 months of work in Toro for two plantation owners who asked for someone to research their high labor turnover and suggest ways to improve the situation. Since Mel knew Rutoro now, he would be the best choice for the job. Mel accepted.

When Mel picked up our mail from the Institute's office, he found a letter from Maman with exciting news. The book he had worked on at the *Musée de l'Homme* in Paris had finally been published with the title *Femmes d'Afrique Noire*. Mel had worked hard on its bibliography and was proud to finally have something in print.

"Congratulations, honey. I wish you a happy and healthy new year and hope your research will continue to go well," I said.

"Happy new year, motek," Mel responded. "Let's toast to our soon-to-be-born baby. May it be healthy."

After Christmas, Mel and I went Chanukah shopping, hoping to find some souvenirs to take back to Europe. One of the arts and crafts shops had an especially enticing window display of African items made of wood, ivory, raffia and clay. In the store, up high on a shelf were about thirty clay sculptures of very similar looking, fine-featured Maasai heads. One of them was especially aristocratic looking. Both Mel and I fell immediately in love with it.

"How much is that one?" Mel asked.

"I am sorry. That one is no longer for sale. A customer has already put a deposit on it," the store owner replied.

"If the buyer changes his mind, please give us a call," we said, and left.

I was relieved when we were invited to a New Year's dinner party, this time at the home of the Stanleys. They had organized a ballroom dinner dance in the senior common room of Makerere College. It was extremely hot that day, and I felt pretty uncomfortable. As soon as Mel set foot on the dance floor, my usually quiet and reserved husband turned into a playful, outgoing and uninhibited man. In spite of my large belly, I managed to dance the waltz with him.

The two tea plantation owners, both in Toro, were very anxious for Mel to do this study. So it was decided with Aidan that Mel would do the studies immediately, thus postponing his remaining research in other Ugandan tribes until he was done with the plantations. By the second week of January, while I waited in Kampala for the birth of our child, he left with Akiki and was gone for several weeks. To get help for myself, we had hired an *ayah* (nanny) to help me with the household and to take care of Ilana and the soon-to-be-born baby.

These *ayahs* were women from any tribe, who came to Kampala to earn money as nannies; they usually spoke enough English to make their way and be understood. The *ayah* who came was a young woman in her late twenties, pretty and pleasant. She was an invaluable help to me, especially for babysitting, so that I felt I could accept any invitation that came my way; I knew she was good with Ilana and a reliable presence when I wasn't there. She had several years of experience.

My due date was February 21. Mel was planning to be back so he could attend the birth. I prayed he would be home when I went into labor; that's all I asked for.

Now that Ilana was in nursery school and Mel was gone, I decided to sign up for sewing lessons at Singer's three mornings a week. The teacher was a young, vivacious Indian lady who wore the most beautiful, colorful silk saris. The sewing machines were not yet electric and I learned to sew on a treadle machine. The first item I made was a dress for Ilana.

I also started Swahili lessons. It was not as difficult as I thought it would be, since I spoke basic Rutoro. If you could speak Swahili, you could be understood by many tribal people all over East Africa. This was far from my Interpreters' School days in Geneva years earlier. Every day I rushed to the Institute's office, hoping to find a letter from Mel. He had just left but I already missed him. That day I was lucky:

My dearest Motek,

We have arrived at the tea plantation and have settled in. Akiki takes good care of me and the people here are very nice and cooperative. We have a nice room. I have started to interview the plantation's managers and laborers. The laborers understand why I am here and they feel that I am on their side. Therefore I can write down their questions and answers during the interviews. No more hiding in the latrines to take notes!

Yesterday I got invited to the Mukama's 33rd anniversary celebration of his accession to the throne. The king was surrounded by gorgeous women. Some of them were his daughters. I heard from a relatively reliable source that the Mukama has at least eight wives. Supposedly he has more than 30 children. As you see, honey, I miss no opportunity to do my research. I miss you very much...

Our friends knew that I was alone, so they looked after me and invited me over. It was wonderful to live in a caring community. Time flew by after all. I was 8 ½ months pregnant and anxiously awaiting Mel's return. In the evening, as soon as Ilana was in bed, I always wrote to Mel.

Dear Motek,

I am longing for you as never before. I am counting the hours until I see you again — 192 hours to be exact. It seems like an eternity. Ilana speaks an awful mixture of English, French and Rutoro. Please do not postpone your coming back. I am jittery enough as is. The doctor said that there is a good chance the baby will come on the 21st.

Four days before my due date, Mel came back. He was very tanned. I was so happy and relieved. We started thinking of names for either a boy or a girl.

"Do you think the baby will be white?" I asked Mel, facetiously. And we laughed.

On February 20, 1961, at 12:40 p.m. our baby was born at Nakasero hospital in Kampala. Mel never left my side. I could not have dreamt of a better pregnancy or an easier delivery.

"It's a girl!" Mel exclaimed. He was ecstatic and glowing.

The nurse cleaned the baby and placed her in my arms. With her dark hair, velvety skin and most adorable feet she reminded me of a little China doll.

"Doesn't the baby look like a miniature version of your mom?" I said.

"She does," he replied. "She is the best early birthday present I could have hoped for."

"What shall we name her?" I asked.

"To me it is important that the name will be pronounced the same in English, French and Hebrew," Mel said.

"I agree."

"How about Tamar?" he said. "It means *palm tree* in Hebrew."

"And Alisa as a middle name. It means *happy*," I answered.

"Tamar Alisa Perlman. I like that," he agreed. "I will send a telegram to Papa and Maman and to my mother right away, to give them the good news."

Later that afternoon, Mel walked in with a magnificent bouquet of gladioli. He had placed an announcement in the *Uganda Argus* and applied for an American birth certificate at the American consulate.

I stayed in the hospital for five days. After my difficulties breastfeeding Ilana, I had tried, for months, to toughen my nipples with a toothbrush dipped in a mixture of alcohol and glycerine. Unfortunately, when I put Tamar to my breast and she started sucking, it hurt unbearably. So I asked for her to be started on the bottle. My doctor gave me hell for not breastfeeding, especially since I was a pediatric nurse and I "should know better." I was very unhappy I couldn't breastfeed and I explained my problem to her. When Mel came to visit me again, he said happily, "Guess what! The shopkeeper called me this morning. We got our Maasai!" I was thrilled.

Just in time for Mel's 28th birthday, I came home with the baby. Ilana was so excited to finally get to see her little sister. She was in awe of this real-life doll.

I handed Mel a book of African photographs that I had purchased while he was away.

"Happy birthday, honey," I wished him.

"This is magnificent!" Mel exclaimed, as he flipped through a few pages.

The next day we had a champagne lunch with the Rollinses to celebrate Mel and Tamar.

"A new American research fellow arrived with his wife and four children. They are about to leave for the bush and have many questions. They want to meet you and are coming for tea this afternoon."

"Now *we* are the old folks with experience," Mel added.

I asked Mel if we could invite Papa and Maman to visit us, since we had not seen one another for almost 2 years. He agreed and said that the summer would be a good time in terms of his work.

Then Mel had to leave again. The political situation in the independent Congo Republic had deteriorated, following its declaration of independence on June 30, 1960. Many refugees were crossing the border, hoping to find shelter in Uganda. Several American missionaries from the Congo were now living at the Institute.

Mel was again gone for several weeks. When he came back I had good news for him.

"Papa and Maman have accepted our invitation! They are planning to come for three weeks toward the end of July. We can celebrate our 5th and their 30th anniversary together."

We decided we could take them to the western province of Uganda to see Murchison Falls, the game park, and the Ruwenzori Mountains. We wanted to take them to Bwenzi and Kikonda where we used to live, to the Muko rest house in Kigezi and maybe the Karamoja district, the most primitive in Uganda. We thought of taking them to meet our friends, the White Fathers. Entebbe with its beautiful botanical gardens and Lake Victoria were also on our agenda.

I was so looking forward to the time when Mel would not have to leave again. Every moment we spent together was so precious. When he came home this time I said to him, "You know Mel, a woman is more fertile a few months after she has given birth. Since we are staying in Africa longer than planned, it might be a good time to have a third child. Who knows? It just might be a boy this time."

Mel thought for a moment.

"It makes sense after the difficulty we had conceiving Tamar. Actually a friend of ours told me something rather interesting the other day. He said if a couple wants a baby boy, the woman has to reach her orgasm before the man. Apparently male sperm are lazy and travel more slowly. So they need a head start to get to the egg first." We laughed heartily and started putting our theory into practice.

The weather was so beautiful that we decided to have a picnic with friends on the grassy shores of Lake Victoria. Equipped with picnic basket and blanket we left. There I placed our six-week old baby on the blanket. Ilana climbed trees, hung and swung from the branches. I was just happy to be close to Mel, and enjoyed the warm sunshine. Unfortunately we could not swim in the lake, because it was infested with bilharzia, a tropical parasitic worm that lives in fresh-water lakes and rivers, infecting millions of Africans, causing diarrhea and organ damage.

I could tell that Mel had a lot on his mind. Since he would no longer receive paychecks from the Institute once we left Africa it was time to apply for grants, so we would have income during our year in Oxford while he finished his PhD thesis. He started to apply for grants to various American foundations.

After Passover, Mel and Akiki returned to Teso and Lango for another month.

On May 18, 1961, I turned 29. Mel had managed to come back just in time to celebrate with me. When I walked into the living room, there were a couple of nicely wrapped presents on the table. Ilana was sitting next to Mel, impatiently waiting to find out what was in the boxes. "Happy birthday, motek!" Mel gave me a big hug. I opened one of the presents. I found a tiny gold-plated watch in one box, and a little, locally made, rafia purse in the other. That evening, just the two of us enjoyed a special dinner in a Kampala restaurant.

"I really miss listening to classical music," I remarked.

The next day we bought a Philips gramophone with four batteries just in case we ever had to go back to the bush. Mel hoped he would come back to Uganda in a few years, perhaps by himself just for a few weeks, to follow up with all the friends he had made in Toro. This was not to happen in the end — by 1970, Idi Amin came to power in Uganda, and it was no longer a safe place for "Europeans."

In June, Mel and I were invited to the ceremony of the Kabaka (king of Buganda). He was going to appoint his new chiefs and confirm his heirs. After the ceremony, the king's musicians, dressed in their traditional native costumes, entertained us with an impressive drum concert. Hearing so many drums playing at the same time with different rhythms was exhilarating and powerful.

A letter arrived from Papa. An editing machine was waiting for Mel in Paris as his belated birthday gift. Mel was excited — now he would be able to edit and splice all his individual films together and put them on one big reel. Included was a letter from Maman, telling us that Ernest was on his way to Algeria. He had been drafted as part of his mandatory military service. The Algerians were fighting for their independence from France and war was raging there but, fortunately, he had a desk job. In about two weeks Papa and Maman were going to land in Entebbe. I quickly put one last letter in the mail.

If you still have some room after you pack everything, Maman, a baguette and a camembert would make us extremely happy.

Mel was planning to take a two-week vacation to spend time with them. We were also planning a wine and cheese party in their honor so that Papa and Maman could meet our friends. I was looking forward to my parents' visit.

We were at the Entebbe airport to welcome them. We watched my parents walk down the stairs of the plane. They looked happy and relaxed, and were holding two baguettes and a plastic bag. We were so excited to see one another after two years.

"How was the flight?" I asked. Maman laughed. "Actually we did not get much sleep with those two ripe camemberts in the overhead compartment. I was so scared that they would smell up the whole plane and make everyone uncomfortable, even though I had packed them in several layers of plastic. In the middle of the night I heard Papa mumble, *"Oh, que la nuit est longue pour les camemberts!"* (So long is the night for the camemberts!)

When Mel opened the door to the apartment, Ilana ran toward us. "These are Dadi and Grandmi, my Papa and my Maman," I told her. The *ayah* was holding Tamar. I placed the baby in Maman's extended arms.

"She is so cute and she looks so different from Ilana. She takes after your family, Mel."

Papa, on the other hand, was not easily enthused by a five-month old baby. While Mel chatted with Papa and Maman, I made coffee for our travelers, put one of the baguettes into the oven and unwrapped one of the camemberts from its multiple layers of plastic. It started to run immediately and smelled to high heaven. Then I walked with the hot crusty baguette and the cheese into the living room, and Mel and I had the feast of a lifetime. Even four-year old Ilana loved it.

Needless to say we had to catch up on many things.

"How are Ernest and Raymond?"

"Ernest is fine. Thank goodness, he is not among the fighting troops in Algeria and Raymond still lives with us. He is doing well in medical school," Maman replied.

"And Maman is going to be the new President of the Paris WIZO chapter, starting in the fall," Papa added proudly.

"That's wonderful, Maman," I exclaimed. "You really deserve it. I know how much the WIZO means to you. Are you happy about it?"

"I am, but many women in the WIZO don't like me because of my German accent. They would prefer a French native as president."

"That's really too bad. I am sure that they will appreciate you once you start. After all the majority elected you."

"Congratulations, Maman," Mel added. "This is a very important undertaking, and I know that you are capable, and worthy of the responsibility."

"I have more good news," Papa added. "We're building a vacation home in La Hauteville, a little village about an hour south of Paris. Hopefully it will be ready by the time you get back from Africa." "We have some good news as well," I said, feeling slightly embarrassed, because it was so soon. "I am pregnant again. Medicine man magic! We are hoping it will be a boy this time!"

Papa and Maman looked at each other and smiled. They were happy for us, and once this news was out we could relax.

After a few days of rest, we took several little trips according to our planned agenda, always returning to Kampala between trips, so that my parents could also spend some time with the children, whom we had left with our *ayah* and Akiki. On one of our day trips we came upon a white line crossing the road — the *Equator!* Mel stopped the car. We got out and stood on the equator, 5,000 feet above sea level! The sky was a bit grey that day and it was drizzling. What a memory!

Papa and Maman returned home, very happy to have visited us.

Around September 1961, I began to wear my pregnancy clothes again, and started to feel the baby kick.

"Guess what, Ilana. You are going to have another little brother or sister soon."

"I want a little brother," Ilana exclaimed.

"Well, you have to ask the good Lord for that, *ma chérie*. We can't do it alone," I replied.

Just before Mel had to leave again to continue with his comparative research, he received three letters — one from the Social Science Research Council. He had been granted a $2,800 stipend. Though he was happy about this grant, it was not enough to cover our expenses for an entire academic year. Mel was hoping to receive additional funds from other sources.

The second letter was from the owner of one of the two tea plantations, thanking him for his excellent analysis and recommendations. The third letter was from Dr. Beattie, complimenting Mel for his excellent work. That meant a lot to Mel.

It rained so much that several roads were closed. At the beginning of 1961, Kenya suffered from a drought, and now it was suffering from catastrophic floods. The Red Cross and other organizations were working very hard. I was so relieved when he was back safely, just in time for Chanukah and New Year's Eve. He had to make a big detour to avoid the flooded and muddy roads. We celebrated the New Year with a glass of champagne at midnight.

In the first week of January, Mel left for the conference in Nairobi. When he returned ten days later, he was a happy man.

"It was one of the best conferences in almost three years," he said. "We also visited the Nairobi Game Park and saw eight lions, twenty yards from the car." Mel spoiled all three of us. Each of the girls got a toy and I received a miniature perfume vaporizer for my handbag and a magnificent record of Israeli songs.

"The doctor thinks the baby might come early," I said.

"In that case I will rearrange my schedule so I can stay in town. I can use this time to write up my latest Toro research."

On Saturday afternoon, January 27, I had tea with Grace, a friend of ours, across the street from our apartment. At 8 p.m. I was not feeling well and went to bed. Much to my surprise, my water broke at midnight. Mel drove me to Nakasero hospital immediately.

At two in the morning, the worst part of labor began. Thank God, Mel was with me once more, and the midwife asked him to hold my legs down. Two and a half hours later, on Sunday, January 28, 1962, the baby was born, earlier than planned and four months before our flight back to Europe. "It's a boy!" Mel exclaimed. "The theory worked!" and the midwife added: "Next time, Mr. Perlman, you will be able to do the delivery yourself." She had not seen many fathers involved with their wives' labor.

We were thrilled to have a son. He was so funny-looking. His head was shaped like a cone and he had a scrunched up, little old face. I cradled him in my arms with so much love, saying, "*Mon pauvre fils!* (my poor son) what have I done to you?"

"How lucky and grateful can one be?" Mel said. "He has your mouth and my dimple and nose." While I was in the hospital, our *ayah* took care of Tamar and Ilana. Mel did the shopping. When he put Ilana to bed that night, she said to him, "Thank you for my little brother."

The next day, a surgeon circumcised our little boy, because there was no *mohel* here. We named him David Eytan. My dream of having all my children before my 30th birthday had come true. Mel immediately sent a telegram to my parents and to his mother to tell them the good news. Papa and Maman wrote back very quickly. They had just returned from their vacation in Switzerland and walked into their apartment with their luggage, when Papa's office called with the news of the telegram. They were so over-joyed to hear they had a healthy grandson that they hugged each other with such force that they both fell over the umbrella stand and broke it.

On January 30, David's birth was announced in the *Uganda Argus* paper. Mel went to the American consulate to claim American citizenship for his son.

Two days after giving birth, I was released from the hospital. I had had three easy pregnancies, and three normal deliveries. I felt so blessed and thanked God for my good fortune! I could not wait to see Ilana and Tamar's faces. Tamar had just taken her first steps. Ilana was happy to have another doll to play with. I felt so great that I went shopping in town, where I ran into a friend.

"You look fabulous," she said. She could not believe that I had just had my third child two days ago.

On February 20, we celebrated Tamar's first birthday and Mel's 29th ahead of time, since he had to leave again. He had to finish his comparative study in other tribes of Uganda. We would be separated for two months — fortunately, for the last time — and now I had three children!

While Mel was gone I received an update from Paris:

The war in Algeria will finally come to an end and Ernest just came back from his military service on March 3rd. He will start working for the Cabinet Plasseraud at the end of April as a chemical patent attorney. Raymond is almost a doctor. Maman is in Israel for the Conference Mondiale of WIZO and is happy to visit Grossmama as well.

Ilana counted the days until her Papa would return. Mel and I were tired of being constantly separated. In March he returned sooner than expected and received magnificent news — a second grant, this time from the National Science Foundation. Together with the Social Science Research Council stipend, we had enough money to get us through our year in Oxford. With God's help, all five of us would be back in Paris in a few weeks.

Mel booked a flight for us to leave from Entebbe on May 12, 1962, arriving in Paris a day later. Worried about what would happen after Uganda gained independence, many Europeans were leaving Kampala.

We were invited for the Seder by Dr. Posznanski, a British professor, and his Ugandan wife, who had become our friends over the years. We were glad to have some Jewish ritual in our lives. We also saw Professor and Mrs. Jelliffe again.

Our Family of five in 1962

In mid-April Mel took me on a little vacation to Karamoja. We felt comfortable leaving our two babies with our *ayah* and Ilana with her best friend from nursery school. Akiki came with us as our interpreter. By the end of the day, after a 260-mile-drive we finally arrived.

In the distance, a few round huts with straw roofs appeared. A few dark, skinny cows were standing on the flat, dry and soiled grounds. Proud and naked Karamojong men with elaborate hairstyles, made of grey clay, were walking around, holding long staffs in their hands. Some were carrying unusual, rectangular wooden objects with them.

"I wonder what those are for," I said to Mel.

The women's breasts were exposed and they wore elaborate, multi-colored bead necklaces. Some went from shoulder to shoulder. The Karamojong were all very thin. Their legs looked like sticks, but overall their bodies seemed healthy and strong.

One of the African warrior nomads noticed us and greeted us with a warm smile. With Akiki's help, we asked him what this little wooden object was that he was carrying. He explained that this was a portable stool that he used as a headrest to protect his hair when he lay down.

"Akiki, the women are wearing so many different types of necklaces. Do they mean something?" Mel asked.

Akiki asked one of the women. She replied, "The number of strands and colors show marital status," Akiki translated. "Married women wear many colorful bead necklaces around their necks and waists, while unmarried girls wear only blue beads around their waists."

There was one stark-naked African with a staff in his hand who stood out to us.

"Akiki, can you ask him if we can take a photo with him and Adyeri?" Mel asked.

The naked man proudly agreed.

When we returned home, tired from the long drive, our children greeted us happily.

It was time to return to Europe. Our departure was bittersweet. Uganda had been a fascinating adventure and the country had been good to us. We added two children to our family, Mel did all the research he needed to write his thesis, and we had money for the following year. Our future looked very bright.

CHAPTER 9

BERKELEY: A PROFESSOR'S WIFE

We returned to Oxford where we re-adjusted to western life. Just a few more months and Mel would be done with his PhD. This second time in Oxford I was much less lonely. Au pairs were inexpensive and many were looking to stay with a family in exchange for room and board to learn English. Imogen, a nice German student, moved in with us. At first I was a little hesitant to live in such close contact with a German girl, but she was a great help and I enjoyed her company, especially since Mel was always either at the University or working on his thesis in the living room. We talked a lot. She was appalled when I told her what we had gone through during the war. Somehow she did not know any of this. She told me she never learned anything in school about the war, only that Germany lost it.

It was time to apply for a teaching position for the next academic year. Mel sent out letters to several universities in the States and to the Hebrew University in Jerusalem. The day of the oral exam was approaching. Then, one day in June, it was finally time to defend his thesis in front of the professors. This was the day he had worked so hard for, the last seven years. For the next two hours I could not stop thinking of my husband. He really deserved to pass. Finally he came home, beaming with pride, exuding unusual confidence.

"After two hours of tough questioning, one of the three professors got up, shook my hand and said, 'Congratulations, Dr. Perlman!'"

Mel grabbed me and twirled me around. Our three children were looking at us with big eyes, wondering what had just happened.

"I passed! I have a PhD! I am soooooo happy, Eva!"

"Mazel Tov! I am so proud of you!"

We were exhilarated. It had been a long haul!

Soon two letters arrived, one from University of California, Berkeley

165

and one from Jerusalem, offering Mel a teaching position as an assistant professor in their respective Social Anthropology departments.

"My dear Mel, if I were you, I would go to Berkeley," Dr. Beattie suggested. "This opportunity comes only once in a lifetime. You can always go to Jerusalem later."

This was such a difficult decision — a lot harder than deciding to get married! We wanted to live in Israel and the Hebrew University came to Mel with an offer. But Berkeley — the prestigious American university — was offering a $7,000 salary!

We thought, talked and reflected for many hours, and finally Mel took Dr. Beattie's advice and made plans to go to Berkeley. We feverishly and happily prepared for another move. We said goodbye to Oxford where we had lived those memorable years.

In August 1963, we sailed on the Queen Elizabeth to New York where we boarded a train and arrived in Berkeley a couple of days later.

The house we rented was within walking distance of the university. We had to purchase some furniture and, for the first time, a small television set. I had grown up without television and I loved our new set. We bought some unfinished chests of drawers and a buffet, hoping to buy something better in the future. We also rented a painting of sailboats — with option to buy — for the dining room wall above the buffet, so the walls would not look so bare. Mel started to prepare for classes right away. He went to the university every day and got to know his colleagues in the Department of Social Anthropology at Kroeber Hall. While he was gone, I got us settled, took care of the children and managed our finances. We enjoyed Mel's fixed salary. Even though we had only one bank account, we had two checkbooks and two registers to keep track of our expenses. When he handed me his check I added it to my checkbook, and then subtracted from my register whatever amount he needed for the month, and he added it to his. The system worked beautifully. We soon managed to buy a second-hand Ford Falcon.

Now that Mel was a professor, we had to get accustomed to our new social status. Professors started inviting us to dinner parties.

"Eva, what would you like to drink? Port, martini, beer, orange juice?" one of our hosts asked me.

"Martini, please," I replied, thinking that it was a sweet wine, similar to the port they call a Martini in France. Half a glass later I nearly passed out. Later someone explained to me that, if a woman orders a Martini in the United States, people assume that she is a heavy drinker. I never asked for that one again!

In the presence of so many highly educated professors I felt very intimidated so I stayed quiet, and was happy to bask in Mel's shadow and to watch him blossom in his chosen career. He enjoyed teaching and he liked his colleagues. The students loved and admired him. He was an inordinately patient teacher. While he built his career, I became a typical American housewife. My job was to raise our children, take them to the playground and wait for them to grow up.

On November 22, 1963, at one o'clock in the afternoon I was standing at my washing machine when I heard the shocking news on the radio: President Kennedy had been shot. I was devastated. How could this happen? I listened intently for an hour, hoping that he would be saved at the hospital, but it wasn't to be. America had lost its president! Mel came home grieving for our country and the Kennedy family. We watched TV for hours. Even Ilana, at the age of six, understood it was a tragic day.

A year later, in the early spring of 1964, we could afford to buy a one and a half story home in the Berkeley hills, with a large bay window and a gorgeous view of the Golden Gate Bridge. I decorated the house with the many artifacts we had brought back from Uganda. The ivory tusk canoe found a place on the mantel and the African stools went in front of the fireplace. Half a floor up were the bedrooms and Mel's office. Ilana and Tamar shared a room while David had his own, into which we put our newly-purchased piano, so Ilana could take lessons. The back stairs that led to David's room soon became the "secret" stairs and the attic was the children's favorite play area. All their toys and games were up there and Mel could not wait to install an electric train for David. Mel's office had big windows and a beautiful view into the back yard with lemon trees and flowers. Finally he had a permanent place to keep all his precious books that had traveled so many places with us. Outside the back door was a lovely patio. For the first time we felt really settled. Now we could raise our children according to our Jewish traditions and celebrate the holidays.

On Friday nights, we gathered in our cozy breakfast nook to celebrate the beginning of Shabbat. I lit the two candles on the three-branch candle holder from Grossmama, which Maman had found in the trunk, and recited the Hebrew blessing. Mel took a glass of wine in one hand and his prayer book in the other and welcomed the Sabbath with the *kiddush*, ending with the blessings over the wine and bread.

The children enjoyed the festive atmosphere and the scent of warm challah. I prepared fish the way I remembered Maman preparing it when I was growing up. For dessert I served *flammeri*, a special fluffy vanilla custard, with strawberry syrup.

Money was tight. After paying the mortgage, $115 per month, we had just enough for food, essentials and stamps to write to Bobbe (Mel's mother) in Kansas City, Mel's father in Colorado Springs, Papa and Maman in Paris and our family in Israel.

On August 16, Ilana turned seven. Despite our financial situation, Mel and I managed to celebrate birthdays with quite a few gifts. I baked a cake. We all sat in the breakfast nook and watched Ilana open her presents (very carefully so I could recycle the wrapping paper).

Just around the corner from our house was Cragmont Elementary School where Ilana started 2nd grade. We enrolled *les petits* (the little ones), three-year old Tamar and two-year old David, in a nursery school that was run by parents. I volunteered at the school one day a week so we saved a lot on tuition. While many other mothers prepared their children's lunches, I felt that it was good for *les petits* to learn to prepare their own. They quickly learned to make peanut butter sandwiches, wrap them in wax paper and put them in a paper bag with a banana, an apple and a napkin.

Mel and I continued to keep up with our promise to raise our children bilingually. I spoke exclusively to them in French and Mel spoke to them mainly in English. Now that they had started school and everyone spoke English around us, it was much more challenging for me, but I insisted they speak to me in French. If they didn't, I refused to respond or simply put my hands over my ears and said, *"Je ne comprends pas l'anglais."* It was tough for them too, but I held my ground and French remained the primary language at home. By now Mel spoke it also very well, and even knew some slang, the kind you never learn in school.

Mel had grown up in a large, conservative Jewish family with lots of cousins, so he took it for granted that we would send our children to Sunday school. Maman had been very rigid about ritual, which caused me to rebel against conservative religion, so I suggested we join a reform temple. Temple Beth El was just six minutes away by car. It was a small temple and we liked Rabbi Abrams. We became members and Ilana started Sunday and

Hebrew school. Even though we did not attend services regularly and I did not keep a kosher kitchen, we observed Jewish holidays and festivals and I never brought pork or shellfish into our home.

As our second academic year began in September 1964, Mel and I were looking forward to celebrating our first Rosh Hashanah in our new home. I made *gefilte fish*, chicken soup and a honey cake. The children helped to bake a round challah to symbolize the New Year rounding off nicely. I set the table and we dipped apples into honey and wished one another a sweet new year. Ten days later we observed Yom Kippur, the holiest day on the Jewish calendar. Dressed in white our family went to the synagogue on the eve of Yom Kippur. The cantor sang the *Kol Nidrei* prayer and it moved me deeply. The rabbi asked us to reflect on the past year of our lives and ask for forgiveness. Have we helped others when we had the chance? What are we committed to improving in the coming year? The next morning, we went to services and stayed a good part of the day. While Mel and I fasted, I had to take the children home to feed them. As the sun set, when three stars were visible in the sky, we asked God to inscribe us in the *Book of Life* for the coming year.

I had grown up listening to opera music, and I loved it. San Francisco was about one hour away and had a beautiful opera house.

"What do you think about getting an annual subscription to the San Francisco Opera? The season starts in September," I said to Mel.

"Sounds like a good idea," he said.

I was excited, but then I realized we could not really afford to also pay for all the babysitting that this would require. I had heard of a neighborhood co-op where parents traded babysitting time on a point system, so I contacted them immediately and we became part of the group. I loved to babysit for others at night because, once the children were in bed, I could do my own thing — write letters, knit, repair socks or catch up on reading. In fact, I soon realized that I got a lot more done while babysitting out than when I stayed at home. I also babysat for our neighbor across the street. She knew that Mel and I loved classical music and opera.

"By the way, *Pêcheurs de Perles* by Bizet will be transmitted live on the radio from the New York Opera House on Saturday morning. You should listen to it," she suggested.

Of course I remembered that beautiful opera. I saw it in Milan at La Scala, but I hadn't heard it since and Mel had never heard it. That Saturday morning we turned on the radio to hear *"Je crois entendre encore"* sung by Nikolai Gedda, an incredible counter tenor who could sing very high notes. We were overwhelmed by the beautiful music. We immediately bought the record and added it to our growing collection. From that day on we spent every Saturday morning listening to the Texaco-sponsored opera. Opera music became part of our family's daily life.

We continued to be invited to dinner parties. The Montefiores, a wealthy English professor and his wife, invited us to their mansion. I had never been in such a house. His servants served us a sumptuous dinner in a chandeliered dining room with sterling silverware, exquisite china and Bohemian crystal glasses. How could I ever invite these people to our modest home and find the right company to invite with them?

Every professor had invited us over to his house at least once. Now it was time to reciprocate. That made me nervous, especially when I remembered my fiasco in Kampala. How could I quickly learn to cook well? I had heard of Julia Child's popular cooking show so I started watching her religiously every week. She had gone to cooking school in France and was able to adapt French cooking to the everyday American kitchen. Her book *Mastering the Art of French Cooking* was a hit — and a great help for me. I was confident that if I followed her timeless and foolproof recipes to the letter, I would become an excellent cook. I planned my first dinner party.

My menu was chicken livers on crackers, *coq au vin* with parsley potatoes, green peas with butter, green salad, brandy snaps for dessert, and coffee and liqueur to finish off.

The party was a great success and I felt encouraged to plan my next one. Mel was so proud of me. To make sure that I did not invite the same couples again together and that I would not offer the same menu, I kept a record of the dishes I served, the guests I had invited and the dress I wore. I also wrote down how the evening went — the mood, what had worked and what had not. In this case I wrote: *'This first dinner was a complete success, but the conversation dragged a bit.* After subsequent dinners, I wrote: *'very enjoyable evening'* or *'our guests were extremely well matched'*... *'lively evening'*... *'guests warmed up gradually.'*

By the time the last guests had left, I was exhausted. After all, the preparation for this dinner party had kept me busy for two full days cleaning the house, shopping for the meal and cooking as much as I could the day before, setting the table and finishing up cooking the day of the dinner party.

Mel was always very perceptive and sweet. Seeing the stack of dishes and my tired expression, he put Chopin's *Nocturnes* on the record player and then came into the kitchen to help me clean up. I washed the dishes and he dried them. I could not stand the idea of getting up in the morning and facing the mess of the night before. It gave us an opportunity to chat about the evening. That was about the only time Mel came into the kitchen; I did not expect him to help with chores at other times. Soon we had about three or four dinner parties a month until we had invited all the people who had invited us.

I quickly figured out that it required the same amount of work to make dinner for six as it did for twelve. My chicken livers on crackers, bouillabaisse, brandy snaps, and coffee eclairs were a hit, so I served this same menu as often as I could, but never to the same guests.

Professor Meisel's wife baked the most delicious challah and she was kind enough to share her recipe with me. That next Friday, when Ilana and *les petits* were at school, I tried out her recipe for Shabbat dinner. It turned out delicious. Whenever I made Shabbat dinner with meat or chicken, I made the challah dough with water and oil only, so as not to mix dairy and meat in the same meal.

Mel's passion and only hobby was photography. He managed to carve out some time to set up a darkroom in our basement. He spent hours in there developing pictures. Except for the red light bulb it was pitch dark in the room. Every once in a while I went downstairs to see how he was doing and brought him a cup of tea. I admired his patience and his perfectionism, but being in a dark room without windows made me feel uneasy and I could never stay very long.

To perfect his skill, Mel took a class in photography by correspondence. As part of his homework, the school sent him a black and white negative of a portrait of Winston Churchill. Mel's task was to produce the best print possible. I found him surrounded by various prints of the same portrait. I could not tell the difference, but it took many prints for him to be finally satisfied with one.

He also had to photograph a subject with perspective, so he dressed our children warmly and took them to the nearby park, equipped with crayons, toys and our three African stools. He set up the chairs diagonally at various distances and took photos with his Rolleiflex while they were drawing. The children were very patient and cooperative subjects.

Photography Assignment

During the 1964 fall semester, about a year after we had moved to Berkeley, Mel came home looking disturbed.

"There was a sit-in on campus today. The students are protesting against the status quo. They are upset because they are not allowed to be politically active on campus." This started a period of significant unrest on the Berkeley campus, when free speech was severely restricted.

Christmas 1964. It was freezing cold outside. That particular day reminded me of Oxford. We enjoyed spending time with each other in our cozy, warm home. I hated going out in the cold. To make sure that the children got some fresh air every day regardless of the weather, I bundled them up in their coats, hats, gloves and boots and told them, "Run around the block twice! When you get back you'll get some ice cream." Fifteen minutes later they returned out of breath with red cheeks, happy to get the promised treat.

The year had gone by really fast. Again it was New Year's Eve. I made jelly doughnuts, just as Maman had always done. Ilana helped. We made about 60 or 70 donuts. On the first of January we gave many away to friends and neighbors to wish them a sweet New Year.

In January David turned three. We gave him a fluffy toy dog with floppy ears and tail. Holding it by one ear while sucking his thumb, he dragged his new friend with him everywhere. Soon it looked grimy, but David loved it anyway, and wouldn't let go.

Mel's mother Bertha (Bobbe) came to visit for six weeks. She baked huge chocolate chip cookies. We all loved them. Bobbe was an easy guest to please. I took her everywhere with me — shopping, yoga, nursery school. In our home, she spent most of her time reading.

When I picked Mel up from the university at the end of the day, he looked concerned.

"Things are getting worse every day," he said as he sat down in the car. "The students are becoming more vocal. They disturb classes and campus life. Professors can't even talk to each other anymore. I was walking through the grounds with a colleague and a policeman told us to go our separate ways. God knows how this will end. If things continue like this, I think we may have to move somewhere else."

Soon civil rights demonstrations were replaced with anti-war rallies. Student and civil rights activist Mario Savio became the most charismatic speaker on campus and leader of the Free Speech Movement. Strikes and demonstrations on university campuses were becoming the order of the day all over the country. Young people were fighting for civil rights and the end of segregation. Folk singer Joan Baez was an outspoken social justice activist and her song, *We Shall Overcome,* was on the radio all the time as a key anthem of the civil rights movement. The Free Speech Movement was the hot topic at the next dinner to which we were invited. There was also a lot of discontent about the Vietnam War.

"That Mario Savio really knows how to arouse the crowd into a frenzy," one of the professors remarked. I stayed quiet as usual, listening attentively, until one of the professors told a joke. I could not help myself and reciprocated with another. Jokes continued flying back and forth between that professor and me.

"Eva, I am discovering a new side to you!" the hostess remarked, surprised. Mel seemed happy that I was coming out of my shell, animating the party.

With all the demonstrations on campus, Mel was relieved when he was off for the summer of 1965. In August Papa and Maman came to visit us in Berkeley and to welcome them, Mel and I had a big wine and cheese party with all our new friends. They had exciting news.

"Ernest is getting married in December!" Maman was so happy. "Her name is Annie. She is beautiful, very smart and a neuropsychiatrist."

"What exciting news! I am so happy for him," I said.

In December the five of us flew to Paris to attend the wedding. At the Charles de Gaulle airport, Mel asked a porter to help with our luggage. When David heard the porter answer in French, he looked at me, surprised, and said, *"Il parle Français!"* (He speaks French!). That was a huge discovery for him. Our children started to understand why I had insisted they speak French with me. Although they all spoke English when they had to, my parents and brothers were happy they could speak French with our children, who in turn could understand everything and were happy to be able to communicate.

We were delighted to meet Annie and her parents. I was so happy that Ernest had found his soulmate. She was indeed an incredibly beautiful bride, and Ernest was so happy and handsome in tails and top hat. It was quite a family reunion! Grossmama had come from Israel. My daughters looked elegant in their red velvet dresses with white lace and David was adorable with his suit and bow tie. Mel and I looked pretty good too, if I do say so myself. Mel wore a tuxedo, I wore a sleeveless pink dress, high heels and elbow length white gloves! We had come a long way since Uganda.

We celebrated New Year's Eve at Annie's parents' house. Our families merged nicely.

Raymond was by this time dating a lovely, slender, dark-haired young woman named Monique, and I wondered if we would soon come back for another wedding,

When we returned to Berkeley, David turned four and Mel gave him a spinning top. I watched David follow Mel to the patio outside. Mel wrapped the string around the top and then showed David how to throw it down a certain way. David watched intently. Then it was his turn to try. He tried and tried, but he could not figure out how to do it. He got so frustrated that he stomped his feet on the ground, but Mel did not let him give up. He kept encouraging him very patiently, coaching him all along. Finally perseverance and stubbornness paid off. Both came back into the house glowing with pride. David had finally conquered the spinning top! His other birthday present was a new toy dog and he willingly gave up the old, dirty one.

Whenever Mel had a free minute he loved to teach the girls how to play chess. David was eager to learn too. Soon all three children were so good that Mel bought each of them their own chessboard and organized tournaments. Mel took turns playing against each child, all three sitting in a row.

Tamar came up with cute remarks. I watched one day a Public Television program about a baby's birth with the children. It was pretty graphic. In order to minimize the pain of the mother that might negatively influence my daughters, 8 and 5, I emphasized for them the difficult passage of the baby through the narrow birth canal. When all was done, Tamar exclaimed: " Oh boy, I wouldn't want to be born!" Another time, she said:"Wow! Maman was born in Germany, Papa was born in Texas, Ilana was born in Paris, thank goodness we all met in Kampala!"

It was hard to believe that we had been married for ten years. In July 1966, to celebrate our 10th wedding anniversary, Mel and I took a three-day trip to Carmel, just the two of us. Friends watched our children. It had been a while since we had time to ourselves. It was a beautiful summer day and we took a walk on the beach. While we were walking, Mel began speaking, carefully choosing his words. "I know that you are extremely busy with the children and you really do everything to keep me happy, honey, but I hoped that you would have a more interesting life of your own, so that you could develop and grow as a person."

I had not expected this at all, but I knew he had a point. I was not intellectually-minded but more of a pragmatic person, a contented housewife and mother, taking care of my family every day and not living in the world of ideas as he did. I was not sure if this is what he meant, but it is how I understood him at the time: I wasn't a stimulating wife. The other professors' wives could talk politics, had degrees, and always seemed to have something interesting to say.

"You are right," I said after a moment. "I would like to be a more exciting wife for you and I will try my best."

Mel stopped, took my hands in his and then said with his kind and gentle voice, "I love you, Eva. I hope you can find something you enjoy doing, learning, or pursuing beyond taking care of the children and me."

We continued walking in silence. Although he had put it mildly, I was hurt. In that moment, his words left me with deep sadness. It would take a long time for me to fully understand. Decades later, I think I understood what he really meant. He was encouraging me to become all that I could be — not that he necessarily needed another intellectual partner. He had plenty at the university. But he wanted to support me to develop my full potential in my own right. Back at home life continued as usual, but I kept thinking of ways to improve myself and those thoughts did not leave me.

We were invited to a French professor's house. It was amazing. The Louis XIV red velvet armchairs were beautiful to look at, but uncomfortable to sit on. Proudly the professor served us a magnificent, rich dinner — homemade liver pâté, cold salmon with homemade mayonnaise and rum baba topped with lots of whipping cream. That night I was really sick with indigestion. The following year we were again invited to his home, and served the exact same dinner. This time I ate a lot less and did not get sick. It showed me the necessity of continuing to keep accurate records of the meals that I served at our dinner parties.

In August, all five of us went camping in Yosemite. It was an inexpensive vacation. We ate at the cafeteria and bought four meals for the five of us — to save money. I made sure that Mel and the children had enough to eat and I lost some weight, which I was not unhappy about. I taught eight-year old Ilana and five-year old Tamar to knit. "I want to knit, too," four-year old David piped up, so I gave him knitting needles and he learned as well.

Once a month the faculty wives met for tea at the International House in Berkeley. Once a year each wife had to volunteer and serve the tea.

"Ladies, what can I serve you?" I asked as I approached a table with two older ladies. As soon as I turned around, I could not remember what they had ordered, because I had not listened. Embarrassed I had to apologize and ask again. Waitressing was definitely not my specialty.

For New Year's Eve 1966, one of the professors was planning to have a costume party and Mel and I were invited.

"Let's go as a Toro couple," I suggested. "We can wear the outfits we brought back from Africa." At that time, it was not politically incorrect.

"I like that idea," Mel replied with a subtle smile.

Party time came. I put on the long, pink, flowery dress I had brought back from Toro and the large, colorful African wrap that I draped around myself. As an accent I wore the ivory bracelet Mel had bought me in the

Belgian Congo. I hid my blond hair under a black kerchief. Mel wore regular pants and a long, white embroidered caftan from Uganda and a suit jacket, just like the African men wore in the bush. Then I darkened our faces and arms with black makeup. Equipped with an authentic spear and a beaded pipe from Uganda, Mel walked out of the door and I followed him, carrying a woven basket on my head filled with my homemade doughnuts.

Our hosts opened the door. We stood there without smiling, since the Batoro people never smiled for photographs. When our host looked at us he was puzzled. It was obvious that he did not immediately recognize us.

"Mel and Eva," I said.

"Really? You look fantastic!" he exclaimed and laughed heartily. We were ushered into the living room. Other guests in costumes were chatting or sipping wine.

"*Oraire ota, Amoti?*" (How are you?) I asked Mel, staying in character.

"*Kurungi, Adyeri, webale muno,*" (Well, Adyeri, thank you) he replied.

"*Abomuka baliyo?*" (Are the people at home fine?)

"*Eh, baliyo.*" (They are.)

To top it off I cited the Rutoro proverb we learned.

"*Mpora mpora ekahikia omunyongorozi ha iziba.*" Of course no one understood, but everyone clapped.

"Well done!" one of the guests remarked.

The next day the hostess called.

"You won't believe this! One of our guests said as he was leaving, "You know, I have never seen an African woman with blue eyes!"

This was the first day of 1967. My thoughts went back to the conversation I had with Mel in Carmel. What could I possibly do to improve myself? Now that all three children were in school I had more time to myself. Maybe I could take some adult education classes.

The next day I went and got a course catalogue of local classes. As I flipped through the pages, a class in pattern drafting caught my attention. To create basic patterns, and then learn to copy any dress or skirt from a magazine or a store window and adapt it to my size, excited me. I could improve on what I had learned in Kampala. Interior decorating and yoga sounded interesting as well. I promptly signed up for all three courses. Mel was pleased.

I had worried for a while about how we could invite the Montefiores to our home for dinner. I had been very intimidated by their lavish dinner the previous year. When Mel came home from work one day he said, "Honey, Professor Jelliffe (from the hospital in Kampala) and Dr. Beattie are in town. We should invite them for dinner with the Montefiores. They are of the same academic standing."

"That sounds fantastic! We should do it," I replied.

By then I had gotten used to preparing several good dinners for professors and I felt more at ease. My repertoire of tasty meals learned from Julia Child had been tested on various guests, so I immediately took out my dinner diary and began to carefully create the menu. My croque-en-bouche, multi-layered cream puffs filled with vanilla custard held together with caramel, had been well received when I tried it before. This time I wanted to do something even more special, so I stuck the cream puffs together in the shape of Africa in honor of our African experts. When I placed the sweet dessert on the dinner table, Dr. Beattie's eyes lit up.

"What a piece of art," he said. "I feel honored."

It was a huge success. Mel was very proud of me.

We continued to get regular mail from my parents. Maman wrote that Raymond was getting married! We were so happy for him and Monique. He was the last child to move out. We booked our flight to Paris with two stopovers, one in Colorado Springs so that we could visit Mel's father and his wife Marie, and one in Kansas City to visit Bobbe and the rest of Mel's family. We were glad when we finally landed in Paris in early September 1967. Papa, Maman and my brothers were so excited to see us. Maman was wearing a beautiful new gold necklace.

"What a beautiful jewel," I complimented her.

"It's from Papa," she said proudly.

After that I never saw her without it.

For the religious wedding we all gathered in a synagogue in Lyon where Monique's family lived. My daughters looked lovely in their blue and green matching dresses and David in his tuxedo. They behaved very well. I was so proud of them and I wanted Maman to be proud of me. I will always remember the wedding luncheon *Chez la Mère Barnier* and the *fromage blanc*, which I still dream about. We always had a great time in Paris. Both my brothers are fortunate to still be married to their first loves, well over 50 years later.

A few days after the wedding we returned to Berkeley as Mel had to teach.

"Eva, would you be interested in teaching French in the afternoons?" one of the parents of Cragmont Elementary asked me when I dropped off the children.

"Sure," I replied. "That sounds like fun."

We could certainly use a little extra income and since my nursing certificate was not accepted in the U.S. this seemed like a good part-time job. I also enjoyed the classes I was attending.

One evening Mel and I had plans to go out, but no one from our babysitting co-op was available. After making a few phone calls, the 13-year-old daughter of one of the co-op members was happy to help out. When we came home that night Ilana was upset.

"I could have done a better job myself," she reported. "Instead of watching *les petits* in the bathtub, the girl played with our magic soap and wasted a lot of it!"

"Well, maybe you can babysit from now on when we are not far away," Mel suggested.

Ilana was proud and *les petits* knew they had to behave when Ilana was in charge and I knew they would.

In our mailbox I found a large manila envelope with a Swiss stamp. I pulled out a letter and a delicate little booklet that Maman made while on vacation in Switzerland, entitled *Le Grand Secret*. Inside were poems and fine, detailed watercolor illustrations of colorful wildflowers that she had collected in alpine meadows. Maman explained why Swiss chocolate was the best in the world. It was made with the most fragrant and best quality milk, produced by Swiss cows that feasted on the best grasses and wildflowers. Her love for flowers and drawing could be felt on every page.

When I read her letter I was quite amused. She wrote that their hotel manager was an irritating and disagreeable man who had no customer service skills, and that she had never seen him smile. Many guests disliked him. A few days before the end of December he announced that there would be a costume party after dinner on New Year's Eve and that every guest was invited to dress accordingly.

She wrote:

"We did not have any costumes with us, but I had no problem creating outfits for Papa and myself with what was available in our room. I asked Papa to put on his black coat. Then I transformed two white

towels into a hat and a neck roll. He looked quite fetching in his costume. Next I took the lampshade from the night table and put it on my head, draping it with the sheer window curtain like a veil over my face. The curtain rod became my magic wand. On the way to the party, we passed by the unpleasant manager. When I saw him, I smiled and touched him lightly on the shoulder with my curtain rod, saying with my sweetest voice, "Bonsoir, Monsieur ! Je suis la fée Mélusine (I am the fairy Mélusine). When I touch you with my magic wand you will become the most amiable man ever." He became indeed most charming on the spot, and stayed that way until we checked out of the hotel."

Maman never ceased to amaze me with her creativity and I admired her for it.

It was the beginning of 1968. That same month David turned six, but this time we did not give him a new doggie.

"David, you are a big boy now," I said. "Maybe it's time to lay the doggie to rest. This is really a toy for babies. What do you think?"

He thought for a moment, looked at the other toys and then, without hesitation, surrendered his poor dirty dog for good.

I continued to explore opportunities for self-development. The pattern drafting, interior design and yoga classes had been a lot of fun and very educational. As soon as the new course catalogue came out, I looked through it to see what other classes might speak to me. A ten-week course in *Achieving Your Personal Style* caught my attention. The objective of the course was to understand your personal style and how it would enhance your individuality. The course consisted of lectures, workshops, home projects and individual counseling. Since my 36th birthday was nearing in May, I asked Mel if the class could be my birthday present. On May 18th, he spoiled me with a course registration. I was excited.

The course started with having our colors done. I was looking forward to this and had an appointment at the Claremont Hotel for a one-on-one consultation.

When I arrived, I met a man in his early forties with long hair and a sweet smile sitting in front of a mountain of fabric swatches. I had been told that he was an artist and color expert. He was to determine what "my" colors would be to wear in various settings.

Part of the course was the study of visual awareness, and introspection into who we were, our moods and our feelings. We had to figure out what made us unique. The instructor explained that people fall into four main categories or *harmonies* - spring, summer, autumn and winter. When the mailman came to our door with a large envelope in his hand I knew it had to be the results of the analysis. I opened it right away. *"You are Spring,"* I read. *"Your colors are radiant, light and bright. They appear to have an inner illumination, a kind of sunlit luminosity, which stems from your blue eyes, which have a refreshing childlike innocence. Your accent adds to your charm and beauty. You look somewhat like a more innocent, young Michele Morgan."* I was enchanted with this description.

I felt oddly validated. I liked the qualities associated with spring, especially the word *spontaneous*. Now I understood why Maman was sometimes annoyed by me when I was a teenager. As I got easily excited and threw my arms in the air with enthusiasm, Maman would say, *"Eva, calme-toi, tu n'es pas à la Comédie Française"* (Calm down, you are not performing on stage). "Behave like *une jeune fille de bonne famille"* (a young lady from a good family). She wanted me to be sedate, quiet and soft-spoken at all times. After reading this analysis, I felt like I had been given permission to be myself and to break out of my shell without feeling immodest, or guilty for not behaving according to my mother's idea of the "right" social behavior. I *was* animated and there was *nothing* wrong with that. I finally felt free to be me. In contrast to my mother, Mel had always let me be *me* and he had helped me to become more confident. In fact, he liked my vivacity and enthusiasm, as he was so calm, cool and collected. I used to say, "We complement each other perfectly. If we had both been like me, our marriage may have exploded, and had we been more like him, our life may have been too quiet."

I started to wear makeup for the first time. In my pattern drafting class I created my own patterns and made some new clothes in pastel shades based on what I had learned in the course. I had a lovely Israeli necklace and I made a princess-style dress in a light pink with a neckline to show off the necklace. The dress was lovely. "Oh, that's a good color on you! You look wonderful!" Mel said. He was thrilled to see me coming into my own. Unfortunately, I wanted to outsmart the "dry clean only" instructions and I washed the dress. The fabric was ruined and I had to throw the dress away!

By the end of the course I knew myself better and had become much more confident in the way I showed myself to the world.

It was our fifth year in the United States and I thought that we would stay forever, so I applied for U.S. citizenship. I wanted to vote and to feel that I belonged. I had to learn about the government and an official interviewed me to see how well I spoke English. It was pretty easy. He asked me who the governor of California was! I became a proud United States citizen in the second half of 1968 and automatically lost my French citizenship. I tried a few years later to reclaim it to have dual citizenship, but I was told that I had only been naturalized French. I was not a French citizen by birth and therefore I was not eligible.

At that time, the Berkeley School Board decided after much debate to support desegregation of the schools. An environment that lessened prejudice and discrimination was the goal. The racial makeup of Berkeley's elementary schools changed dramatically overnight. On September 10, yellow school buses started bringing black children to schools in white neighborhoods and vice versa. Ilana, 11, was still in 6th grade at our little elementary school around the corner from our house, together with Tamar and David. The desegregation had little impact on them this first year.

However, when Ilana entered 7th grade the following September, at Martin Luther King Junior Middle School, the desegregation hit closer to home. Unfortunately, the children had not been taught to understand one another. Besides racial strife, puberty added its own problems for budding teenagers. Ilana had never encountered such tension in school before. On the surface she understood the reason for integration, but she did not understand why it brought about so much tension. Black and white teenagers played pranks on each other. Ilana came home frantic.

"Maman," she said, "you won't believe what happened in school today. A white girl was standing at her locker and a black student came behind her and cut off one of her beautiful long braids! Everyday there is a fire in a garbage can. I am afraid to go to school."

Cragmont Elementary School also had some black students. At dinner Tamar kept bringing up her new friend Phyllis.

"Is your friend black or white?" I asked out of curiosity. Six year-old Tamar thought for a moment, then responded with a puzzled look on her face, "I don't know." She was completely color-blind and I understood then that if we mixed children at an early age, integration would work.

We did our best to expose our children to new things during these times. Two summers in a row we went to two camps in northern California.

Each time we spent a week in a beautiful forest of pine trees and did a lot of walking. The children really enjoyed those vacations and living outside all day. One winter we drove to Lake Tahoe to give them the joy of playing in the snow, which they had never seen. In the summer of 1968, *The Magic Flute* was being performed at the Greek Theater in Berkeley. We all went and enjoyed it, and it reinforced our children's love for opera.

Mel started the academic year again in September 1969. When I went to pick him up at 5 p.m., he was not at the south gate where he usually waited. All the gates were barricaded. Concerned I drove around, looking for another entrance. Finally I saw him standing on the sidewalk looking distraught.

"The students demonstrated again today," he said as he got into the car. "It got so out of control that the police had to use tear gas to disperse the crowds." The very next day, Mel came home looking worried.

"We had a department meeting today. I will not be given tenure next year," he said. "After next June I will be out of a job."

"Why? What happened?" I was shocked.

"*Publish or perish* is the motto at Berkeley. I have written a few articles, but I have not published enough. I have contributed chapters in various books, but I still have not written up my Uganda research in a book of my own. To get tenure in Berkeley, you have to publish, publish, publish and I have devoted my time to teaching and to the students instead." I felt sad and anxious for Mel, but excited at the same time. A new adventure?

Mel immediately applied to several universities in the eastern United States and Canada. Before long he received an invitation to an interview for an associate professorship at Brock University in St. Catharines, Ontario, Canada. I loved the idea of moving to Canada, in the Toronto area. It was closer to France! Living in Berkeley had been interesting and pleasant, but if they didn't want Mel anymore, I was just as happy to move away. Mel was perhaps not the most brilliant man, but he was intelligent, a deep thinker and a very hard worker. He reminded me of the La Fontaine fable *The Tortoise and the Hare*. Consistency, perseverance and not letting yourself be distracted from your goal worked better than brilliance and lack of focus.

Mel went to St. Catharines, Canada, by himself for the interview and was offered the position at Brock University. He liked the campus, the department and his future colleagues, and got a realtor to show him a few homes. Soon he called me from Canada.

"Motek, I found a beautiful two-story Tudor-style house with five bed-rooms on a lovely, wide, tree-lined street for $40,000. St. Catharines is only sixty miles southeast of Toronto. What do you think? Should I buy it?"

"If you like it, honey, I know I will like it too. Go ahead and buy it!" I answered without hesitation. It was April 18, 1970. Mel and I could make life-changing decisions in a minute over the phone!

A week later Mel was back. He liked everything about Brock and St. Catharines.

"The bus stop is just around the corner from our house. It won't take me longer than ten minutes to get to work. "The good news is that St. Catharines has a large francophone population. And not far from our house there is a French Catholic public school, The Immaculate Conception. I think our children may have a good chance of being accepted," Mel added.

The next few days I spent getting our house ready for sale. If we painted it, it would look much nicer and it might be easier to sell. With that idea in mind I got into our Ford Falcon with the intention to buy some paint at a big warehouse. At an intersection without stop signs or traffic lights, in the middle of nowhere, a car that I had not seen came at me at a ninety-degree angle and before I knew it I was hit. I held on to the steering wheel for dear life as my car flipped over and I landed on my back on its ceiling. I had not worn my seat belt. On the other hand, had I used it, I now would be hanging upside down. My heart was pounding. In a state of shock I just lay there waiting. Hopefully someone would pass by and call the police. After what seemed an eternity I heard a police car. The policeman got the door open and pulled me out. Luckily, although shaken, I was alright. I was very grateful that I had gotten away with just a big bruise on my hip. The policeman took me home.

I really felt the need to go to the junkyard and take a look at our Falcon. When I saw the car, a pile of twisted metal, all I could think was, '*How on earth did I get out uninjured?*' I felt incredibly lucky and thankful. What a miracle! With the insurance money we purchased a brand new Volvo station wagon for $4,000 with superior safety features for the long trip ahead of us.

Just three months before our departure, and her 13th birthday, Ilana became a Bat Mitzvah on May 9. She led the entire service and did exceed-ingly well. Mel and I were very proud of her.

We were ready to move again.

CHAPTER 10

A NEW LIFE IN CANADA

In August 1970, we were on our way to Canada in our new Volvo station wagon, crossing the country from west to east. Almost 3,800 miles lay ahead of us. The car was packed to the ceiling and we sat very cramped. Since several of Mel's relatives lived along the way, we were planning to visit them. We had not seen them for a while.

In Colorado Springs, we stopped to visit Mel's father and his wife Marie. They were happy to be our tour guides for a few days and took us to see several caves. The children loved the tram ride to Pikes Peak. We also visited the U.S. Air Force Academy Cadet Chapel, a modern architectural masterpiece of glass and aluminum spires.

By this time we were all grateful for the air conditioning in our new car — the temperature was well over 100 degrees Fahrenheit. On the way to Kansas City, Missouri, to see Bobbe we visited an Indian reservation where we bought some Navajo jewelry. A few days later we continued our northeast journey to Terre Haute, Indiana to spend a little time with Mel's brother Ralph and his wife Elizabeth. Mel was very close to his brother, although they did not see each other very often.

Early in the morning we left Terre Haute and by midday we reached Detroit. A terrific summer storm was pummeling our car, making visibility very difficult. Mel and the children were fast asleep. Just one more bridge over the Detroit River and we were in Windsor, Canada. It was an incredible feeling. Here the lawns were green and the atmosphere was peaceful and serene.

Five hours later we reached our destination: St. Catharines, a pleasant provincial town of about 100,000 inhabitants on the southern shore of Lake Ontario. It was the home of multiple ethnic groups, it had a General Motors factory, a university, and two large hospitals. We were all looking forward to getting out of the car so we could stretch our legs.

By the time we reached Hillcrest Avenue, it was already getting dark. Mel stopped in front of our new home, a two-story brick house with a big lawn surrounded by tall trees. A long driveway led to the garage in the back. I loved it at first sight.

Our Home on Hillcrest Avenue

The next day the moving van arrived with our furniture and new appliances and we settled into our five-bedroom home. We all loved it. While the children and I unpacked, Mel focused on setting up his office. He was to start teaching in Brock University's Sociology department in two weeks.

As soon as we had a free moment, we met with the principal of the French Catholic school.

"Do you speak French at home?" the principal asked.

"Yes, we do," Mel replied.

"Then we'll be happy to accept your children. Do you want them to attend the religious classes or would you prefer they go to the library and do their homework instead?"

"Ask the children," we answered in unison. We wanted them to have a well-rounded education and learning about other religions was fine with us.

At a parent-teacher conference a few months later the teacher asked me, "Have you taught your son anything about Catholicism?"

"No," I said. "Why do you ask?"

"Well, the other day in religious class your son was the only one who knew the correct answer," the teacher remarked. We laughed and I realized then that David had decided to attend religious classes.

We were excited to celebrate our first Shabbat and spend time together making challah. When Ilana saw me gather the ingredients, she said, "Maman, can I try to make it by myself this time?"

"You sure can," I said.

I handed her the recipe and left her alone. After a while she called me "Maman, the dough does not seem to rise. What can I do?" "Well, either the water or the milk was too hot and killed the yeast." We still tried to bake the dough. When I took it out of the oven, it was hard as a rock.

"Maman, I made rock challah," Ilana remarked. We both laughed.

Life in Canada was very pleasant. The countryside was beautiful, green and clean. After the tumultuous years in Berkeley we cherished the peaceful and serene atmosphere. Brock was a young university and Mel enjoyed teaching there.

The first few months I felt very lonely in St. Catharines. The children were at school and Mel at the university, so I signed up for a class in pattern drafting, hoping to meet some women who had the same interests I had. The male teacher sold his own designs. Several of us liked his cape and asked him for the pattern.

"Buy the cape and you can copy the pattern," he replied.

I didn't like him and stopped going after three months. He was so different from my Berkeley teacher, who would have given the shirt off her back — and the pattern for it! — if we had asked her.

We had been spoiled with the weather in Africa and California and now we had to adjust to a bitterly cold winter. When I looked out the window one morning in December, three inches of snow had fallen during the night. Our long driveway was covered and needed to be shoveled, so Mel put on several layers of clothing — first a shirt and tie, then a warm sweater and a suit jacket over it, and his black leather coat. He also put on a leather hat, wrapped a scarf around his neck and slipped his hands into leather gloves. Twenty minutes later he came back in. His glasses fogged up, his nose was red and running. He hugged me and went off to his classes.

I checked the employment section of the local newspaper every week and I always saw the same ad several weeks in a row:

Looking for a smiling person to assist me in my fast-growing business. Two hours a day can earn you $45 a week. Call for an interview.

How come this advertiser could not find *one* smiling person in all of St. Catharines? I called and was invited for an interview. A distributor for Fashion Two Twenty, a network marketing company like Mary Kay in the U.S., was looking for a beauty consultant.

"I love your smile and would love to have you on my team," the lady said. "I will train you to use our products. You will learn to give facials and apply make-up. I think you would be very good at this."

An hour later I walked out, highly motivated with my new investment, a skincare glamour case. I started to take better care of my skin and apply makeup daily. Since leaving Berkeley I had stopped using makeup. Mel noticed my new appearance.

"You look very nice," he smiled.

I had to find women who were willing to host a makeup party at their home. A friend agreed to host my first show. While I gave her a facial in front of her guests, I talked about the products and explained how to use them. By the end of the party, I got my first orders and booked my next show. Meeting women and helping them look and feel pretty was rewarding. The company also had a few products for men such as a special aftershave lotion called *Mystery*. I loved its smell and gave a bottle to Mel. He loved it too.

Every week the company put on contests and the distributor with the highest sales received a prize. Soon I was the top salesperson of the week. With every success I felt more confident and more motivated. To further motivate the sales team, our local leader, Wynne, put together a weekly bulletin called *Spotlight*. She wrote about each distributor's sales activities and highlighted unique personality traits of those who had done very well. I read:

> *Eva Perlman is an ever shining light and a pacesetter. She does not allow setbacks or lassitude to undermine her self-discipline or cause her to abandon her goal. She keeps her mind on the target and goes forward unswervingly.*

After a year of hard work I was a regional award winner. My reward for outstanding achievements was a diamond and gold bracelet. Mel was very proud of me. This job did wonders for my self-confidence.

One Saturday morning I went to the market with no makeup on. The merchant at the stand where I always bought my vegetables, looked at me with concern and said, "Have you just come out of the hospital?" I made sure to never again go anywhere without makeup!

That year Papa sent us five plane tickets and we flew to Paris in the summer.

"Eva, you always wanted to go to Italy with Mel," Papa said as he handed me two airline tickets and some cash. "For the next ten days Maman and I will take care of the children. Go and have a good time." I was overjoyed. Papa was always so thoughtful, giving and loving. He knew how much I wanted to go to Italy with my husband. Mel had missed a beautiful vacation when we met. This trip felt like a second honeymoon. In love like newly-weds we walked hand in hand through the busy streets and plazas of Rome. We visited the Colosseum, Fontana di Trevi, the Forum, the many churches, cathedrals and museums and treated ourselves to two Verdi operas, *Aida* and *Rigoletto*. Sitting under the stars in the ruins of an old castle, the *Terme di Caracalla*, we enjoyed the spectacularly lit ruins while the greatest opera singers performed right in front of our eyes. To witness Radames, the hero of *Aida*, return home victoriously after defeating his enemies, standing in a Roman carriage drawn by twelve powerful horses, galloping side by side at full speed towards the audience, then stopping just in time at the edge of the stage, literally took our breath away!

We soon found out that the most authentic Italian restaurants with the most reasonable prices were located in the cool basements a few steps below the streets. This was where the locals ate. Here the jovial owner and chef served guests himself, usually wearing a large apron over his corpulent body. We preferred to eat frugally and spend our money on souvenirs like a little glass whale that we named Aida and special wine glasses for Shabbat.

In the *Santa Croce* district in Florence, not far from downtown, we visited the Great Synagogue.

On the way to Venice, our bus stopped in Ravenna for lunch. The city is known for its beautiful early Christian mosaics, which I had seen with my parents years ago, and I wanted to share them with Mel. They had left a lasting impression on me. To this day I remember the brilliant, rich colors and gold accents. Many of the scenes depict victory of eternal life over death. When Mel and I looked up to the cupola in one of the churches, we saw countless stars embedded in a stunning royal blue ceiling. While the other passengers ate at a restaurant, we literally ran from one church to the next, hoping to see as many mosaics as we could. Even though we had no lunch that day, our eyes had a feast.

From our hotel room in Venice we had a view of the Rialto Bridge and the Grand Canal. I could have stayed for hours at our window watching the world go by on the water, the tourists, the gondolas, the water taxis, the firemen, the police. I was so grateful to my parents for having made this trip possible for us.

Filled with wonderful memories we returned to Paris. The children had a great time with Papa and Maman and made their own memories.

"What did you do while we were gone?" I asked them.

"We visited the *Châteaux de la Loire,*" they exclaimed enthusiastically in unison. "We were gone for four days with Dadi and Grandmi!" That trip with their grandparents would remain unforgettable for them.

I noticed several new paintings on my parents' walls. One was of a rose in subdued beige, brown and green colors. "Do you like it?" Maman asked me. "It was painted by a wonderful Jewish artist called Benn. He is originally from Bialystok, Russia. We met him at a gallery exhibition a few months ago. He and his wife Ghera survived the war by hiding in a cellar. For two years they never saw the light of day. During that time Benn began to illustrate Psalms from the Bible. The Psalms and verses inspired him to create many drawings. After the war he created beautiful paintings from these drawings, mostly in soft, dark or light pastel colors."

Maman placed on the living room coffee table a large, heavy box with the inscription in golden letters *62 Psalms and Verses of the Bible.* Carefully she took out one reproduction.

"Psalm 121, verse 1 - *I lift my eyes unto the mountains. Where will my help come from?*" she read.

"Aren't these beautiful? They touched me deeply."

I was impressed by the way the artist had captured the emotion of despair with a few simple lines and dark, subdued colors. We went through the entire box.

"I would love to meet Benn," I said. "Can we buy a box too? What do you think, Mel?"

"I would love that," he replied.

"Let me see what I can do," Maman offered.

The following week the four of us visited the artist's studio. A white-haired man in his sixties, wearing a white lab coat, stained with oil paint, opened the door.

"Please come in," he said in a soft voice.

He introduced us to a flamboyant woman, dressed in colorful exotic clothes. A scarf covered her unruly, curly black hair.

"This is Ghera, my wife."

She looked like a gypsy. We followed them into their living room, where paintings were leaning against the walls everywhere, depicting biblical themes, landscapes and political figures. There were also many paintings of women who all looked like his wife Ghera. It was obvious she was his muse.

"I always carry a little notebook in my shirt pocket," he said. "Many times a verse or a psalm and a sketch appear in my mind's eye when I am riding the subway or walking somewhere. One day I would like to see my 200 biblical paintings displayed in a museum in Israel."

I was not only impressed by his great talent, but also by his modesty and humility.

"Could we buy one of your boxes of sixty-two psalms?"

"You have to ask Ghera. She takes care of the business."

She sold us a box. We thanked them for allowing us to stop by.

"You are lucky that she let you buy a box," Maman said to us afterwards. If she doesn't like you, she won't sell to you or she inflates the price so much that it becomes unaffordable.

"Behind every successful man is a great woman," I commented back in the car.

Before leaving Paris, we stopped by Raymond and Monique's beautiful apartment, opposite luscious gardens. One of the rooms served as his medical office. It was hard to believe my little brother, the former weatherman and lover of flowers, was now a respectable physician.

When we returned Mel hired a contractor to add a big office to the back of the house, with windows and French doors that opened into the garden. It took just a few weeks and his office was ready, bright and sunny. Mel was so happy to sit behind his oak desk with two lovely off-white swivel lamps, surrounded by his books. He was always in his office if he was not at the university, sitting in his armchair reading, or at his desk typing on his IBM electric typewriter which had replaced the old faithful Olivetti, that had served us through England and Africa. Every so often I looked through the glass door and asked, "Would you like a cup of tea, honey?" Mel looked up and felt his arms. If he was cold he would say, "Yes, please. Thank you."

The children were growing up. They understood that they could not barge into Mel's office whenever they wanted, but if they knocked and had a question regarding homework they were always welcome. Mel listened attentively, then walked over to his bookshelves and pulled out two or three books relating to their questions. The children found out it might take some time before they could leave the office, because Mel would get really into it and pull out more and more books.

Mel was working on his book, *Family Life in Uganda,* using general systems theory to explain the changes in marriage and family. I proofread his writings in the breakfast room. I had never heard of general systems theory before, so I walked into his office and asked him. Mel's eyes lit up. Even though he appeared calm and professorial on the outside, I could hear excitement in his voice as he answered, "It's a new theory that explains that all the individual components must work together to make a system work. It can be applied to various fields such as biology, anthropology or society. "

"Is the human body such a system?" I asked, trying to understand what he was saying.

"Yes. All of the body's organs work together in harmony. If only one is incapacitated, the whole system would break down. I want to use it to explain marriage and family life in my book."

Mel began to read all the books he could find on the subject. Every week a new book seemed to come out that dealt with this topic. Soon it was the hot topic among the intellectuals at the university.

Our home had a huge basement with several rooms. One was our recreation room, another the laundry room. The furnace room, which had no windows, was pitch black; Mel had established his darkroom there. I did not like to go down to the basement to do my laundry, unless Mel or the children were around.

Twice a year Mel left for two, three or four days to attend an anthropological conference in a major city in the United States. I started missing him a month before he left. There was only one thing I looked forward to while he was gone — making milk rice sprinkled with sugar and cinnamon for the children and me — because Mel did not like it.

Life was hectic, but we made sure that we all shared dinner together every day.

"Eva, what would you like to listen to tonight?" Mel asked as he walked over to the record player. Two records with twenty-five best-known and most loved melodies in the world were our favorites.

"How about the 25 Melodies?" I replied as I placed the soup on the table in the breakfast room.

"What opera is this?" Mel asked the children. Every four minutes another piece came on.

"Is it Rigoletto or La Traviata?"

"La Traviata!" Ilana shouted.

"Correct," Mel said.

Then the waltz *Morning Papers* sounded through the room.

"Strauss!" Tamar, 11, and David, 10, shouted in unison.

"Yes, Strauss," I said, "but which waltz is it?"

Silence. None of the three remembered, so I got up and started dancing, gesturing with my arms, pretending to throw 'morning papers' to the front doors of homes, hoping it would help them remember the name. Then Ilana got up and started imitating me. Tamar and David joined in, pretending to throw more papers in the air. Pretty soon we were all dancing and throwing papers, except for Mel. He was sitting in his corner, enjoying the ruckus and chuckling quietly. We had forgotten the soup!

Our love of photography led us to a local camera club of about thirty or forty members who met once a month in a nearby church. We joined and were looking forward to exchanging information with other experienced photographers. Chairs were arranged in a theater-like setting. Four judges, who were also excellent photographers, sat at a separate table. Two of them were members of our club and two came from another club for objectivity. Once everyone had arrived, the lights were dimmed and the first slide was projected on the screen. Everyone watched in silence. After a few minutes the first judge voiced his comments.

"Overall I like the slide, but it's a little over-exposed. I give it a 7."

"I agree, it's over-exposed and the light post is distracting. I give it a 6," the second judge said.

The third judge gave it a 6 as well. The highest grade was ten, but it was rarely given and 6 meant the slide was not worthy to be shown again. The club secretary kept track of the average points for every slide and gave out ribbons for the best work at the next meeting.

To listen to the judges' comments really helped Mel and me become better photographers. I learned to pay attention to detail, to see things I never saw before, and I learned about composition. Soon Mel submitted his slides to international competitions. I competed also, but only in our club. Aside from it being very educational, being members of the photography club was great fun and we made many new friends.

After one of the gatherings, a photographer who had changed his slide based on the suggestions of the judges, submitted the improved version, but to his disappointment, and our amusement, this different group of judges gave it an even lesser grade than it had received before.

"Well, beauty is in the eye of the beholder," Mel said with a little smile.

There was only one synagogue in St. Catharines and it was very conservative, so, in 1972, we helped found *Temple Tikvah* (Hebrew for *hope*). It was a reform temple and we created it together with several Jewish friends mainly from Brock University. One of our founders contacted the rabbinical school in Cincinnati to find out if they knew of a student rabbi who could come part-time to lead our services in St. Catharines and to prepare our children for their bar and bat mitzvahs. They sent Rabbi Kogan, an ordained rabbi, and his wife. He was teaching in Cincinnati and working on a PhD at the University of Toronto. He was clean-shaven, soft-spoken and very likeable. Members took turns hosting the couple in their homes when the Kogans came for Shabbat and various holidays. At first we met in individual homes. After a few months we rented a chapel on Church Street behind a church led by Reverend Asbil. Everybody helped transform the chapel into a synagogue. The crucifixes were replaced with tablets of the Ten Commandments and we hung up an eternal light. The congregation bought a salvaged and restored Torah scroll from Poland and one of our members built a special oak cupboard to house the scroll.

Our Jewish community really liked Rabbi Kogan. He was direct, outspoken, and wise. Twice a month he came for Shabbat from Cincinnati. His services were not boring like those I had attended as a teenager with my parents in Paris. Whenever I sat next to Mel in our temple, I felt closest to him, especially when Rabbi Kogan quoted a psalm that the artist Benn had illustrated. Then Mel and I would look at each other and smile. It was our little secret. Sometimes we invited the Christian members of the church to our service. Our two congregations got on very well. A few years later, Mel and I were asked to lead a full Passover Seder for the church members. I gave them the recipes for a Passover meal, and the dinner was worthy of the best Jewish cook.

St. Catharines' conservative synagogue was having a dinner dance and we were invited. After dinner, couples went on the dance floor to dance the samba, rumba, waltz and tango. Mel loved to dance and he was a good dancer. As soon as he heard the music, he got up from his chair, took me by the hand and led me to the dance floor. I tried to follow him as best I could without stepping on his toes. Then jitterbug music came on. Mel took my right hand and immediately moved his hips back and forth, then shuffled his feet and pulled me toward him. On the dance floor Mel became a different person. Dancing like a pro he bent his knees and led me in a pirouette under his arm as we changed positions. Experiencing my serious professor husband looking almost like a gigolo amused me to no end. I did not recognize him. That night our friends discovered that side of him too and nicknamed him *Twinkle Toes*.

Every year we subscribed to the Toronto opera and got season tickets. We asked our children which operas they wanted to see. This tradition continued even after they went off to university and came home only for the day. We bought extra tickets for friends. After the opera we often had dinner together at the Old Spaghetti Factory before returning home.

During the 1972/73 season, we went to see Verdi's *Rigoletto,* which I had also seen with Mel in Rome. It was one of my most cherished operas because it is a touching story of a father's love for his daughter and the music is unforgettable. I had seen the movie of the opera with Tito Gobbi in the title role several times in Cambridge, England where I spent a summer improving my English before starting language studies in Geneva. The film was playing in a small repertory cinema and I went to see it every day for a week. I found Tito Gobbi's voice and acting extraordinary. Now, while we were sitting in our seats in Toronto waiting for the opera to begin, it was announced over the loudspeakers that Louis Quilico, the excellent Canadian baritone who was scheduled to sing the role of Rigoletto, would not sing that night. Although, for me, he could not compare with my beloved Tito Gobbi, I was looking forward to hearing him. I was disappointed, but much to my surprise his replacement, John Rawnsley, whose name I had never heard before, sounded just like Tito Gobbi. His warm, magnificent voice filled the house. I cried through the entire opera!

At Chanukah Mel and I always made a big splash for the kids. Although we had to watch our money, it was festive, and we particularly enjoyed spoiling the children. Mel and I spoiled each other. He was always so generous, and gave me gifts that he knew I wanted. For example, one day I said to him: "Mel, some day I would love to have a real pearl necklace." The following Saturday, he asked me to get into the car and said, "Let's go find you a pearl necklace."

Usually Bobbe flew in from Kansas City to see us around her birthday in February and stayed for three to four weeks. We always enjoyed her visits, and she loved going with me everywhere. She had a heart of gold. When I prepared dinner, she sat in the living room and read Jewish books. Her diet was limited to cottage cheese and cabbage leaves, peanut butter and butter sandwiches. She ate little at our house, but when we took her to a restaurant, she ate enough for three people, and even took the leftover bread rolls home.

With a family spread out over two continents, letters continued to go back and forth between Canada and Paris. When Ernest came to New York on a business trip in the spring of 1973, he rented a car and came to visit us. During dinner he told us what happened when he wanted to cross the border from the U.S. to Canada.

"The border official checked my passport and asked, "Do you have any food with you?"

"You mean there is no food in Canada?" I answered. "The officer did not think it was funny and searched every inch of my car."

"Well, you do not joke with a border official!" Mel said.

I did not realize how much I had missed Ernest's humor. When it was time for him to leave it was hard to say goodbye.

That summer, Papa and Maman came to visit us for the first time in St. Catharines. They loved our home.

"You seem to get along much better with your mother, Eva," Papa remarked.

"I have learned to keep my mouth shut and try not to have the last word, no matter how I feel."

"I am glad you have come to that understanding," he said. He was relieved.

I received a letter from my friend Marie who had been our neighbor in Berkeley. She was raving about her grandchildren and proudly wrote that she had devoted her whole life to them. I did not feel the same way.

"When you get married and have children of your own, don't expect me to take care of them on a regular basis while you are at work," I told my children. "I want to have my own life with your father when you are grown up."

In early 1974, Mel and I were looking forward to our first annual photography convention in Amherst, Massachusetts. Half of our camera club was going. The children were old enough to take care of themselves for a weekend and friends promised to keep an eye on them. Mel and I had already put together a list of the seminars and workshops we wanted to attend before we started on our 400-mile drive.

The convention was very instructional, entertaining and exciting. For the next 48 hours we ate, slept and dreamt photography with the best photographers in the country. Some had even flown in from abroad. There were about twenty-five workshops to choose from, but we only had twelve time slots.

As soon as we checked into our hotel on Friday around noon, we quickly dropped off our luggage, and ran to attend the first two lectures.

For the rest of the weekend Mel and I rushed from one workshop to the next. Whenever we ran into one of our club members, we asked what they had seen to make sure we would not miss the best ones. We kept reshuffling our agenda. The weekend flew by in an atmosphere of enthusiasm and excitement.

On our drive back home the sky began to look ominous. Big black and grey clouds were moving in, covering the sun. The light and atmosphere begged to be captured. Mel wanted to find a suitable foreground so we drove around the countryside for a good twenty minutes. Then we came upon a barn, next to a huge tree, lit by a ray of sunshine that was peeking through the clouds. Mel got out of the car and snapped the photograph just at the right moment.

"This photograph reminds me of Ansel Adams!" a friend later remarked when he saw it hanging in our home. It was the best compliment anyone could have given Mel. Life was truly wonderful.

In June 1974, Maman called from Paris. Her voice sounded unusually serious. "Eva, I don't want you to worry, but Papa had a heart attack. He is in the hospital. The doctors are confident he will recover completely."

Still, I was terribly concerned. My dear, loving and caring Papa was ill and he was only 72. I called Maman every other day. I was relieved to hear that Papa was recovering nicely. At the end of June, Maman called. "Papa has been moved to a renowned cardiology clinic in Evecquemont. His doctor is optimistic. The hospital is just 24 miles west of Paris. I can visit him every day."

The next day she called again.

"Papa is doing so well that the doctor is allowing him to go on vacation to Switzerland, his favorite country, but not higher than 3,000 feet above sea level. Papa is so excited that he wants me to pick up some brochures from the travel agency right away. As I was leaving today his phone rang. It was a colleague of his. I heard Papa say, 'Don't worry, Pierre, you know I'm always at your disposal.' That's a very good sign. He seems to be his old self again." I was so relieved to hear that Papa was working again, even from his hospital bed.

The next morning, a Friday, the phone rang again. This time Maman sounded terrible.

"Eva — Papa is gone," she said, her voice faltering. "He died quietly, suddenly and without suffering in his armchair while waiting for his breakfast."

I broke down, I was devastated.

"The funeral will be next Tuesday. It will give you time to get here."

While crying, I called Mel at the university. "My beautiful Papa is gone." "I'll be home right away," he said.

For the first time in my life I had to face the loss of someone I deeply loved. The next day, as I was running a last minute errand before leaving for France, I saw a man much older than 72 crossing the street slowly with a cane, in obvious pain. *Why was he alive, yet Papa was dead?* I thought angrily. Papa had always taken care of himself. For many years he had taken short naps after lunch. He had taken long walks on weekends, and he had eaten Maman's healthy cuisine. To help myself I finally rationalized, "If he had not done all the right things, he could have died of a heart attack in his fifties or sixties." Still, I was grieving.

Fortunately our three children were already at Camp Massad for the summer and well cared for. We let them know we were on our way to Paris. They were, of course, shocked and sad to hear the news.

When Mel and I arrived at the Paris airport, my strong mother looked pale, fragile and spent. With tears in her eyes she told us in detail what had happened.

"When I opened the door to Papa's hospital room the next morning with the travel brochures in my hand, he was not there and his bed had been cleared. Frantically, I ran into the empty hallways looking for someone to tell me where he was. 'Where is my husband?' I called in anguish. Finally I found a nurse. 'Oh, he expired at 8 a.m. this morning,' she told me, matter-of-factly. I was overwhelmed with grief. My whole world had fallen apart. I stood there, alone. No one offered me a chair, or a cup of coffee. Somehow I managed to call Ernest and Raymond. Forlorn and grieving, I waited for them. I was just glad that your Papa did not suffer."

It was a blessing for him, but a terrible shock for the rest of us, and an unbearable loss, especially for Maman. Papa and Maman had been happily married for forty-three years and Maman had always depended greatly on Papa for support and companionship.

As soon as we arrived, I needed to see Papa to believe that he was gone, so on Monday, three days after he died, Maman, Mel and I went to the hospital. He was in a special cooling room, covered with a white sheet. All I could see was his face. As hard as it was to see Papa like this, it helped me to get closure.

On Tuesday we buried him in Le Vésinet above his parents. Papa had been a very kind and ethical human being. He had always been there for me and I could count on him one hundred percent. He had been a gentle, smart and generous man, just a beautiful human being.

For the next seven days we sat *shiva*. Family and friends stopped by to bring food and support us in our grief. The rabbi came in the evening. Enough people came to make up a *minyan* (10 people) so we could say *Kaddish*, praising God and praying for peace.

When Benn heard that Papa had died, he painted a special biblical verse for Maman:

"Our soul has escaped as a bird out of the snare of the hunters; the snare is broken, and we are free." Psalms 124:7

Maman was deeply moved and hung the painting on her wall.

Bobbe came to visit again, this time in the summer. It was 1975. As a special treat we took her and the children to Artpark in Lewiston, New York, an outdoor theater, to see the musical *Hello, Dolly!* It was just on the other side of the border about fifteen miles from St. Catharines. At the border an officer looked inside the car and asked Mel "Where were you born, sir?"

"In Pampa, Texas," he replied.

Then he looked at Bobbe, who was now in her eighties and asked the same question.

"Russia," she answered with a gruff voice.

"Your papers, please!" the officer demanded.

Bobbe foraged in her handbag and pulled out her marriage certificate with a picture of herself when she was twenty-three. The border officer inspected it and gave it back to her with a puzzled look.

"And where were *you* born?" he then asked me.

"In Berlin, Germany," I replied.

Now even more puzzled he turned to Ilana and asked her,

"Where were you born?"

"In Paris, France," she replied and before the officer could ask again, Tamar and David piped up in unison, "In Kampala, Uganda."

At this point he was so dumbstruck he forgot to get his most important question answered: i.e. where we were going. He simply gestured, "Just go!"

We all laughed. What an international bunch we were!

My Fashion Two Twenty cosmetic business was doing well, but I no longer found it interesting. I was ready for a new challenge. At 43 I still hadn't found my calling. The Canadian government had established an adult counseling center that offered a series of aptitude tests, so I decided to go.

"Mrs. Perlman, you tested so high in everything, you can do whatever you want," the counselor concluded after he reviewed my results. "*That's not helpful*," I thought. After all this testing I was back at square one. When the interviewer saw my puzzled look he said: "Maybe you should look through the Niagara College and Brock University course catalogues and see if anything appeals to you." I followed his advice and got the catalogues. As I flipped through the pages, I was drawn to a two-year business program. Mel was very supportive. I enrolled immediately.

Niagara College was in Welland, 12 miles from St. Catharines. When I walked into the classroom the first day I noticed how young my classmates were. They were dressed in jeans and most young men wore long hair and a beard. Compared to them I looked very conservative. In every class I sat in the front row, ready to absorb everything. I especially loved the accounting classes. The teacher was a tall, good-looking man, very kind and patient, who taught with great enthusiasm. He explained things clearly, gave many examples, and always included his own experiences. He made accounting sound fascinating. As soon as he finished explaining one topic my hand was up, ready to ask the next question. "What if…?"

"Eva," he said, "Give me five minutes and I'll get to that." I was very motivated to do my best. As soon as the bell rang, my classmates rushed out, while I stayed behind to get yet another burning question answered. I loved working with figures.

Before long I knew that I wanted to become an accountant. *I should have gone to business school instead of becoming a nurse when I was young,* I thought, *but in my day, girls became nurses or teachers.* When we had a free hour, my classmates congregated in the hallways, drinking beer and chatting. I went to the library to study.

As it happened, I started studying at Niagara College at the same time Ilana started at Brock. It was fun to discuss at dinner what we learned during the day! Tamar and David were now going to the French high school in Welland and took the school bus every day.

In January 1976, Ilana spoke to us about what she wanted to do next.

"As part of the university studies, students are encouraged to spend a year abroad. I would love to go to Israel for my second year and study at the Hebrew University in Jerusalem, just like Papa did," she said, excited. "It is such an essential part of our family history and, of course, I want to spend time in Israel and get to know the country and my Israeli family better." She had learned about Israel for many years in Hebrew school, as well as from Mel, me and my mother. The WIZO ladies were not the only ones my mother influenced! We did not need convincing, but Ilana continued enthusiastically, "I can get credit for it and if I attend an *Ulpan* (an intensive Hebrew course) I will improve my Hebrew."

Mel and I loved the idea. Although our lives had evolved differently and we had not gone to live in Israel ourselves, we had succeeded in transmitting the love of Israel to our children. As an added bonus, Ilana would get to know Grossmama, Uncle Alfred and his children. That summer Ilana flew to Israel. Her absence left a big void in our family, but she wrote to us regularly and kept us informed about her experiences, her classes and the family.

As it turned out, 1976 would become a very special year abroad for all of us. After six years of teaching, Mel was eligible for a sabbatical. Mel wanted to go to London to do research at the School of Oriental and African Studies. Tamar, David and I were happy to live in London for a year, and I was glad to give up my Fashion Two Twenty cosmetic business altogether.

Once again, I was ready for a new adventure. I put my studies at Niagara College on hold for a year.

That September all four of us arrived in London. Professors from all over the world lived in the same apartment complex across from Regent's Park in northwest London. It was a beautiful area close to public transportation. We met people from Canada, Australia and New Zealand. Tamar, 15, and David, 14, attended a local high school and Mel was busy doing his research, so I found work at the British Library. The customs official at our entry into England had stamped my passport with a stamp that somehow allowed me to work. While filing documents was tedious, it kept me busy. Living in London on an American salary was quite comfortable. What a different experience this was, compared to our first year of marriage in Oxford twenty years earlier!

In October Maman went to Israel to attend a big party for Grossmama's 90th birthday. Then they both returned to Paris together and called us to say hello. They loved each other and quarreled sometimes. "Grossmama still gets up every morning at 6 a.m. to transcribe the Hebrew bible into Braille," Maman reported.

"Wow. That is quite remarkable," I commented.

From London it was much closer and less expensive to fly to Israel. Tamar and David had never been. Christmas vacation was coming up. We all missed Ilana and wanted to see her and Uncle Alfred and his new wife. Sadly, my aunt Tsilli had passed away prematurely from cancer. Alfred had remarried; his new wife Hanna had come to Israel from Argentina. And we had not seen my cousins Judy and Gadi for a long time.

Mel bought us plane tickets. A few days before we left, Maman called from Paris again.

"I have very sad news. Grossmama died of kidney failure this morning. Three days ago she was not feeling well, so I took her to the hospital. She slipped into a coma. She did not suffer."

"Mel just bought tickets to visit Ilana in Israel," I said.

What a strange coincidence! Now we could all be at Grossmama's funeral! Maman made special arrangements to take her body to Israel.

The day of the funeral, the sun was shining and it was comfortably warm. Ilana came from Jerusalem and met us at the entrance of the cemetery. It felt so good to see her despite the sad circumstances. Only a handful of close family members attended. Together we walked to the gravesite. The hole had already been dug and the coffin stood next to it. According to the Torah *'we come from dust and must return to dust.'* In Israel, a body is buried without a coffin. When the gravediggers broke the seal of the coffin, Maman sobbed. To her, breaking the seal was a desecration of her mother's remains. Mel and I held her close and tried to console her while the two men carefully took out Grossmama's body, which was just wrapped in a white shroud, symbol of purity. They laid her in the ground and covered her with soil. The rabbi said a few prayers and we all said *Kaddish*. We were very sad, but glad to be together and able to support one another.

After the funeral, we gathered in Uncle Alfred's apartment. Six languages were flying around — French, English, German, Hebrew, Yiddish and Spanish. I was proud to introduce David and Tamar to the family and happy to meet Hanna who seemed to take good care of Uncle Alfred. She spoke Spanish, Yiddish and some Hebrew. I had difficulty communicating with her because my Hebrew was rusty and my Spanish poor.

At one point my cousin remarked, "You have it easy in Canada. Why don't you come here and help us defend our country. Every day we put our lives on the line." I felt offended and guilty at the same time.

"Mel and I wanted to come live here when we met, but life has taken us on a different path," I said in our defense, trying to stay calm. Maybe my cousin had a point.

The next day, Ilana took us to her dormitory in Jerusalem. When her friend, a reserved and quiet young man with a mass of red, curly hair walked in, Mel was standing on a chair in the corner, taking pictures. He was so focused on what he was doing that he barely paid attention to what Ilana said: "This is Mark. He's from California. He is also studying here for a year." Later that day, when we were alone, she said, "Unfortunately he seems only interested in his studies."

Before returning to London, we visited Tina and Hilde who had been instrumental in bringing Mel and me together. They were thrilled to meet our children and to see that Mel and I were still very much in love after twenty years.

Just before our year in London was up, Ilana came to visit us. Her year in Israel was over and she would continue her studies at York University in Toronto. She brought her "friend" Mark with her. His year in Israel was over as well, and he was on his way back to Los Angeles to continue his own university studies.

It was becoming more and more obvious that Mark was not just any friend, but that our daughter had strong feelings for him, and that this relationship might be a serious one.

That summer, before returning to Canada, we were able to join Ernest and Annie, my brother and sister-in-law, and my nephew Daniel, on a short trip to Spain with our three children. We visited the marvelous *Alhambra* in Granada, and the sites in Seville, Toledo and Madrid. It was fun to be with my brother and his family and we enjoyed Spain very much. In August 1977, we all returned to St. Catharines and picked up our Canadian lives after the adventures of living abroad for a year. As Mel and I helped Ilana move into her dormitory at York, I thought to myself, *'How lucky she is to live and study on such a beautiful campus. She can design her own life and study what interests her.'* I wished I could have had such an experience. I reflected back on my life at that age. I had moved to Switzerland at 18. Yes, I also had lived away from home for a year, but I had been much too immature to really appreciate it.

Tamar and David returned to the French high school, Mel started to teach again and I continued my second year at Niagara College. Mark and Ilana stayed in touch by mail. We were kind of relieved that Mark lived far away so Ilana would focus on her studies. For the time being, it was a long distance relationship.

One day, Mel came home with a book he had borrowed from the public library — Halsman's *Sight and Insight.*

"Take a look at this book, Eva. It's superb," he said. "I am amazed how this photographer captures the essence of a person in a portrait!"

We sat down in the living room and Mel opened the book carefully. Inside were full- page black and white portraits of over a hundred of the best known people in the world, including Albert Einstein, Winston Churchill, Mae West, Pablo Picasso, Dustin Hoffman, Humphrey Bogart, Joan Baez, Elizabeth Taylor and Woody Allen. I was just as impressed as Mel. "I wish I could buy this book, but it is out of print," he said when we reached the last page. Over the next few days he contacted several bookstores, but the answer was always the same — the book was unavailable.

Fifteen-year old David loved to practice tennis against a wall at a school in our neighborhood. Every so often a ball landed on the flat roof of the school. One morning at 5 a.m. the phone rang. I jumped out of bed. Bleary-eyed and drowsy I picked up the telephone.

"Mrs. Perlman, this is officer Armstrong. Do you know where your son is?"

"In his bed of course. Where else would he be?"

"No, Mrs. Perlman, he is here at the police station. We found him climbing on the roof of the elementary school on Highland Avenue!"

"Oh, for heaven's sake!" I exclaimed. "He was probably trying to retrieve his tennis balls." Thus, I confirmed his story.

When I looked out of the window, I saw my son coming toward our house, carrying our long, heavy ladder over his shoulder.

"David, what happened?"

"I just wanted to get my tennis balls. I figured no one would see me if I went early in the morning. I'm sorry, Maman. A woman living across the school saw me and called the police."

We did not say much more. His trip to the police station in a police car had been embarrassing enough.

"Can Mark spend Rosh Hashanah with us?" Ilana asked us when she called from Toronto. Mel and I were not surprised.

"And by the way, he is a vegetarian," she said. "A vegetarian?" I repeated, surprised. "I have no idea what a vegetarian eats." After we hung up I wracked my brain as to what I could possibly prepare for all of us to eat. All I could think of were fruits and vegetables, eggs and nuts.

"Mark is a vegetarian," I told Mel. "What am I going to cook?"

Mel did not have an answer, the kitchen was my department. Finally I settled on spinach and hard-boiled eggs in cheese sauce.

When they arrived the day of Rosh Hashanah, it was pretty obvious that the two were in love. But Mel was skeptical. After the meal Ilana and I went to clean the kitchen leaving the two men alone so they could get to know each other. From the kitchen we heard Mel ask Mark question after question in his mild-mannered, soft-spoken way. I could tell he was choosing his words carefully.

"What plans do you have for the future?" I heard Mel ask.

"I am thinking of becoming a librarian or a dietitian, Professor Perlman," Mark replied.

He sounded like a nice fellow, but still Mel seemed a bit concerned about Ilana's future.

"Don't worry, Papa. I am definitely going to finish my B.A. in linguistics in Toronto," Ilana promised.

During the Christmas vacation and the following Passover, Mark came again. "I have decided to get a master's degree and eventually a PhD in nutrition and pharmacology, Professor Perlman," Mark said. We liked the idea.

Mark seemed to feel more comfortable. This time he also asked Mel about his work and Mel's answers became longer and longer. They also began to spend some time in the darkroom. We became fond of Mark, and imagined he would likely become our son-in-law.

In June of 1978, I graduated from Niagara College with a diploma in business management. Toward the end of the year, employers came to the college to recruit new employees, and all those long-haired students were suddenly well-shaven and dressed appropriately. I hardly recognized them. While many of my colleagues got jobs, I enrolled in a third year to specialize in financial management. It would give me several exemptions from courses for the accounting degree if my grades were high enough. A few more courses and I could become an accountant!

That summer, Ilana flew to Los Angeles for two months to be with Mark. Within a day, they called to say they were engaged! We rejoiced.

Mel and I flew to Paris to visit my family. Maman lent us her car and we drove all the way to Norway, which, we had been told, was a very beautiful country. Unfortunately, we had to travel through Germany. I still felt uncomfortable and scared, and did not want to set foot in that country, so we slept one night in Holland just before the German border and next day drove non-stop through Germany, to sleep across the next border in Denmark! Norway is indeed a very beautiful country. From one little place called Hell, we sent a postcard to Maman of a fiery sunset and the words 'Greetings from Hell.' We returned from Europe, just in time to receive bad news.

It was my brother Raymond, on the phone from Paris.

"Maman is in the hospital with a broken hip. Two days ago a motorcyclist passed by her in broad daylight and grabbed her handbag. She tried to hold on to it and was thrown to the ground. She had surgery and she will stay in the hospital for a few weeks. She should be okay." I was relieved.

Now that Maman was stuck in the hospital with nothing to do, I thought it might be the perfect opportunity to get her to write down a few memories from the war years. I called Ilana and told her what had happened.

"Grandmi always told me that no one would be interested in her war stories, but if you write to her, now that she is bedridden, and show real interest, she might open up and share her memories with you. Tell her you wish she would write them down for your family, and even for your future children." Ilana wrote to her. Several weeks later, she received a letter from Maman with the only story she was ever willing to write. It was the story of the bicycle accident in the Vercors.

Later that summer, we traveled with Ernest, Annie and Daniel. They came to Canada and we even met up with the newly engaged couple in Vancouver.

Mark came again for Rosh Hashanah and once again I served him spinach with eggs.

I still did not know what else to cook, but I placed a small bowl of nuts by his dinner plate to make sure he had enough nutrients.

The African Woman

While Ilana helped me in the kitchen, Mel asked Mark to follow him to his office. Their conversations were growing in length and in depth. The more it became clear to Mel that Mark was truly interested, the more he opened up to him. Before long Mark was reading Mel's papers and the two were discussing general systems theory and photography. Mel came alive when he could discuss these topics with someone who was genuinely interested and qualified. They spent more and more time together in the darkroom. Mel was happy to have found a willing student who, unlike me, seemed to be just as patient to come up with that perfect print as he was. We had not seen Mark and Mel for a few hours, so Ilana and I went downstairs to the darkroom to see what they were doing. When we opened the door slightly we heard Mel say, "I am having a really hard time with this African woman." Mel was working on a print. He had taken her photograph while we lived in Uganda, one foot from her face with his Rolleiflex.

"Why are you having such a hard time with this print, Professor Perlman?" Mark asked.

"You see her bright, white teeth and the white bead necklace she is wearing around her neck and the black fly on her forehead? When I try to darken the white areas a little, because they are too bright, everything around them becomes too dark."

Ilana and I were happy that the two were enjoying each other's company and that Mark was becoming part of our family. Soon he would no longer call Mel Professor Perlman, but Papa.

Back upstairs Mel showed Halsman's *Sight and Insight* book to Mark.

"Do you know of any art book stores in Los Angeles where I might still get a copy of this book? We can't find it anywhere," Mel asked.

Soon Mark had to fly back to California and now we all missed him, not just Ilana.

A year later, in June of 1979, I graduated with honors in Financial Management. At the same time Ilana graduated from York University. I was exempt from seven courses because of my good grades and had to take only six more courses, two a year, to pass the final exam and become a full-fledged Certified Management Accountant (CMA).

I got an accounting job at the Shaver Hospital, located opposite Brock

The New Graduate   *Mel and Eva in 1980*

University, on the hill. It was a hospital for the chronically ill. While I worked there as an accountant, I took night classes.

We got busy making preparations for the wedding, as Mark and Ilana planned to get married at *Temple Tikvah* in St. Catharines. It was to be quite a family reunion. On August 26, the temple was festively decorated with every seat taken, and a hundred and twenty familiar faces looked toward us in great anticipation. At the end of the aisle, at the entrance to the *chuppah*, Mark was glowing, standing with his parents, next to Rabbi Kogan. Since the days that I started reading fairytales I had always believed in love and marriage and I had found everything I had ever dreamed of in mine, so I was hoping that our daughter would find the same fulfillment with Mark. To me, being happily married was the best way to live. Mel and I walked Ilana down the aisle to the *chuppah*. Rabbi Kogan, who had by now known our family for several years, gave a very personal speech. After the blessings and the exchange of rings, Mark and Ilana sealed their marriage with the traditional breaking of the glass. They were showered with good wishes and left the next day for their honeymoon, before settling in Los Angeles in their own apartment.

Shortly after the wedding, in September, Mel and I helped Tamar settle in her dorm at the University of Waterloo. A year later in 1980, David started his university studies, also in Waterloo. Our home was now an empty nest, and it felt very strange.

Mel suggested we should supplement the small life insurance policy he had through Brock, so we purchased a $250,000 life insurance policy. The monthly premiums would go up every year but after ten years, the interest would cover the premiums and we would not have to pay any more monthly fees. It sounded affordable and I thought it was a good idea.

Every month Mel faithfully submitted two black and white and two color prints to *Photo Life* Magazine, which had announced a 10-month competition with the theme of Youth and Leisure. He won nothing for nine months, but he was determined to win a camera for me since the one Papa had given me had been stolen in New York. We chose two more prints carefully for the last month. A few weeks later Mel got a call.

"Congratulations, Mr. Perlman. You have won first prize in the black and white competition of *Photo Life* Magazine!" Mel was ecstatic in his quiet way. "In fact," she continued, "the judges had a hard time deciding between two photographs, not realizing they were both yours!" He won a two-week trip to Hawaii for two, a color enlarger and $2,000 spending money!

Photography Contest winner

Mel started winning many accolades and awards for his *Cobbler in Nazareth* and his *African Woman* in various international salon competitions. Both pictures were featured on competition catalogue covers.

Thinking that we were destined to live in Canada for the rest of our lives and knowing that we wanted to go back to London for the second sabbatical, I applied for Canadian citizenship. As a Canadian citizen I would be allowed to work in London, as Canada still had ties with Great Britain.

In May 1982, to prepare for the final exam to become a certified management accountant, our teacher had us review various exams from previous years.

"Look for the bonus!" he kept saying. "It might be hidden somewhere in the write-up that you will get." If the company is still paying a large bonus to a president who retired years ago, say $300,000 annually, it might be a major burden for a struggling company and it would be your responsibility as an accountant to bring this to the owner's attention. By early 1982, I had taken all required night courses to write the final exam. Everybody kept saying, "Eva, don't worry, you'll pass." But that was not how *I* felt.

The day of the four-hour exam the teacher passed out a package of twenty pages, which included a write-up of the company, its management, its financials and other statements, various tables and graphs. At the end of the twenty pages it said:

You have been hired to analyze this company and write a report with your recommendations on how to improve its bottom line.

I felt overwhelmed. There was so much information to plough through that I was worried I would run out of time. I spent quite a while analyzing the company's financial statements and investments. As I was reading through the many pages, I noticed the bonus fleetingly, but then I forgot all about it. At some point I was so frustrated that I wanted to give up and walk out of the room altogether, but then I commanded myself, "Eva, don't be a fool! You finish this, and you do the best you can!"

Finally I came up with a few suggestions to make the company financially more stable. Once I was done with the analysis, I began to work on the write-up, making sure that I did not make any spelling errors, that my writing was flawless and to the point, that the titles were underlined properly so that my presentation was visually appealing.

"How did you do?" I asked a friend when it was all over.

"I practically only wrote about the bonus," she answered.

Oh my God! The bonus! What had I done? Why hadn't I made a note of it immediately when I spotted it? After all this exhausting work I will fail, I thought. I had done everything. I had worked on the presentation exceedingly well. Everything was well organized. I dotted my i's and crossed my t's, but in the end I forgot THE most important point — the bonus.

While I was waiting for the results that would come two months later, Mel and I went on vacation to Algonquin Park in Northern Canada. David stayed at home. He had taken on a summer job at Shaver Hospital.

"David, I am expecting a letter from the Society of Management Accountants of Canada," I said. "Please open it immediately when it gets here and call our hotel with the result. I need 60% to pass. Please don't tell the hotel person my grade. Just say 'Friday' if I Failed or 'Saturday' if I Succeeded."

Everyday Mel and I hiked and took pictures in the park and every day I stopped by the reception desk for messages. This particular day the August sunset had been spectacular and Mel could not stop taking pictures, so we returned to the hotel quite late. We had just gotten into bed when I realized we hadn't retrieved our messages.

"I'll go see," Mel offered.

He quickly got dressed and went to the reception desk. He came back with a quizzical smile on his face.

"Well, Eva, what answer were you hoping for?"

"Saturday?" I replied softly and hesitantly. Mel nodded.

"Are you sure?" I replied. I simply could not believe it.

"I wonder what grade I got," I said. "Let's call David right now."

I quickly got dressed and rushed down to the bar to make the call.

"What did I get, David?" I asked.

"Sixty!" he said. "Congratulations!"

I had passed by the skin of my teeth. Had I talked about the bonus, I would have gotten 80! But to get 60 while forgetting the bonus was a miracle. Not only was I so very happy to have passed, but also I could hardly have faced another grueling exam. It was absolutely the most difficult thing I have ever done.

In October 1982, the Society of Management Accountants organized a big gala in a Toronto hotel in honor of the new graduates. At the age of 50 I had become a certified management accountant. Mel was so proud of me for my hard work, dedication and success. I remembered our walk on the beach in Carmel and his encouragement that I grow as a person. I took those words to heart and now I too was proud of myself.

It was Chanukah 1984, and Mel and I were excited to celebrate this special time with all three of our children and their respective partners. Tamar and Brian, David and Tish lived close to us. Ilana and Mark flew in from California. They all arrived on the third night of Chanukah. As soon as Mel saw Mark, he went to get the latest chapter of his book and asked Mark to review it. I could tell that Mark felt honored. The two had grown to know and respect each other. We enjoyed a lovely traditional Chanukah dinner, including homemade latkes and applesauce.

After dinner everyone helped wash dishes and then fetched their gifts and arranged them in the living room. Mel was pleased with every present. Every once in a while we heard him say, "Ohhhh," after opening one of his presents. It was his subtle and subdued way to show that he was pleased. Then Mark handed Mel his gift.

"Wow!" Mel said softly. It was *Sight and Insight* by photographer Philippe Halsman.

Though he rarely displayed emotion, Mel got choked up. Mark had been determined to find a copy at any cost. It took contacting thirty used bookstores all over the United States!

To pass the time between Chanukah and New Year's Eve, we wanted to do something special and fun together, and decided to prepare skits. Each couple had a few hours to prepare. Ilana and Mark decided to imitate Mel and me. She showed up, dressed in a blouse and skirt of mine, followed by Mark wearing Mel's famous leather hat and two of his sweaters, his jacket, a winter coat and tie. He carried twelve books. With a deadly serious face, he set up a blackboard. Then he began to draw all kinds of lines and data, explaining systems theory. Mel, usually a quiet giggler, laughed out loud and hard. Only rarely have I ever seen him react with such visible joy.

The few days together passed by very quickly. Unlike other Jewish families who ate doughnuts during Chanukah, we made them on December 31st to welcome the New Year at midnight so it would be as sweet and round as the doughnut. It was a tradition Maman had embraced from Grossmama. I rolled out the dough and then cut out rounds with a small glass. Ilana and Tamar enjoyed filling them with jelly. The jelly had to be right in the middle or it would ooze out while being fried. I took them out of the hot oil, and my daughters tossed them on a plate with sugar and then arranged them on a serving platter. At midnight we welcomed the New Year with a glass of champagne and a doughnut. The next day I gave a dozen to our neighbors and wished them a Happy New Year.

After these few exciting days with the family, Mel and I had to get used to an empty house again.

In March 1985, Ilana called with exciting news. They were pregnant! Mel and I were ecstatic. Our first grandchild! I immediately called Maman. She was excited to become a great-grandmother.

Maman had news too. She had sold her Avenue Niel apartment and planned to move to a smaller apartment the following week. I was happy for her. It was a good move. My brothers lived only twenty minutes away and saw her regularly.

Every two months, Mel and I drove about 60 miles to spend a day in Toronto. Our first stop was usually the World's Biggest Bookstore. Then, after a quick pizza or croissant lunch at the neighboring mall, we went to see one of the new, usually foreign, movies, which would most likely not make it to St. Catharines. On our way to the movie theater we passed a record store. Since we still had time, we checked out the opera section. There I spotted a friend from our local opera guild in St. Catharines.

"Hi, Irene! What are *you* doing here?" I exclaimed.

"We came to hear Kathleen Battle tonight," she replied.

"Where?"

"At Roy Thomson Hall."

By now Mel was a true aficionado of opera and Kathleen Battle, a lyric coloratura soprano, was one of our favorite singers. She had a clear and stunning voice and could sing the highest notes with great ease.

"Mel!" I said excitedly. "Let's call and see if we can still get tickets for tonight."

"Ok, *you* call!" he replied even though he knew that I hated to use a public phone.

"Please, Mel, *please, you* call!" I begged.

"No, *you* call," came his seemingly indifferent reply. I could not understand his lack of enthusiasm. I tried another way to convince him, "Okay, let's go to the movie theater and buy our tickets first and then we'll make the call," I suggested.

Mel did not react. I knew that there was a public phone and soda machine in the lounge of the cinema. We bought our tickets and went into the lounge. Mel would still not cooperate. In total desperation I fished a quarter out of my wallet and went to the phone myself. As I was about to put my quarter into the slot, Mel took the receiver out of my hand, and hung it up. Then he opened his coat. In the inside pocket, he had two tickets for that concert! I could not believe how sweet he was!

The singer was so magnificent I was moved to tears and when I looked at Mel, he had a tear in his eye as well. We were so attuned to each other that we were deeply moved by the same thing at the same time.

The months passed quickly and on September 1, 1985, three weeks early, our first grandchild was born. She was named after Mark's mother,

Diane Ruth, who, tragically, had passed away suddenly a few years earlier. We bought our first video player and Mark and Ilana sent us tapes so we could watch the baby grow. Naturally, she was the cutest baby we had ever seen! Due to Mel's teaching schedule, we had to wait for three months until they arrived in St. Catharines for Diane's first Chanukah. Mel had a new subject for his photography!

David married Tish and Tamar married Brian within two months of each other in 1986 — David in July and Tamar in September. To our surprise both chose non-Jewish partners whom they met while they were students. It stirred up a lot of emotion, especially for Mel. We wished them well and hoped they would be happy.

Ilana and Mark visited us again. It was such fun to have a baby in the house. When I walked into the kitchen I found Mel lying on the floor, absorbed in taking pictures of his granddaughter. It seemed so out of character for the usually calm, cool and collected professor. Every time Diane moved an inch, he was right there to snap another picture, captivated by this new little miracle in our lives.

Passover 1987 was extra special. Our whole family made the effort to come together at our house in St. Catharines. All three of our children came with their families: Ilana and Mark with Diane, Tamar and Brian, and David and Tish. Even Maman flew in from France to meet her new eighteen month-old great-granddaughter. Everyone was so excited to see Maman and little Diane, and we were very happy to be together. As part of the preparations for the Seder, Mel put a revered *Haggadah* (the special book relating the story of Passover) on the chest near our dining table. This particular *Haggadah*, beautifully illustrated and leather-bound, was published in Amsterdam in 1695. It belonged to Gottfried Sender, a former student, then colleague, of my grandfather, Joseph Gutmann. Gottfried was a soldier in World War I. During a furlough in 1915, he was invited to the Seder at my grandparents' home in Germany. He brought with him this *Haggadah* and entrusted it to my grandfather for safekeeping, saying:

"If I do not come back from the war, I would like you to continue to pass on this *Haggadah* from generation to generation in your family as it has been passed down in mine." He returned to the war and sadly never came back.

In time, my grandfather gave the *Haggadah* to my parents who kept it for many years and shared it at every Seder with their guests, remembering

Gottfried Sender and my grandfather. Many years later, after my father passed away, my mother remained the sole guardian of the precious book. When she became President of Hadassah WIZO in Paris, she was in charge of preparing several Holiday display tables for their annual fundraiser. There was a Shabbat table, a Rosh Hashanah table, and of course a Passover table on which Maman placed the Amsterdam *Haggadah*. During the event, my mother was called to the table where two elderly ladies stood crying.

"Whose *Haggadah* is this?" they asked.

"It is mine," my mother replied and explained how it came to be hers. The two ladies told her that Gottfried was their younger brother and they always wondered what had happened to that *Haggadah*. My mother immediately offered it to them, but they refused, thanked her and said, "You keep it. We have no one to pass it down to." This treasured *Haggadah* is now in Mark and Ilana's home where we celebrate the Seder every year, and where the Amsterdam *Haggadah* of 1695 will continue to be passed down in our family.

I had spent the last few days cleaning the house and preparing food for this great holiday. Spring and happiness were in the air. For this festive Seder I had decorated the long dinner table with daffodils and taken out our candlesticks and most precious silver. We all sat down at the table. After I lit the candles, Mel lifted the first of four glasses of wine, and recited the *Kiddush* and *Shehechiyanu*.

"Blessed are you, Lord, King of the Universe, who has kept us alive so we can now celebrate this season together. Thank you for making it possible to have a four-generation Seder, with Maman and little Diane with us." Mel was so moved that he choked up and could hardly finish the blessing.

What we didn't know was that this would be the last Passover we would all celebrate together.

Life in Canada had been good to us for seventeen years. The children were living their own lives and Mel and I were happy living like newlyweds after 31 years of marriage in our lovely Tudor style home in St. Catharines.

Mel's monthly life insurance premiums were increasing steadily. Although Mel had three more years to pay before the interest would cover the monthly dues, I re-evaluated our finances and said to Mel, "You know, we are paying so much for that life insurance. Maybe we should invest our money somewhere else since you are in good health. The house is paid off and if, God forbid, something were to happen to you, I would still have your pension from Brock."

Mel agreed. We gave up the expensive $250,000 life insurance policy and cashed it in for $21,000. We began investing with a stockbroker.

CHAPTER 11

IN SICKNESS AND IN HEALTH

In July 1987, three months after our beautiful Passover together we looked forward to returning to Amherst for the annual photography convention. Mel had been suffering from migraines and lower back pain for years, but was generally in good health. The day before our departure he was not himself. He was unusually weak and had to lie down on the couch to rest.

"You look pale, Mel," I said, concerned. "Are you sure you want to go to Amherst?"

"You know how much I love to go there. I'll be fine," he replied.

So we left. We spent the night in Albany. Mel didn't eat much. After dinner we went to bed so we could leave early the next morning. We had another 150 miles ahead of us.

The convention was a winner. Mel managed to see everything he wanted to see, but unlike former years, he was happy to return home.

"Tomorrow morning I am going to see Dr. Geffen," he said.

When Mel undressed that evening, I gasped. His shoulders were covered with enormous bruises as if he had been in a horrendous car accident. The next morning Mel went to see the doctor. At noon, he called me at work.

"Eva, please come home immediately. No time for questions."

I knew by the tone of his voice that something was drastically wrong, so I hurried home, feeling scared. He sat me down and spoke softly.

"The doctor did a blood test. I have leukemia. I have to go to McMasters University Hospital in Hamilton immediately. They have a bed waiting for me."

Oh my God! He had been in good health all his life except for this past week. I was terrified.

Forty-five miles and fifty-five minutes later we arrived at the hospital. A nurse took us immediately to the Hematology Department. Mel was in bed when the doctor walked in.

"I am Dr. Brain, the head of the department," he introduced himself. "Dr. Geffen called me. You have been diagnosed with acute myeloid leukemia. It's a form of cancer that starts in the bone marrow and shows up in an unusually high count of white blood cells. There is risk of hemorrhage and/or blood clotting. We have no time to lose. After the blood test we'll start chemotherapy immediately."

"What is my prognosis?" Mel asked calmly.

"I cannot tell at this point, Mr. Perlman. Let's hope for the best," the doctor answered. "You were lucky. Very often patients come to the emergency room because they are bleeding to death."

The thought of losing Mel made me nauseous. I stayed and watched in agony while the nurses got Mel ready for the aggressive chemotherapy treatment. The surgeon implanted a catheter in Mel's chest so they could do transfusions and draw blood without having to prick him each time. He was very weak.

While Mel received the treatment, the doctor dropped in often to check up on him. They discovered they had both graduated from Oxford, creating an immediate bond between them.

"I like Dr. Brain and I trust him," Mel said.

Our lives changed overnight. I gave up my accounting job immediately to spend my days with Mel at the hospital. Every day I drove back and forth between St. Catharines and Hamilton. Every day I sat at his bedside, keeping him company until it got dark, watching as he had constant tests and transfusions of platelets and red blood cells. He did not speak much. Both of us held on to the hope that these treatments would bring him back to health. Sometimes I read or knitted by his bedside. Never did a complaint pass Mel's lips. It moves me to tears to this day to think how accepting and calm he was. Maybe he wanted to keep me from worrying.

Tamar and Brian arrived from Waterloo, David and Tish from Oshawa, and Ilana, Mark and baby Diane from California. Twice daily we drove to spend the day with Mel. All of us were anxious and scared, but in Mel's presence we tried to be cheerful.

Two weeks later, Mark and Ilana reluctantly headed back to the airport to return to LA. As I sat at Mel's bedside I suddenly noticed that he had become unresponsive. I called the nurse immediately and he was wheeled away for some tests. Time stood still while I waited for him to return. Finally the door opened and Dr. Brain walked in, looking very serious.

"I am very sorry, Mrs. Perlman, your husband has a kidney hemorrhage and is in a coma. We transferred him to intensive care. I don't know at this point if he will make it."

My heart almost stopped beating.

I rushed to the nearest public phone and asked the operator to connect me with the Detroit airport immediately, where I managed to have Mark and Ilana paged over the loud-speakers. Mark came to the phone and I told him what had happened.

"We are coming back immediately," Mark replied. I was so thankful that I reached them before they boarded their plane.

My children found me outside the intensive care unit. I was a wreck.

"Papa is bleeding. Obviously they cannot operate on him. The intensive care doctor said he has only a five percent chance of surviving," I said.

We waited patiently. In spite of the severity of the situation, we were still hoping for a miracle. For the next few days Mark and Ilana stayed with me until they had to go home. Thank goodness Tamar and David were nearby.

For two and a half weeks I sat in intensive care next to Mel's hospital bed, watching him lie motionless and unconscious. I touched his hand, but there was no reaction. I hoped he would wake up and the nightmare would be over. I wanted everything to be back to normal. A catheter drained his urine into a bottle at the foot of his bed. Every day I watched that bottle. At first the urine was bright red. Then it slowly became more pink. It gave me some hope. Were his kidneys getting better? One morning, when I came in, the color of his urine looked normal. Then, after 17 days, Mel regained consciousness — miraculously. "You are a lucky man, Mr. Perlman. Your leukemia is in remission. It looks like the chemotherapy has worked," the doctor reported. "Your kidneys look normal again on the x-rays. It's unbelievable! Your weight on the mattress stopped the hemorrhage."

Mel thanked the doctor softly. He was exhausted and very weak, but grateful to be alive. He had lost twenty pounds and looked like *un petit tas de misère* (a little heap of misery). I truly admired his composure and his courage.

As soon as Maman heard that Mel was out of intensive care, she flew in from France. It was August. She loved him like a son. Now both of us sat at his bedside from early morning until it was time to go home. I was grateful to have Maman by my side. One day she asked the nurse for a basin with warm water.

"Can you sit up, Mel?" she asked.

Mel pulled the cover aside and sat up on the side of his bed. When the nurse came back with the basin, Maman said, "Put your feet into the water, Mel. I'll give you a pedicure."

Then she bent down, washed his feet and dried them with a towel. I was very touched by how kind, attentive and soft she could be, a side of her that she did not often show.

"Thank you, Maman," he said. "That is so kind of you."

Her only request was that I take her to McDonald's so she could try a hamburger for the first time. It turned out she especially loved the French fries.

After six weeks in the hospital, with a catheter still in his chest, Mel had recovered enough to go home. The doctor showed me how to administer medication daily through the catheter. He also recommended that Mel drink Ensure to regain some of the weight he had lost.

Mel was overjoyed to be home. He spent most of the day in his leather armchair in the living room. Every month I took him to the hospital for a blood test, and transfusion if necessary. It was summer so Mel had time off from teaching and told the university that he would have to take the fall term off.

Toward the end of November I took Mel to the hospital for the usual blood test. Dr. Brain had good news for us.

"I am satisfied with your husband's progress. We can take out the catheter. Why don't you go on a vacation for the holidays? A change of scenery will do him good. "

Mel suggested Puerto Vallarta.

"That may not be a good idea," Dr. Brain answered. "You want to be close to an American hospital. Their hospitals may not be equipped with what you might need."

"What about Tampa, Florida then?" I suggested. "It's nice and warm and we don't have to worry about hospitals."

All three of us agreed on Tampa and we left for a week. It was great to see Mel strong enough to get on a plane. Every day we took a walk on the beach, holding hands, watching the waves, the seagulls and the pelicans on the beach, beak to beak. I photographed the pelicans and called the photo *Honeymoon in Florida*. Mel also took a few pictures, but he was not as focused as he usually was. Every 15 minutes he had to sit down. In the afternoons he took extended naps, but he managed to go to the movies with me. He lacked the strength to do anything else. His fatigue worried me. By the end of the week he seemed to have made a little progress.

After we returned home, our children came to celebrate Chanukah with their recovering father.

"Papa, you are going to have another grandchild," Ilana said excitedly. "We hope that you both will come for the birth of the baby."

Mel and I were overjoyed.

By January 1988, Mel's health had improved enough for him to resume teaching for the spring semester. Even though it took a lot out of him, he made significant progress on his book *Marriage and Family Life in Uganda*. Miraculously, his monthly blood tests remained normal.

The fear that the leukemia could come back was always on my mind. I am certain it was on his mind as well, but we never talked about it. Yet, I felt that it was important to find out where he would want to be buried, so one morning while we were still in bed, I asked him this sensitive question indirectly.

"If I die before you, where will you bury me?"

Mel looked at me, and without hesitation, he answered, "In L.A. of course."

That answer gave me the peace of mind I needed. We had agreed some time ago that we would move to Los Angeles once Mel retired. We loved the idea of living where the sun was always shining and living close to at least one of our children.

Five months later, he was done with teaching until the fall. We were planning to go to California in the summer for the birth of our second grandchild. He had just finished correcting all his students' papers and handed in their grades to the Brock administration. It was the end of the first week in May. The next day as Mel was getting dressed, "Eva! My right leg is blue," he said.

Frightened, I called Dr. Geffen right away.

"Get him to St. Catharines General Hospital immediately! I'll be there in ten minutes," he said.

The blood test showed that the leukemia was back in full force.

"Take Mel back to Dr. Brain's department at McMaster in Hamilton immediately," our doctor said. As soon as we arrived, a new catheter was implanted in his chest, but the bleeding could not be stopped completely at the point of entry. Mel had to get chemotherapy again.

"If we can get him into remission again, I may want to send him to Johns Hopkins in the U.S. for treatment of his bone marrow," Dr. Brain said.

"What do you mean *if*, doctor?" I asked. He didn't answer. I knew that at 55, Mel was too old for a bone marrow transplant. But...could his marrow be treated?

As soon as Mel was admitted and his room set up, he asked me to bring him his precious books so he could focus on his work. Soon his room looked like his office — piled with books and journals. He wanted to continue writing. Once again I spent my days at the hospital. His room was bright and full of sunshine. The curtains were wide open. Tamar and David came to spend a day with Mel every weekend. Years later, Tamar told me of the wonderful conversation she had with her dad about the chapter he was writing. He asked Tamar if she had ever experienced discrimination in the technology field. She told him she felt very fortunate that she had not, that she was very comfortable as a woman in the tech field. He was happy to hear this. The status of women in any society was always one of his main interests.

Mel was in good spirits, sitting in his bed in his pajamas, reading.

"Eva, can I dictate my new chapter to you?" he asked.

"Of course," I said. "I would love to take notes for you."

I pulled my chair next to his bed and began to write down his dictation while he was receiving chemotherapy from the drip above the bed. Every twenty minutes a nurse or doctor would check on him or draw blood. We did not stop working until it was dark outside and time for me to go home and type up my notes for him. We kept busy, avoiding conversations about the possibility of an inevitable outcome. Every day for the next week he dictated and I wrote.

On Wednesday, May 18, 1988, Mel welcomed me with a big smile.

"Mazel Tov, honey, happy birthday!"

I sat down next to him, and Mel handed me a letter. I opened it and began to read:

Congratulations, my darling honey... It ended with: *I will love you always, your Mel*

When I looked up, Mel had tears in his eyes and so did I.

The next day I came with good news. "The whole family is coming to spend the weekend with us, Tamar, Brian, David and even Ernest, who is on a business trip in New York!" I told Mel. Ilana was eight months pregnant and could not fly.

Two days later, we were all gathered around Mel who was sitting up, talking excitedly about the chapter he was writing.

That night Ilana called. "How is Papa today?" she asked. "He is in good spirits. He even sat up in bed and happily did some work."

Ilana was able to speak with Mel briefly. His voice cracked with emotion as he told her how sorry he was that he would not be able to fly to California to meet the new baby.

I was very worried because the bleeding around the catheter, although light, would not stop, but I said nothing and acted happy.

The next day, I arrived later than usual because I had to take Ernest to the airport to catch his flight back to Paris. When I walked into the room, the curtains were drawn and Mel was lying in his bed in semi-darkness.

"The light is bothering me," he said as he saw the worried look on my face. "I have such a bad headache."

I noticed that one of his pupils was dilated and much bigger than the other. That scared me because my nursing background told me that something was wrong in his brain. I feared that it could be a hemorrhage again, in the brain this time. The doctor entered, followed by his students. He examined Mel.

"One of his pupils is very dilated," he told the students. "Stick out your tongue, please, Mr. Perlman."

Mel tried, but he could only nod his head.

"Stick out your tongue, Dr. Perlman," he repeated a bit louder, but again Mel only nodded. It was obvious that he could not do what he was asked to do.

"We have to take an x-ray of his brain right away," the doctor concluded, and the nurses rushed him to radiology. I waited nervously.

About twenty minutes later Dr. Brain returned and asked me to follow him to his office.

"I just got the results of the x-rays, Mrs. Perlman. I am sorry to inform you that most of your husband's brain is filled with blood. Either he is going to stop breathing or his heart will stop. It is just a matter of time."

I tried to take this in.

"Do you want me to try to resuscitate him when that happens?" he asked me.

My voice was breaking, full of tears. "No. If his brain is filled with blood, how can he possibly live?"

I walked back to Mel's room, crying. There he lay, the love of my life, in a coma, again.

"I love you, Mel," I said, gently holding his hand as I was looking into his beautiful face. "I will always love you."

I knew the fight was over. Heavy-hearted I called Ilana in Los Angeles.

"Ilana, Papa is in a coma. Please buy a double plot at the Jewish cemetery."

We both cried as I filled her in about what had happened during the last 24 hours. I left it up to her and Mark to make the necessary arrangements. I went home and packed an overnight bag.

The next morning at 5 a.m., Victoria Day in Canada, the phone woke me up. With shaky hands I picked up the receiver. It was the nurse.

"Your husband is in very bad shape. If you still want to see him alive, come right away." It was the worst nightmare of my life.

I immediately called Tamar and David, then hurried to the hospital with my nightgown and toothbrush. All three of us arrived at the same time. When we opened the door to Mel's room, he was still breathing. I touched his forehead and his hand. He was boiling hot. The temperature center in his brain was no longer functioning. We stayed all day. That night Tamar and David went home. I had just placed my bag in the room next to Mel's and put on my nightgown when the nurse knocked on the door. It was 10 p.m.

"Mrs. Perlman, your husband has just expired."

I had expected it, but not that quickly. It hit me hard. I rushed into his room. He was still hot and his face was flushed, but he looked peaceful. It was May 23, 1988. Mel was only 55 years old and I was a widow at 56. We had been married almost 32 years.

I called our children and Maman, then drove home to St. Catharines alone and distraught, trying to see the road through my tears. My life seemed over. Although it was close to midnight, I called Peter, the president of our Temple.

"I am so sorry," Peter said. "Where is your husband's body?"

"Still at the hospital," I answered.

"I will call the *Chevra Kadisha* (Holy Society) immediately. They will pick up Mel's body and prepare it for burial," Peter reassured me.

I was numb, but I kept on going as if in a trance. So many decisions had to be made in a very short time. Early the next morning Tamar came. Together we went to the funeral home to choose a casket. Peter was waiting for us. Walking through the large room with all the different coffins was heartbreaking. We chose a simple pine casket that Mel would have wanted, without brass fixtures or other metal adornments. The casket had to be specially sealed to be flown to Los Angeles.

Tamar took care of everything. She was an invaluable help and a pillar of strength for me. She called Rabbi Kogan in Cincinnati to ask if he would come to St. Catharines to hold a memorial service at Temple Tikvah, and then do the funeral in Los Angeles a few days later. She called our relatives in France — Maman, Ernest and Raymond — Mel's brother in Terre Haute, Indiana, and his family in Kansas City — as well as our friends in St. Catharines. They all came to our home with food and to express their condolences. We sat together and shared memories of Mel. Mark and Ilana were devastated that they could not come; Ilana was now eight and a half months pregnant. Maman arrived from France, as well as Mel's brother Ralph, just in time.

Rabbi Kogan led the memorial service. The temple was packed with friends, professors, some of Mel's students, our doctor, our dentist and his staff, our financial advisor and many others whose lives Mel had touched and who came to pay their final respects. Many spoke and remembered something moving or funny that Mel had said or done. One lady remembered Mel's nickname, *Twinkle Toes*. Rabbi Kogan spoke of his friendship with Mel. I was deeply moved when he referred to me as the 'bride of his youth.'

I did not know how I would go on. The chapter on 32 years of marriage had forever closed. I would never be able to reminisce with Mel about all the special things we had experienced: our life in Africa, Oxford, London, California, our many joys at particular times in particular places. I would never again buy him a shirt or a tie. All that was history. What I was left with were memories.

"How am I ever going to get over this?" I asked Rabbi Kogan.

"You don't get *over* it, Eva. You get *through* it."

After the memorial service in St. Catharines, we flew to Los Angeles for the funeral at Mount Sinai. I was grateful that Maman, Tamar and David traveled with me. Ilana was so big that I was afraid she might go into labor any minute. She was so sad and uncomfortable.

On May 27, four days after Mel died, we gathered in the chapel at Mount Sinai in the Hollywood Hills. I sat in the first row next to my closest family. Many of Mark and Ilana's friends and extended family came. The closed casket was in front of us. The thought of Mel's body in it was unbearable.

I wondered if I would ever wake up from this nightmare.

Mark got up and delivered the most moving eulogy:

"*Robert Anderson wrote the following in* I never Sang For My Father." He began to read:

"*Death ends a life,*
but it does not end a relationship,
which struggles on in the survivor's mind
towards some resolution which it may never find."

What I have to say here today represents part of my struggle. It is not my intention to eulogize Mel Perlman. There are others, more qualified and more articulate, who will sing his praises and list his accomplishments in the days and years to come. For me it is enough to know that he exemplified the highest ideals of Jewish life as described in the Book of Micah: "He has told you what is good and what God requires of you, but to act justly, to love kindness, and to walk humbly with your God." (Micah 6:8)

Rather than eulogizing my father-in-law, I prefer to share some memories of the twelve years we knew each other. During those years, I earned a place in his heart and he earned a place in mine. In the beginning I called him Professor Perlman, but long before he died I came to call him "Papa" in every sense of the word.

I'm sure it was a surprise when I showed up in Canada for Rosh Hashanah. At the end of my first meal in St. Catharines, everyone mysteriously disappeared except Papa. This was my first introduction to the mild-mannered, soft-spoken "Grand Inquisitor" who spoke slowly, chose his words carefully and asked me thousands of tough questions over the years. At the time I thought he was still trying to get rid of me, but, as time passed, I realized that this was his way of showing genuine interest in someone. Those first questions were simple enough. Essentially, what are your plans for the rest of your life...and be specific!

I could not help but chuckle at that remark as Mark had painted such a perfect picture of Mel. Mark continued:

> *A Perlman tradition on holidays was to put on little plays. Inevitably my contribution would be a parody of Papa. I would spend hours developing systems' diagrams for a five-minute play. It meant a lot to see Papa laugh and for him to understand the subtleties in my diagrams.*
>
> *He did not wallow in self-pity when he found out he had leukemia. It was merely a nuisance keeping him from his work. We found his hospital room as we would find his office — piled high with books and journals. Even though he was often very tired in the months following his chemotherapy treatments, he took great pride in the fact that he had returned to teach another semester and that he was making significant progress on his book. A week before he died, Papa had dictated eight pages of a new chapter to Maman.*
>
> *I would like to close with these words from Thornton Wilder:*

"All that we can know about those we have loved and lost, is that they would wish us to remember them with a more intensified realization of their reality. What is essential does not die but clarifies.

The highest tribute we can pay to the dead is not grief but gratitude."

Mount Sinai Memorial Park
Los Angeles, California
11 Sivan 5748 / May 27, 1988

Silently we all got into our cars and drove to the gravesite at the top of Mount Sinai cemetery. The view was spectacular, the landscape serene. There was life on the freeway down below. It was a warm and sunny day. As we recited the *Kaddish*, the coffin was slowly lowered into the ground. I picked up the shovel and threw dirt on the coffin. I felt like I was throwing my heart down there too.

I looked at Ilana. She was about to give birth and I was saying goodbye to the love of my life who would never know his new grandchild. Grief and joy, hand in hand. After the funeral we started the *Shiva*, the seven days of mourning, at Mark and Ilana's home in Northridge. Their friends and extended family stopped by with food every night to say *Kaddish* with Rabbi Kogan. It was a consolation to have our own family Rabbi from Temple Tikvah with us.

Ilana was well past her due date, so she and I took brisk walks up the hilly streets around her house to try to start labor. It was a long two weeks, but we were all together, and it felt good to be four generations in the house, waiting, waiting for joy to interrupt our grief. Finally Ilana went to the hospital and the doctor induced labor. The baby was born, all rosy, plump and beautiful!

"It's a girl!" the doctor announced.

A second girl for Mark and Ilana and a second granddaughter for me. Mark, the proud father, cut the umbilical cord. Then he called his parents and Maman, who were having dinner in Northridge with two and a half year-old Diane, waiting for our news. They rushed to the hospital.

"Mazel Tov! She is beautiful!" they exclaimed in unison as they joyfully gathered around Ilana and the newborn.

A week later we had the naming ceremony in Mark and Ilana's garden. The baby received the Hebrew names Malka Leah, after her grandfather Mel who had passed two weeks before her birth. He had been named Melvin Lee, after his grandmother Malka Leah, so the name had come full circle four generations later. On the birth certificate her English name was Myra. It had been a difficult two weeks, but the new baby brought joy to our bereaved family.

Maman flew back to Paris and I returned to St. Catharines, alone this time — and to an empty house. Everywhere I looked I was reminded of Mel. There were his books, his cup on the desk with his name on it, his office with his beloved armchair, his clothes in the bedroom closet, his razor in the bathroom. Our king-size bed felt so empty now. Yet life went on and I knew I had only two choices — to give up, lie down and wait to die, or to pick myself up and carve out some kind of a new life for myself. I had three wonderful children and two lovely granddaughters. Those were great reasons to continue living.

Every day letters were showing up in my mailbox that brought me some consolation, and touched me deeply. One letter was from Deborah Harrison, a dear friend and colleague of Mel's from Brock University. I opened the letter and read. This is an excerpt:

Dear Eva,

This is just a note to say how sad I have been in the wake of Mel's death. I do understand what you have lost. If any two people had what appeared to be the 'perfect marriage' it was you and Mel. Virtually alone amongst my acquaintanceship, you restored my faith in the institution. It wasn't just that you had managed to derive comfort from living together, and to keep deriving it over a long period (which would have been achievement enough!), you also seemed to get as much of a jubilant kick out of each other's company, day by day, as you did when you first met. If that kind of compatibility happens once in a lifetime, let alone over a whole lifetime, an individual has been truly blessed. And so you and Mel were blessed beyond compare. I remember very happily the times I spent with you as a couple over the years, and can emphatically testify that your joy in one another as a family radiated outwards.

We were blessed to have Mel in the sociology department, too, and fortunate to have him as a colleague. I will not pretend that I agreed with all Mel's views (nor he with mine!), but we had a lot in common as people and never allowed our differences to become personal. Mel's vision of the world operated on a plane considerably above academic and political bickering, and everyone in the university respected him for it. One of the reasons I went into university teaching was that I thought I would work with many people like Mel. I was wrong, alas; I haven't. Universities contain almost as few people of Mel's quality as you would find in Simpson-Sears, and this has been my great disillusionment. Hence I was luckier than I, at first, realized to have Mel as a department-mate. He was the sort of person the phrase 'scholar and gentleman' was meant to describe, and one of the very few. He was not at all self-serving in his approach to departmental affairs, and often seemed to be the one voice of reason in a madhouse. I will always miss his special, thoughtful input. It especially complemented mine, because I was on so many occasions the impulsive character. He

*comprised a very crucial part of the department, and, for me, will be
irreplaceable....*

Love, Deborah

As I put the letter down, I cried my heart out, as much for the loss of
Mel as for how Deborah viewed our marriage and also how he had touched
people's lives, not only in our family, but outside of it as well. He had been
such an influential member in the sociology department. I felt so proud and
privileged to have been his wife and to have spent thirty-two short, yet very
memorable years with this wonderful man.

Letters continued to come and each one moved me deeply in its own
way as each one depicted a different facet of Mel. Two or three letters came
from students who had graduated from Yale at the same time as Mel in 1955.

To this day, 31 years after his death, I receive thank you letters from
Brock students who receive money from the Melvin Perlman Scholarship
Fund, which my children and I established in Mel's memory. Brock invested
the initial money and disburses the interest earned every year in two student
scholarships. The fund has grown considerably over the years.

CHAPTER 12

A WIDOW'S LIFE

Losing Mel was devastating. I was a widow now and had to get used to the idea of being in charge of my own life. It was a challenge at first and felt very uncomfortable. All my married life I had depended on Mel's presence. He had been my rock and I was very happy to live my life in his shadow. Now there was no one by my side with whom to discuss important decisions or face life's problems. I had gone into my marriage straight from my parents' home. For thirty-two years I had lived with Mel as one half of a couple. His life's purpose had been mine. Of course my children continued to support me in every way possible, but they lived their own lives now. Although I was sorry to leave Tamar and David, I was anxious to leave St. Catharines. A fresh start in Los Angeles sounded good, far away from the beautiful home where every room reminded me of Mel.

On the following Valentine's Day, everybody was exchanging flowers, candy and greeting cards. There was love in the air and I was alone, a widow at 56. Mel's birthday was coming up on February 26th. I was not looking forward to that day without him, but Valentine's Day was a day everyone shared and celebrated publicly. It was the saddest day for me.

After 18 years, I had to empty the house — the basement, the darkroom equipment, all the books. I was grateful for the support from Tamar and David. It was an overwhelming job, but it helped take my mind off my grief. I had to decide what was truly precious to me: the records Mel and I had listened to at dinner, Mel's photos, slides and ribbons, the letters we had written to each other in Africa, many of the books, furniture and artwork. I knew that Mel would want me to send his finished and unfinished papers to the School of Oriental and African Studies in London, so I sent them off in two trunks.

The year following Mel's death was the most difficult of my life. Though

I am inclined to be positive and enthusiastic, I struggled. I remembered what Rabbi Kogan said: "You don't get over it. You get through it."

I moved to Sherman Oaks, CA in June 1989. Luckily I had found a beautiful condo, but I felt lonely and lost. What was my life's purpose to be now? What did I really want to do? For a while I just lived from day to day. I ate. I slept. I thought. Should I look for a job? Open my own business? Thankfully I had enough money to take it easy for the time being, although I had lost the $250,000 life insurance policy that we had decided to give up. I would have loved to buy a fixer-upper, and resell it after renovating it, but I did not know anyone who could have worked with me. I also wanted to make new friends and heard of widow and widower support groups. I liked the idea and joined a group that met once a week at Valley Beth Shalom Synagogue in Encino. To meet others who shared the same grief was comforting. Our group facilitator was a kind and understanding psychologist in her late thirties. She created an environment in which everyone felt safe. As we got to know each other, we openly shared our most private thoughts and feelings. I soon realized that we all had very similar fears.

One of the widows said she would feel guilty if she took off her wedding ring. Another said she couldn't get rid of her husband's clothes. Another said she wanted to date again, but felt she was betraying her vow to be faithful. The thought of dating again did not feel right to me either and I could not imagine ever being close to a man again. The psychologist reassured us that we needed to give ourselves time to heal and not feel guilty about anything.

Between Rosh Hashanah and Yom Kippur I visited Mel's grave. In my heart I knew that he would want me to be happy and that he would encourage me to start a new life. As I was standing at his grave, looking at his name on the bronze plaque in the ground, I thought about my own funeral. It had been so hard for all of us to make tough decisions after Mel's death. I wanted to spare my children from going through the same trauma with me, so I decided to make arrangements for my funeral ahead of time.

The thought of working again and having a regular schedule felt good. Public Storage in Glendale was looking for an accountant. I would have something to do and I could meet new people, so I applied for the job. It was a beautiful, modern office building. As I walked into the main office, several women were working at their desks. Through two huge floor-to-ceiling windows I had a beautiful view of the mountains. When I exclaimed, "Oh!" one of the ladies smiled at me. Later, after I got the job, she told me she liked me right away because I was sensitive to the beauty of nature.

Slowly I was getting more comfortable living alone and I began to carve out a life of my own. I reconnected with my old friend Maggy from France who had followed us from Courbevoie to Autrans and now also lived in Los Angeles. Referring to our early years in Courbevoie, when she had to take me to school, she told me that she "hated my guts" because she could not talk freely with her friends when that "brat" was with her. I also reunited with Michèle, Maggy's older sister, who ended up in Los Angeles as well. It was so strange that the three of us, following different paths after the war, should all come to Los Angeles.

On March 4, 1990, I was thrilled to hear that David and Tish had their first child, Lisa, a beautiful baby girl. And on September 27 of the same year, Tamar gave birth to a lovely girl, Rachel Lee, the R in remembrance of Rodolphe Gutmann, my father, and her second name Lee given to her in memory of her grandfather Melvin Lee Perlman.

I flew to Paris in the spring of 1990. The occasion was the 35th reunion of the *Ecole de Puériculture*, the School of Pediatric Nursing from which I graduated in 1955. We all met in a small *château* in the countryside and had a wonderful time getting reacquainted. It was strange that 35 years had passed, and we had no trouble recognizing one another. Besides a few wrinkles, or a light change of weight, we were the same spirits, laughing and loving life.

From France, I flew to Israel. I had not been there since 1976 and Grossmama's funeral. Uncle Alfred took me to the *Yad Vashem* Museum, Israel's largest Holocaust Museum in Jerusalem. It is a magnificent and huge museum, where you can easily spend three days if you want to see everything. It recounts the war years, with all the historical details, and a multitude of videos and survivors' testimonies. It was the first time I saw up close what my family had escaped during the war.

I saw for the first time the Children's Memorial. I entered the hall in complete darkness. All I could see were little blinking stars in the sky. Then I heard the voices:

Mark Kaplan, 8 years old, France... Sophie Levy, 5 years old, Germany... Samuel Rosenblatt, three months old, Poland... It went on and on. I was awe-struck and very emotional. I learned that each morning a caretaker lights new candles that burn until closing time. All those twinkling lights are created with just five candles reflected in mirrors. It is an awe-inspiring place that honors the million and a half children who were murdered during the Holocaust.

The following summer I visited Maman in the *Rue de Courcelles*, her new home. As we were having breakfast one morning Maman blurted out, "*J'ai raté ma vie!*" (I failed my life). I was shocked.

"Maman, we have survived the war thanks to *your* extraordinary bravery, and miraculous luck," I reminded her. "You had a wonderful loving husband and you have healthy, smart and happy children and grandchildren. That is a lot to be grateful for. Why do you feel that way?"

Maman did not respond. That night, when I went to bed, her words kept me awake for hours. Had she never gotten over the fact that she had not become the doctor she had dreamt of being? Had the war traumatized her more than I realized? Maman wanted to do something important in her life and she never felt that she got the recognition she had craved and truly deserved. She had poured her soul into the WIZO, but some women were jealous of her, and she felt that. I had never seen her truly happy for any length of time except when she was playing with her grandchildren or her great-grandchildren. What I felt as a lack of affection from my mother, she more than made up for with my children and their children. She was an amazing great-grandmother. She was very gifted at painting flowers and building things for them, like a little doll house or a grocery store. Maman had all the patience in the world. She was a different person with them from the one I knew.

Unfortunately I never heard Maman express gratitude for her life or pride in her children. To her the glass seemed to be always half empty. That bothered me and prompted me to live my life in a different way, to be grateful and always count my blessings. Even though I understood and had compassion for her, it was not easy to bear her negativity and it did anger and hurt me sometimes. I never learned what prompted her to utter such words. With a heavy heart I flew back to Los Angeles.

David and Tish had a son Daniel on April 24, 1992, and Tamar and Brian welcomed Joel Aaron (for Abe Perlman, Mels' father) on April 24, 1993. Both of my grandsons were born on the same day, one year apart! I was truly blessed.

In July 1992, four years and two months had gone by since Mel passed away and I was slowly willing to entertain the idea of dating again. I missed the love of a man in my life and was longing for someone to put his arms around me and make me feel like a woman again, so I looked through the singles' section of the *Jewish Journal*. A few ads appealed to me. I replied and got a few dates. It was fun and exciting to dress up and feel attractive again for a date. The first man I met was only looking for a woman with a car or money. That was disappointing. My next date came to my condo for a cup of coffee. When I saw this fairly good looking, tall man at my door, I was pleasantly surprised, but when he spent the next 45 minutes telling me about all the things that were wrong with him — his heart, his diabetes, his knee replacements, his teeth falling out — I was thrilled when he was finally ready to leave and I could accompany him to the door.

Again I flipped through the ads. '*A dream come true to all women*' I read. Hmm. I replied to his ad and he came to meet me at my place the next day. When the doorbell rang, I opened the door, ready to greet this man with a big smile. There he was, my dream come true — a tall, bald-headed man with a beard, weighing about 300 pounds, who talked about nothing else but his conquests. Was I thrilled when he was ready to leave? You bet! Still I was not willing to give up. The next candidate invited me to dinner. He spent the whole evening telling me about his deceased wife and how wonderful she had been. With another one, I took a walk in the countryside. We walked and he talked about himself non-stop, never asking me anything about myself. The last one I met was half deaf and half blind. He still drove, but could only make right-hand turns, which often meant making huge detours to get to his desired destination. I heard that older men looking for a companion were interested in either a "nurse or a purse."

I was beginning to doubt I would ever meet anyone I would like in a special way again. Maybe I needed to try another approach. This time I contacted a Jewish matchmaking agency.

"We would love to help you find the perfect man, but we can only represent you after one of our psychologists has evaluated you," the agent informed me. "Are you willing to see the psychologist?"

"Sure," I replied.

A few days later I received the evaluation in the mail:

Eva presented herself as a sure, confident, outgoing, communicative person, even though she says that she is still shy. She appeared cultured and sophisticated, and also stubborn and independent. She spoke openly of her background, her relationships and her interests including movies, good theater, opera and travel. She was casually dressed and made an attractive appearance.

Amused and satisfied with the results I put the evaluation down for a moment, feeling that it made me seem much more attractive than I thought of myself. Then I continued reading the next part, which interested me the most:

The Ideal Person for You

He should be a kind and gentle person who is interested in the well-being of others. He should be a supportive person who is able to compromise and be tolerant. He should be well-educated and enjoy the arts and culture. He should be someone with a positive, fairly happy approach to life. He should have a good sense of humor and be able to laugh at himself and at life. Finally, he should be honest, loyal and committed.

I realized they were describing Mel. I had already met him, married him, spent a wonderful life with him and lost him. I knew then that it was going to be impossible to find such a man again. Mel was my one and only *b'shert*. Needless to say, nothing ever came of this matchmaking attempt, although I had paid a dear fee for the service.

On January 17, 1994, at 4:31 a.m. I woke up suddenly, feeling like I was lying on a moving bed of rocks. *'Earthquake!'* I thought immediately. The building was shaking. Frightened, I jumped out of bed and injured my knee on the corner of the TV set, which had fallen off its stand. I noticed that the wall behind my bed was empty. Where was my precious, glass-framed Rokeby Venus? The jolts had moved my bed far enough from the wall that the picture had fallen straight down behind it. I felt so lucky that it had not shattered over my head. In my living room, everything had fallen out of the built-in bookshelves. In the kitchen the dishwasher stood open. Glassware was scattered everywhere. The refrigerator door was open and its contents were on the floor. Much of my good china, a beautiful wedding present from Monsieur and Madame Plasseraud, with a gold monogram PG (for Perlman/

Gutmann), had broken into a thousand pieces. As I was trying to figure out how I could possibly clean up this mess and where I would be safe, I looked out of my window. The apartment building next door had collapsed on top of all the cars that were parked in the garage underneath!

The phone rang. Thankfully it was still working.

"Eva, are you okay? I just saw on the news that there was a big earthquake in Los Angeles!" My cousin Judy was calling from Israel.

"I am fine," I replied, "but my apartment is a mess. I will call you later." Tamar called also immediately from Canada, very worried. Thank God, Mark and Ilana were alright, although their kitchen was a disaster too.

Then I tried to open my front door. I pushed and pulled, but no matter how hard I tried, the door would not open, so I called my next-door neighbors. They came over immediately. It took two of them pushing from the outside and me pulling from the inside to finally get it open. One aftershock followed another, but at 7:30 a.m. I decided to go to work.

"Eva, what are you doing here?" my boss said. "Go home! If you need help, call me."

By the time I got back, a red ribbon had been placed around my building and all the residents were ordered to move out immediately. I called my boss.

"I need help. My apartment building is no longer safe," I said.

"We'll be right there, Eva," she said.

By 2 a.m. the movers were finally done and the apartment was empty. Just as we were ready to drive off to Mark and Ilana's house, we saw that electric wires crossing above the street had actually fallen over my moving van. One of the movers called the fire department immediately. An hour later the firemen had successfully removed the wires, but now the van would not start. The blinking lights had stayed on for over twelve hours, and the battery was dead. Thankfully Mark and Ilana lived close by. Mark came immediately with jumper cables and started the truck. Finally we were on our way, my belongings went into storage and I lived with Mark and Ilana.

Aftershocks continued. Several times the children and I had to seek shelter under the dining room table. After a while, we got used to the jolts. Soon it became our new habit to gather under the table before bedtime so that I could read a story to the children. Eventually the aftershocks stopped and normal life began again.

About four months after the earthquake, eager to be on my own again, I found a two-bedroom apartment three minutes walking distance from Mark and Ilana's home. I was happy going to work at Ryland Homes, a new job, living within my own four walls again.

That summer I flew to Paris for two weeks to spend time with Maman. She had moved recently to a senior residence in Neuilly and I was curious to see where she was living now. Ernest picked me up at the airport. When I walked into the lobby, I was impressed. The reception area was welcoming. The lounge area was decorated with flowers, armchairs and sofas. Large windows with a view to the garden gave the place an airy feel. The receptionist called Maman.

"Your son and daughter are here," she said.

"*Faites monter, s'il vous plaît*," I heard Maman's voice.

Ernest and I took the elevator to the third floor. Maman was already waiting for us at the door.

"Bonjour, Eva! You look tired!" were the first words that came over her lips.

"How could I not look tired after spending a night on the plane?" I answered, somewhat defensive and disappointed by her remark. I would have preferred to hear her say, "I am so glad to see you!"

Her new place was small, but loîvely. She had her best furniture as well as her artwork and books and I felt at home right away. She even had a small balcony where she could tend to her beloved flowers.

The next evening, Ernest, Raymond and their wives came and we had dinner downstairs in the restaurant. I was wearing a lovely dress. When Maman saw me she said, "Oh, your dress is nice!" Why couldn't she say, "Eva, you look nice in that dress."?

I loved her and I am sure she loved me, but I would have been so happy to get one personal compliment. I felt that I would never measure up to the person she expected me to be.

In the summer of 1995, I had to face another challenge. I had been working for Ryland Homes for four and a half years. I was busy doing the accounting and reinvesting funds for the company's various branches all over Southern California.

"Good morning, Eva," my boss said that morning. "Can we talk in my office for a moment?"

I followed her and sat down behind her desk, facing her.

"I have some not so good news for you. Ryland Homes has decided to eliminate your position. We need to reduce our overhead. From now on the managers of each branch will take care of their own accounting and investments. I am sorry, Eva. We'll give you two months to look for another job, and we will still give you your five-year bonus. We very much appreciate the work you have done for us."

The news did not overly upset me. Yes, it had been a comfortable position, but the prospect of change and a new adventure still excited me.

I soon landed a job at Warner Brothers. I loved movies and working in the entertainment industry sounded exciting. I had just started working there when Maman announced that she was coming to visit. I was excited to have her stay with me in my new apartment. She had a little difficulty walking, but overall she was doing very well at almost 85. Hearing that their great-grandmother was in town, Diane, almost 10, and her 6 year-old sister Myra, stopped by often. We were just around the corner. Maman enjoyed spending time with them. One typical summer afternoon, Maman asked me for some paper, scissors and crayons. Diane and Myra followed her out to the shaded balcony where they all sat down at the garden table. From a distance I watched Maman fold the paper in accordion style and then cut into it. Then she gently pulled the paper apart and a row of little dolls holding hands appeared. The girls squealed with delight. Maman had a big smile on her face. She was so artistic and had a lot more patience than I ever had with my children or grandchildren. How incredibly loving and sweet she could be. As far as I can remember, Maman never played like this with my brothers and me. Of course the circumstances were quite different when we were little. Sometimes things skip a generation.

A year and a half after the Northridge earthquake, the insurance company finally reimbursed me for the condo I had lost. With the money I bought a condo in Encino. Once again it was love at first sight and I moved in.

I quickly became friends with one of my new neighbors, Eleanor, also a widow. She had me over for coffee and I shared a few stories of my life with her. She invited me to a life story writing class and I joined her group. I started writing — how I met my husband, our life in Africa and in England, how we survived the war, etc. Soon I had quite a few stories on paper. Every week I walked in with a new story to share. My classmates seemed to enjoy what I read to them. Sometimes they laughed, sometimes they cried. Their positive and encouraging comments motivated me to write more. Listening to my classmates' stories and to the teacher's positive criticism was also very helpful.

As I sat in my home office one day, reflecting on my life, one question kept coming up for me again and again: Why was I saved when so many other Jews were murdered? My family and I had come so close to being caught by the Nazis several times yet somehow we always escaped — sometimes in the nick of time. I think of it as miraculous. I thought back to when the two Nazis showed up at the doorstep of the yellow house in Autrans and we were forced to live under one roof with them for two weeks. *Was there a higher purpose to our survival, and to mine in particular?*

After six months, I lost my job at Warner Brothers, but it had been such a tough job that I didn't mind at all. I went home, bought a ticket, packed my suitcase and left for Paris. I had no responsibilities at home or at work and could stay longer with Maman. In Paris, I always slept on a mattress on the floor, as Maman had only one single bed. In the daytime, I stood the mattress up against a wall. This time Maman was happy to see me. As usual we had lunch in the restaurant of the residence. Several of her friends came to greet me.

"Nice to see you, Eva. How wonderful that you came from so far to spend time with your mother."

"But Eva is only staying for three weeks!" Maman complained. This upset me. Can't she just be grateful?

Maman and I spent much time talking. Hearing her complain all the time drained my energy. For example, she once mentioned a friend of hers to me, a lady attorney who had a wonderful life and a rewarding career, and died at the age of 101. "Only a dozen people attended her funeral. Isn't that shocking?" she said.

"Maman, she had a long life and outlived most of her friends so nobody was left who remembered her," I tried to console her.

"I guess you have a point," she said reluctantly.

Once or twice a week, Maman visited friends in the hospital who no longer had any family. She fed them and spent time with them until they died. Maman said, "I wish I had younger friends!"

I made a note to myself to make sure I always had younger friends.

The hope of meeting another man had not been on my mind for quite some time when I bumped into a gorgeous, grey-haired man in his early sixties on my building's elevator. He was impeccably dressed in blinding white shorts, white tennis shoes, white socks and a perfectly ironed cotton shirt. He reminded me of the actor Lee Marvin — tall, muscular, strong and healthy looking. *What a gorgeous fellow,* I thought to myself. We both got out of the elevator on the second floor. He turned left, I turned right. A few days later I ran into him again, but neither of us said a word. I saw him a few times at HOA meetings and I knew his name was Gordon.

On September 1, 1998, Diane turned 13. It was Maman's first great-grandchild and my first grandchild to become a *Bat Mitzvah.* Maman and my brothers flew in from France, and Tamar and David came from Canada, all with their children, to celebrate this joyous occasion with us. Even Uncle Alfred came from Israel with his second wife, as well as my cousin Judy. Diane led the service beautifully, chanting all the prayers in Hebrew. When it was time to read from the Torah, there were several people called up to the *bimah.* My mother and Alfred, the two siblings, had not shared an *aliyah* together since 1927 in Driesen, Germany at their *Bar* and *Bat Mitzvah.* We all beamed with pride at Diane, and were grateful for this amazing family reunion.

A friend of mine took a three-day seminar in personal development at the Landmark Forum. Excited, he told me how much it had helped him come to terms with his traumatic past. I was interested in learning more. My relationship with my mother prompted me to think that perhaps it was time to learn to forgive and to let go of any resentment I had carried around with me all these years. He invited me to join him in the course.

Five hundred strangers from all walks of life had gathered in a large hall. Coaches and speakers introduced themselves and explained that this seminar would be very beneficial to those who dared to share their feelings honestly. Participants were invited to come up to the microphone and tell why they were here and what they expected from the course. The thought of speaking in front of so many people made me shake with fear. I had always felt uncomfortable speaking to a group, even to friends in my own living room. Row by row, people went up to the microphone and talked about life-shattering experiences they hoped to overcome. As I listened, I realized their traumas were much worse than mine.

When it was my turn, I took a deep breath and stepped up to the microphone. Surprisingly words came out without any difficulty. In fact, when I was done, I felt relieved. It really had not been such a big deal.

Part of the course was to write a letter to a person we resented, but the letter was not meant to be mailed. I wrote to Maman. Knowing that I would not mail this letter allowed me to tell her exactly how I felt without sugar-coating anything. By the time I was done, I felt a lot better about our relationship and my resentment had diminished. As a specific event came to mind, I tried to look at it from her perspective, which allowed me to be more compassionate towards her. The next day we were asked to call a person we had not spoken to for years. "Have a conversation with them and apologize, if necessary." I don't remember if I called my mother. Some couples taking the course together decided to break up and go their separate ways as they discovered they were incompatible. On the other hand, thanks to this course many relationships were repaired.

I signed up for their leadership course. Participants were asked to plan a project of their own choosing and find a way to get others excited about it to the point where they would agree to be involved. *I could bring the residents in my condo association some joy, fun and laughter*, I thought. Many looked old and miserable to me. I could invite them for coffee and cake in our recreation room on a Sunday afternoon, and to cheer them up I wanted to bring in a comedian I knew from my Rotary Club. I called him immediately.

"Would you be willing to entertain our condo association on a Sunday afternoon?" I asked.

"Sure," he said.

I had found my entertainer. Next I went from door to door to all my neighbors. With great enthusiasm I explained what I was planning to do and asked if they were willing to help me organize the event.

"Thank you for thinking of me, but no, I can't help you. It's a great idea though, Eva. Keep trying," the first one said. I got the same response at every door.

The last neighbor I went to see was a nice gentleman in his 90s.

"Eva, why don't you go and ask Gordon," he suggested. "He might be willing to help you and he lives on your floor."

That handsome fellow I keep running into in the elevator? I thought to myself. *Why not?* So bravely I went to his condo and rang his doorbell.

When he opened the door I had a big smile on my face. "May I ask you a question?"

"Please do," he replied. He invited me in.

I explained my project and he listened attentively.

"I'm sorry. I don't want to help," he said honestly.

But we enjoyed talking with each other and talked for an hour. "It's getting late. Let's go grab a bite!" he suggested.

I had not expected this invitation, but without hesitation I accepted, delighted and flabbergasted at the same time.

We went to Jerry's Deli where we talked about lots of things. I found out he was Jewish and we talked about meeting people and dating.

"Eva, you look unapproachable," he said.

"Why?" I asked, surprised, not expecting his brutally honest remark.

"Well, you are wearing a long skirt, long sleeves and a turtleneck. A woman who is completely covered like this gives a man the message that she is unavailable."

That night I went home floating on cloud nine. The next day I walked out of my apartment in a short skirt and a revealing blouse, hoping to run into my gorgeous neighbor again. To avoid being too obvious I let a few days go by before I invited him over for coffee. It was an awful brew, but he stayed for two hours. He sat on the couch and I in my armchair. There was a sizzle in the air. We were so deeply involved in our conversation that I didn't notice it had gotten dark outside. Sitting in semi-darkness it had not occurred to me to switch on the light.

From then on we met often for coffee. I started to feel confident Gordon was attracted to me as well, though he gave no signals that he wanted to take our relationship further. I decided to take a risk. "What would you think if we both went for an HIV test?"

"Sure," he said matter-of-factly. Without further ado, off we went to Kaiser, holding hands. I was tremendously attracted to him. I was dying to feel his arms around me and longing for a kiss.

Two or three days later the results came. Negative on both counts. I could not wait to get back to his apartment and close the door behind me.

Every morning Gordon prepared a lovely breakfast for us. We spent every night together, had breakfast in the morning and then spent the day doing our own thing. He worked from home investing in the stock market while I was busy with network marketing. This became our exciting routine.

My project to amuse my neighbors had failed miserably, but I had found a much more satisfying way to spend my time.

One day I noticed five pennies in the corner of the elevator. I picked them up thinking someone must have a hole in his pocket. The next day I found a nickel. I couldn't wait to get back into the elevator again to see if there was more money.

As I was reading the new issue of our community's bulletin, *The Gazebo*, a story caught my attention:

The Mystery Continues. Unless you live in the southwest complex of Encino Plaza North, you're probably unaware of events that have been taking place there, more specifically in the elevator of Building A. For the past several months, people entering the elevator have been finding five cents lying on the elevator floor. It's either five pennies or a nickel, placed in the same place every time under the elevator buttons. Does anyone know who's doing this, or do we really want to know? Occupants have said that this is a form of harassment, someone wishing everyone luck, a hole in the pocket, or flaunting someone's wealth?

The following questions are obvious:

Should we allow this to continue and disrupt the continuity of our lives?

Should we investigate this event by checking the fingerprints on the coins?

Should we offer a reward for the identification of this jerk?

Should we retain the services of a private investigator?

Should we refuse to pick up the money when we find it there?

Should we just allow this to continue and enjoy our good fortune?

Please submit all personal conclusions and recommendations to The Gazebo for publication.

We were all quite amused!

Shortly thereafter, when I returned home, I found an out-of-service sign on the elevator door and had to walk up the stairs to my apartment. Attached to my door I found five pennies with a note saying *just so you don't have to take a loss of income!* I was amused to no end. Gordon was the mystery man. I could not wait to see him that evening.

"So you are the one who keeps leaving money in the elevator?" I asked. He smiled, then replied, "People love to find money and I like to make people happy. Just this morning I overheard the two old ladies who live below me talking to each other, saying, "It's fun to find money in the elevator, but I am having a hard time picking it up. It hurts my back."

"You are one of a kind!" I said. We both laughed heartily.

Soon I found out that Gordon had another side as well. He was temperamental and could be very difficult to get along with. He had an explosive and passionate personality, which he controlled very well externally, but if I said the wrong thing, he lashed out.

One day I called Gordon over because I had a problem with my computer. While he was trying to fix it, I asked him a question that had nothing to do with what he was doing.

"Eva, don't talk to me. I can only do one thing at a time!" he lashed out angrily. It caught me by surprise. I understood that I could easily ruffle his feathers. I could have felt hurt, but I decided not to. I had learned when dealing with Maman that there were times when I had to shut up.

Only very few people got to know Gordon's tender side. My family and friends accepted him for who he was. I do not think that Ilana and Tamar liked him very much, but they saw how happy I was and they accepted him. I made great efforts to keep our relationship going because I had a good time with him.

Every so often Gordon and I talked about Mel and reincarnation.

"You know, I am looking forward to meeting Mel again and I will meet you too and we can have a *ménage a trois* up there in the netherworld," I joked.

"If you have two men for yourself, I want two women," he chuckled. We often joked about it.

Gordon offered to take me for a ride on his motorcycle. I was scared, but I went anyway. After he had driven half a block he stopped.

"Eva, stop clinging to me for dear life! I can hardly breathe!"

That was the first and last time he took me for a ride.

One morning Gordon opened the closet in the living room and took out a gun.

"If I ever find out that I have a terminal illness, I will end my life with this," he said without any emotion. "I would not want to live for years in a wheelchair and be totally incapacitated."

I did not know what to make of it. Gordon was five years younger than me, very handsome and in glowing health. Why was he thinking of a terminal illness? It was an odd moment, but, optimistic as I was, I brushed off the possibility that it could ever happen and did not give it another thought. He also showed me a manuscript he had written, and he lent it to me. It was a love story, beautifully written, with great panache and humor.

Gordon always had dollar bills in his pocket or in the glove compartment of his car to give to a beggar or a bag lady. One evening we were having dinner at a restaurant when we saw a homeless woman pass by. Gordon got up immediately. "I'll be right back," he said and rushed out the door. Through the window I saw him run after her and hand her a few dollars.

David was planning to come from Canada to stay with me for a few days. I was looking forward to introducing him to Gordon and the two got along well from the start. Gordon mentioned that he was making large sums of money by investing in the stock market online, not only for himself, but for several friends as well. "I will teach you how to buy and sell stocks online," he said to David. "This way you can work from home."

When I told my friends and neighbors Sharel, Lori and Jane that I was now close friends with Gordon, they seemed surprised.

"Really?" they exclaimed. "You're friends with that know-it-all? He's so arrogant and rude!"

"Well, he's very nice with me," I said in his defense. "In fact, he can be very charming, generous, and loving. Why don't you come over for coffee on Sunday afternoon and I'll invite him as well. You might discover his other side. He can be witty, fun and entertaining."

They came and so did he, impeccably dressed as usual. We sat around the dining room table and I served coffee and cake. He seemed quite comfortable, relaxed and happy in the presence of the ladies.

"Gordon, I think they would enjoy hearing something about your life," I said.

"Well, my parents came from Russia. My father was a physician and I was born in San Diego, where I grew up with a younger brother. I am a civil engineer and I get called after earthquakes to establish whether buildings should be retrofitted or not," he began.

My friends listened politely as Gordon continued, "I've been divorced for twenty-five years. I have two daughters. One is working in San Francisco and the other is in Europe doing research on mad cow disease. They are both doing very well for themselves. We are very close and we call each other at least once a week." Gordon tried to be his best self.

"That's impressive," Lori said.

"Gordon, tell them about the pranks you played on your parents and housekeeper. Tell them about the time you and your brother went into your parents' bedroom," I prodded.

"Well, my brother and I had no business looking into their drawers, but we did anyway. Inside one of them, we found a box with what we thought were several little balloons. So we blew them up, went on the balcony and threw them down into the yard."

We all laughed.

When I picked up my mail I found a letter from Ilana with a French stamp on it. I knew she had flown to Paris for an Amgen meeting, the bio-pharmaceutical company she worked for. She had visited her grandmother. *"Maman, when Grandmi speaks of you to her friends, she speaks with pride and her eyes sparkle. You can be sure that she loves you very much,"* I read. It meant a lot to me, especially since I could not remember one time when Maman had said, "I love you, Eva" or "I am proud of you." I knew she loved me, but she just could not say it. I still harbored a lot of resentment and understood that the Landmark Forum course had not helped me as much as I had hoped it would.

A few months later Raymond called from Paris.

"Maman is not doing well. She can't walk and she sometimes has a hard time remembering. I am afraid she might have Alzheimer's. The other day she showed me a letter from some sweepstakes. It said *Congratulations! You have won a million Euros!* And now Maman is convinced that she has won that money. She is so excited about it. I tried my very best to make her understand," Raymond continued. "Ernest and I showed her the small print, but there is nothing we can say to convince her otherwise. I am very concerned."

"That does not sound good," I replied. "Last time I visited her I also noticed that she had a hard time remembering certain things, but that is quite normal at her age. After all she is almost 89."

Over the next eighteen months, I flew to Paris nine times. Every time I saw Maman, she was a little more forgetful and fragile. I told her about Gordon.

"He is five years younger than me, nice and good-looking."

"I am very happy for you, Eva," she replied. "Does he have money?" She was afraid that he may be taking advantage of me. I reassured her on both points.

One time as I visited Maman, she said to me out of the blue, "Eva, when I die, I do not want you to come to my funeral!" At first I was dumbstruck and speechless. But the next morning, I woke up furious. Maman had told me all my life what to do and what not to do, what to wear and what not to wear. I knew that her illness made her say strange things, but it hurt nevertheless. I knew she meant well. She probably did not want me to fly all the way from California just to bury her. Still, that was a strange way to show her love and concern for me.

My brothers and sisters-in-law visited our mother almost every day. The situation was very difficult for them and I was sorry I couldn't help more. It became clear very quickly that Maman could no longer live alone, so Ernest and Raymond hired three caregivers to take care of her around the clock. Fortunately, we did not have to worry about Maman running away as she was unable to walk more than five minutes before having to sit down and rest.

In February 2001, Raymond called from Neuilly. "Maman is deteriorating rapidly. Either she needs me to bring her some medication or her caregivers have a hard time handling her."

"I am so grateful for all you do for Maman, Raymond," I said. "I will come again as soon as I can." Ernest and Annie also visited Maman often. It was a very difficult time for my brothers and sisters-in-law.

I informed Ilana and Tamar that my mother was getting worse. Myra was turning 13 in June and was preparing her bat mitzvah. It was clear that Maman was not going to be able to come, so in April 2001, two months before Myra's 13th birthday, Ilana, Myra and I flew to France to be with her. She had declined even more since I had last seen her. She was disheveled and pale, and had no longer the strength to move around with her cane or to go down to the restaurant. She preferred to sit in her armchair. Maman had difficulty communicating and reverted to speaking German much of the time.

Myra pulled her chair up, put her Torah portion in front of Maman and began to chant, in her soft and beautiful voice, following the text with her finger, so that Maman could follow. All of a sudden Maman perked up and seemed more lucid. Myra paused.

"Ki" (meaning *as* or *because* in Hebrew), Maman said, filling in the next word. She was following the Hebrew text as Myra chanted.

Ilana took pictures of them, but Maman's face was no longer full of life and sparkle.

The three of us sang *Shalom Rav* and *V'Al Kulam* from the prayer book. Maman seemed to enjoy it. In my mind I traveled back in time to when we lived in Le Vésinet so many years ago, when I listened to Maman singing Schubert melodies while accompanying herself on the piano. She loved to play Brahms, Chopin and many others. These were special moments that had filled my heart with love for classical music. To this day I cherish those moments. It was my first exposure to an array of emotions through music.

Ilana and Myra had to go home, and it was especially hard for Myra, knowing that she probably wouldn't see her great-grandmother again. Just after they left, one of Maman's caretakers called me in the middle of the night.

"Madame Perlman, please come immediately!"

I put on my robe and rushed upstairs. When I opened the door Maman was sitting in her bed, her sheets in disarray, shaking the bars of her bed and crying, "Get me out of this bed!" I tried to calm her down, but to no avail. I called Raymond. The poor guy always seemed to take the brunt of things because he lived five minutes away and he was a doctor. He came immediately and gave her a tranquilizer. Maman relaxed and went to sleep. The next two nights the same thing happened. Finally the three caregivers could no longer handle her. My brothers and I couldn't either. We had no choice but to have Maman admitted to the Georges-Pompidou Hospital in Paris. It broke my heart having to go back to the U.S. under these circumstances. I felt terrible leaving her tied to her bed, completely confused and not understanding why she was there. There was nothing anyone could do to reach her. As soon as I got back, Raymond called me: "If you still want to see Maman alive, you'd better come immediately."

Even though the financial and physical burden of having to constantly fly to France was taking its toll, I arrived at the hospital two days later. Maman was just lying there, more or less comatose.

"*Bonjour, Maman! C'est moi, Eva.*" I took her hand. For a moment she opened her eyes and murmured "Eva!" It was the last word she spoke.

Three days later, on Shabbat, Ilana and Tamar arrived. Maman had always told us: *the Just die on Shabbat.* All day long we sang Hebrew songs to her, hoping that she would let go, but she didn't.

"Many Holocaust survivors have a hard time letting go on their death-bed," her doctor told us. "She is not the only one. They had to have such will power to survive the war that they hang on for dear life."

We all spent days in the hospital at her bedside, my children, Ernest and Raymond and their wives. It was hard to watch Maman transform into a breathing skeleton, because she no longer ate and she had pulled out the needle that gave her water. Ernest's birthday and mine were coming up on May 17 and 18. *With a bit of bad luck she might just die on one of our birthdays,* I thought.

On May 18, 2001, at 5:30 a.m. my daughters and I were awakened by the ringing of the phone. It was the nurse.

"I am sorry to tell you that your mother expired at 5:00 o'clock this morning."

Maman had lasted ten full days without food or water just to die on my birthday. Yet I was thankful that the struggle and suffering had come to an end and she was finally at peace.

According to Maman's wish we buried her next to Papa and his parents in the Le Vésinet cemetery. Ernest, Raymond and their spouses, as well as Ilana, Tamar and I arrived at the gravesite. The slab of marble with Papa's name and the names of my grandparents engraved in golden letters had been moved to the side. The rabbi, a friend of Ernest's, said a few prayers. We said *Kaddish.* I could not cry. It had been such a difficult time for everyone that I felt only relief. As my daughters and I left Paris, a sobering thought came to my mind. I was now the oldest person in the family. *I will be next.*

A month later I went back to France to help clear out Maman's apart-ment. When I arrived, the receptionist handed me a stack of condolence letters with stamps from all parts of the world. Among them was a letter from Madame Micha, one of Maman's best friends from the WIZO.

"I have wonderful memories of your mother," I began to read. *"She was an exceptional woman. I was at a children's Purim party once with my two daughters. I remember how Charlotte had prepared the mothers very carefully to make children's costumes and plan the songs. This party took place in a Paris hotel close to the WIZO headquarters. There was great joy in the hall. The children were very excited and difficult to control. I was calmly sitting at a table watching the scene when I suddenly spotted a lady at the next table. She was clad in dark*

clothing and sitting with her head bowed. She seemed totally unaware of the turmoil around her. She no doubt came with a relative. She was motionless and looked desperately sad. After a while, I approached her and shyly asked the reason of her sadness. She wiped two big tears off her cheek and said to me, "I lost my daughter very recently. She was ten years old, a happy and healthy child, loved by all, an excellent student, affectionate and caring. She died, alas, very suddenly." The woman was inconsolable. Her sister had insisted that she come to that party with her and her nieces, hoping this could perhaps offer her some momentary relief from her grieving. But that atmosphere only made her feel worse. I took her hands in mine and was unable to comfort her. A thought then occurred to me. I advised her to make an appointment with Charlotte Gutmann. She accepted my advice and went to see Charlotte the next day at the WIZO office. I never found out what was said during that meeting. But, that same evening, this lady called me on the telephone, and said to me, "Madame, I want to thank you from the bottom of my heart for suggesting that I talk with Mme. Gutmann. I was at the edge of suicide, but I can now tell you very sincerely and with serenity, I have made peace with life again."

As I put down the letter, tears rolled down my cheeks. How I wished I had heard about this incident when Maman was still alive! We could have talked about this. I could have asked her what she said to that lady. Every letter I read pointed out a different quality of Maman. I did not realize how many lives she had touched throughout the years and just how much she was admired and loved. To look at Maman through the eyes of others helped me greatly to see her in a new light. She had been a remarkable woman — smart, creative, indefatigable, courageous, generous to a fault, and completely devoted to her family, her friends and her volunteer work at the WIZO. She had so many great qualities. For me, she had been a difficult mother, so what?

My brothers and I sorted through her books, her furniture, her paintings, her jewelry and her clothes and divided everything equally among us. As I was clearing out her drawers, I was surprised to find the letter to the Lewins, her relatives in Cape Town, South Africa, that she had dictated to me a year earlier when she could no longer write herself. She obviously forgot to mail it. I decided to keep it in case I wanted to contact them some day.

Gordon was happy to see me when I came back. He told me he had lost $800,000 in one day. I suspected he may be exaggerating, and I was not overly concerned. *He is dealing with millions; he'll gain the money back*, I thought.

He started complaining of headaches.

On the morning of September 11, 2001, Gordon and I were having breakfast together in his apartment with the TV on when we watched a plane fly toward the Twin Towers of New York's World Trade Center and plough right into it. "Oh my God!" A second plane followed, crashing into the second tower, which exploded into flames. Both towers came crashing down. We were shocked beyond belief. It seemed unreal. What a tragedy! We couldn't believe what we saw as it was happening. Security was heightened everywhere. The world was in mourning and would never be the same.

A month after 9/11, Gordon's headaches became more severe. I went to see him in the middle of the day. His door was never locked and I just let myself in. He looked terrible, distressed and sick, sitting at his computer, as if he had aged twenty years overnight. What had happened to the gorgeous smile that I loved?

"I went to see the doctor," he said. "I have a brain tumor."

I was terrified.

"They can't operate. If they did, I could end up paralyzed or a vegetable for the rest of my life."

The following week he told me that he got a second opinion. The result was the same. The memories of seeing Mel suffer from cancer had never faded. Being diagnosed with brain cancer seemed even worse. I understood his despair. What could I do to help? Fortunately, David had planned to come visit the following week. Knowing that he and Gordon were close, I was hoping that he could talk him out of doing something irrational.

I remembered how Gordon had told me some time ago that he would end his life if he were ever diagnosed with a terminal illness. Knowing that he had a gun, I was very concerned and decided to call the suicide line.

"We cannot help unless he calls himself," I was told. I begged Gordon to call the suicide line himself, but he did not call. I offered to take him to the City of Hope, but he declined. In early October, David arrived.

"Gordon says he has a deadly brain tumor," I said, feeling scared and helpless. "I am afraid he will kill himself. He has a gun." I wanted David to help me assess the situation and if possible, dissuade Gordon from his plan. Gordon was delighted to see David, and he became his normal self and in a good mood. Dressed impeccably in a light blue shirt, dark blue shorts and white tennis shoes, he looked like he was on vacation.

"Let's go have some ice cream," he suggested.

The three of us walked to the drugstore together, cracking jokes and having a good time. Back at the apartment, David followed Gordon to his closet. It was filled with hats of all kinds. Gordon took out a cowboy hat and put it on, while David donned a Bavarian felt hat. They laughed heartily and were having a blast. It was a bitter-sweet time, though, because I feared these could be our last happy days together. Toward the end of the evening David carefully addressed the sensitive issue.

"Gordon, Eva told me you are sick."

"Yes, and I can't accept the idea of living the rest of my life incapacitated. There is nothing to be done. It's time for me to go. I have made up my mind," he said matter-of-factly.

"Gordon, we love you and we don't want to lose you. There must be a solution," I said, still hoping we could change his mind.

It became clear to me there was nothing we could do to deter him from his plan. We talked for another two hours and by 11 p.m. we said good night. I knew Gordon had some sleeping pills. David and I went back to my apartment. As hard as it was, I had to accept his decision.

As soon as I woke up the next morning I said to David, "Please go check on Gordon."

I was frightened of what he might report. Two minutes later David was back with a smile on his face.

"Gordon is sleeping very peacefully."

I was relieved.

David and I spent the next day with our family. I felt restless the entire day, wondering what Gordon was up to. That night, as soon as we got back, I rushed over to see him. He looked sleepy.

"I took sleeping pills last night after you left and slept for 24 hours like a baby, but here I am again, back to my troubles and my pain," he said, almost annoyed.

I was relieved. David and I went to Shabbat dinner at Mark and Ilana's. We did not talk about Gordon. I did not want to burden them with my problems. There was nothing they could do anyway.

Later that evening we came back to my garage. Gordon's car was in its usual spot, but the windows were wide open. "David, please go check his car," I said.

"The car is empty," he reported a minute later. "There are two pillows on the back seat with indentations of a body that must have rested on them."

We rushed upstairs and opened the door to Gordon's apartment. He was sitting on his couch, looking forlorn.

"Why did you leave your car windows open?" I asked.

"I just could not take the smell of the exhaust, so I broke out of the car," he replied, disappointed.

He had actually tried to kill himself with the exhaust! *How did I get myself involved in this?* I wished that I would soon wake up from this nightmare. David was flying back to Canada the next morning.

As we returned to my apartment I said to David, "I am afraid that Gordon will try his gun next. I wish you could stay longer." The next morning, I took David to the airport. I went to see Ilana and the girls. I did not mention anything to Ilana about Gordon. By the time I got back it was getting dark. My heart was beating fast as I opened his door slightly. In the dim light projected by the TV, I could barely make out Gordon, sitting on the couch, holding something shiny in his hand. On his right cheek was a dark spot. His abdomen was still moving. I rushed to my apartment and dialed 911.

"I am afraid my neighbor tried to commit suicide," I said, out of breath. "Please come immediately!"

I was waiting in my apartment with the door wide open. Twenty minutes later the fire truck arrived with the paramedics. They rushed into Gordon's apartment. Sometime later they came out, carrying Gordon on a stretcher.

"We are taking him to the Encino hospital. I doubt he'll make it," one of the paramedics said. "There were two letters on the coffee table. We'll take them with us as well." I wondered to whom Gordon had written.

Half an hour later I called the hospital — Gordon had expired. It was October 20, 2001. I immediately called Mark and Ilana.

"Gordon just killed himself. Can you please come to the Encino hospital right away? I need to see him one last time. I can't do this by myself."

They came immediately. Gordon looked peaceful. The stress of the last few weeks had left his face and he again looked very handsome, lying there on the hospital bed in his impeccable clothes. I could not believe that he had actually taken his life.

"Goodbye, Gordon," I whispered. "May you rest in peace."

For the last two and a half years Gordon and I had a great time together. I would always remember him in a special way. Mark and Ilana stood by me quietly. I was glad they came. It was a sad end to another chapter of my life.

"Are you next of kin?" one of the nurses interrupted my thoughts.

"No," I said.

"Do you know any of his family? Whom should we call?"

"I know that he has two daughters, but I have never met them. All I know is that they don't live close by," I replied. "I'll see if I can find their numbers."

"If there are no next of kin, his body will be sent to a hospital in downtown L.A. for autopsy and cremation," the nurse informed me. "If you want to retrieve his ashes you will need to get written permission from next of kin."

I went to his apartment to look for his phone book, hoping to find his daughters' numbers. It was on the kitchen counter. I checked every page and could not find their names, but I *did* find the name of his cousin in Sacramento, whom I had met once before. Then I closed the door of his apartment for good. At home I called his cousin.

"This is Eva, Gordon's friend and neighbor," I said. "I am so sorry to tell you that Gordon has taken his own life."

"I am so sorry for you, Eva," she replied, not seeming overly saddened by the news. "That's really too bad."

"Could you please contact his daughters and tell them what happened?"

"Yes, I will," she said. "I will come down next month to visit my relatives and we can have lunch if you wish."

"I would like that," I replied.

A few days later, to my utmost surprise, the autopsy revealed that Gordon had been in perfect health and there was no sign of a brain tumor. How could that be? He had been so convincing. I had believed him beyond a shadow of a doubt. *How many other things had he told me that were untrue, and why?*

On my way to the elevator the following week, I noticed there was some activity in Gordon's apartment. The door was open and a man was moving some furniture out. He was the owner of the apartment. He informed me that the tenant hadn't paid his rent for the past two months.

Had Gordon really lost all his money in the stock market and died penniless? Was this what drove him to kill himself? I was sad and felt guilty that I hadn't taken his financial loss more seriously.

Eventually Gordon's cousin came to the Valley, and we had lunch together.

"Gordon told me he had an inoperable brain tumor, but the autopsy revealed he was in perfect health. How is that possible?" I asked.

"I don't know. All I know is that Gordon had a rough childhood," she said. "His parents idolized his older brother, so he always felt like he didn't matter and he suffered from it greatly. As a child he was unwanted, unloved and abused. No one really wanted to be around him. Even his daughters have not spoken to him for years."

"What? He told me he spoke with them regularly."

"No. He didn't have any contact with any of his relatives except me."

"He told me he was the son of Russian parents, and that his father was a doctor and they lived in San Diego."

"That is true," she confirmed.

My mind went back to the day I walked into his apartment and found him in front of his computer, looking devastated. Had he really invested for his friends? Had he lost their money, too? Could that be the reason he shot himself? Had he spun himself into a cocoon of lies that ended up choking him? I didn't know what to believe.

Before she left, Gordon's cousin gave me the email address of Gordon's youngest daughter Jacie.

I wrote to Jacie and told her how sorry I was that she had lost her father. I told her about our relationship, that he had been very good to me and that I was hoping to meet her one day. I assured her that he did love his daughters.

Before long she wrote back giving me permission to retrieve his ashes from USC Medical Center. She was glad to hear that someone had loved her father.

Nine months later I went to the USC Medical Center with her letter in hand. I was handed a plain, surprisingly heavy, cardboard box and two letters. These were the letters that the paramedics had found on Gordon's coffee table and taken with them the day they picked him up. One letter was addressed to his daughters and the other one to me. I put the box down and opened one letter:

My Eva,

I need to write this note to you and share my feelings for you. I have never met anyone that I have had this comfortable and passionate love for. Knowing and loving you has proven to me that there is a God and that he is on my side to give me someone like you. My 63 years have been paid in full just by having you for two and a half years. God bless you.

Love,
G.

I was moved to tears. His actions had shown me in so many ways that he had indeed loved me, but he had never verbalized it while he was alive. Filled with emotion I picked up the heavy box and carried it to the car, cradling it in my arms.

I opened the second letter.

My children,

May God bless you both. May you love each other forever. Love and enjoy each other and share your happiness together. May your happiness and love be at least equal to mine with Eva Perlman and her family. They are the most beautiful people beyond our comprehension. I have always loved you.

Dad

It was important to me to have a ceremony for Gordon. I wanted to remember his life, say Kaddish and scatter his ashes in the mountains he loved. My friends Sharel and Lori helped me put together a booklet of songs, poems and prayers. We were joined by his daughter Jacie and Gordon's motorcycle buddy, Mac. We gathered in my living room.

"I am so glad to meet the people who really cared for my father," Jacie said. "You are the first in the last fourteen years. Very few people got to know my father's heart. He had built a wall around himself." We shared stories about Gordon and honored his memory.

Then we followed Mac to a beautiful lookout on Mulholland in the Santa Monica Mountains past the Rock Store where Gordon used to hang out with his biking friends. It was his favorite spot, a large dirt area by the roadside where vehicles could stop to enjoy the view of Conejo Valley. We said *Kaddish* as motorcycles roared by. I opened the box and scattered Gordon's ashes into the canyon. The wind was so strong it blew them right back on us. If Gordon was watching from above, he probably had a good laugh.

I invited Jacie and her family to dinner and I got to meet and spend time with the grandchildren he never knew.

Soon thereafter, I received healing news. Brian and Tamar were moving to California with their children to be near us. Rachel was 11 and Joel 8. They arrived in January 2002. It was wonderful to have them closer, especially after a difficult year. A couple of years later, I was thrilled to attend Rachel's Bat Mitzvah. Also David, who had been divorced for several years, got happily remarried to a lovely woman named Marilyn, and gained a stepson, Evan.

CHAPTER 13

TRAVEL ADVENTURES

Mel, Maman and Gordon had passed away. I had retired from regular work and network marketing was allowing me to have a flexible work schedule. I really needed a change of scenery. Why not take some time off to contemplate what I wanted to do with the rest of my life?

Our Feng Shui teacher suggested that we all go to China together. After a 15-hour flight from Los Angeles, we landed in Beijing in northeastern China. Everything was so colorful and different there, the people, the buildings, the unbelievable traffic.

The next few days we spent exploring Beijing, the Forbidden City and the Chinese Imperial Palace of the Ming Dynasty in the center of Beijing. North of the city we climbed The Great Wall of China. The steps were a foot high and not everyone in our group was able to climb them. From the top we could see the wall meandering through the countryside and the view was breathtaking. Then we flew to Xi'an, about 600 miles southwest of the capital, to see the famous Terracotta Warriors who protected the tomb of the first emperor and were supposed to accompany him into the afterlife. In Xi'an archeologists had excavated hundreds of life-size terracotta soldiers. For more than 2,000 years they had been covered with soil. It is considered to be one of the most important archeological finds in the world. These stone figures, all standing at attention, looked amazingly real in their uniforms. Some soldiers had their hands open, others made a fist; some had no head, some had no arms, but the ensemble, neatly arranged in perfect rows, was an incredibly impressive sight.

In Guelin we boarded a ferry and traveled slowly down the winding Li River between differently shaped, tall mountains with rounded peaks partly hidden by fog. These mountains were superimposed on several levels into the distance. It was a photographer's dream come true. We passed by bamboo forests, small villages and fishermen in their boats, water buffaloes swimming in the river, and women doing their laundry along the river bank. I had seen fantastic pictures of this landscape at the camera club, but to experience it with my own eyes was breathtaking. At every turn there was another incredible view of the tall, dramatic limestone mountains. I took at least a hundred pictures.

Shanghai was our last stop before returning to the United States. It is a modern city, which was a refuge for many Jews during WWII.

A few weeks later, in August 2002, my friend Eileen (Mark's stepmother) and I flew to Vancouver to take an Alaskan cruise. As I was standing on the deck watching the trail of foam the ship was leaving behind, I took a deep breath, filling my lungs with fresh, clean air and listening to the sea gulls that were following us. We cruised through the Inside Passage, between the mainland and dozens of small islands covered with pine trees.

We stopped in Juneau, the capital of Alaska. It could only be reached by helicopter, ship or train. Eileen and I took a helicopter ride to the Mendenhall Glacier. Looking down and seeing the ground three miles below was frightening, but the view was magnificent — a stunning landscape of mountains and lakes, the blue sky above, and the light-blue crevices of the glacier below. After spending some time on the glacier, the helicopter picked us up again. We hiked through the Tongass National Forest, a rainforest of ferns, mosses, lichens, spruce and fir trees. Bald eagles flew overhead to their nests.

On our way back toward Vancouver we went on shore in Sitka, the oldest and fourth largest city in Alaska, a former Russian port, bordered by high, snow-capped mountains to the east and the Pacific Ocean in the west. The rain did not deter us from taking a boat trip to see wildlife, humpback whales, sea otters, sea lions and seals.

As our ship sailed back home through the Inside Passage, I watched the sun go down behind the mountains, casting its orange glow on the dark blue water. Killer whales were playing in the waves.

We were treated to special lectures on the ship by a young man, Michael M., who lived in the Alaskan wilderness for two years. I met him after one of his talks and we became friends. When I came home, I received an email from Michael. I was delighted.

*"My friend Corbett owns a lodge in Arusha National Park, Tanzania.
He is planning a safari for next February. I am going and I would be
delighted if you would consider joining us."*

I felt so privileged that he would invite me. I had been on safari before,
when we lived in Uganda. After a short moment of hesitation I thought,
Why not? When a good opportunity comes my way, I know I'd better grab
it. Others might analyze the situation, and then, when they are ready for it,
the opportunity is gone. It's like trying to photograph whales! I had relatives
in Cape Town whom I had never met. Maybe this was my chance to go meet
them in person. Maman had talked about them often. Her cousin Harry Lewin
had emigrated from Germany to Cape Town to escape the Holocaust, and she
had gone to see them in 1985, and to attend Harry's grandson's *Bar Mitzvah*.

I immediately sent an email back to Michael, accepting his invitation.
Then I looked for the letter that Maman had dictated to me when she could
no longer write herself. Thank goodness she had forgotten to mail it at the
time or I would not have had their address. I wrote to them in hopes of
going to see them before joining the safari. Soon their son Alfred (Alfie)
answered. He informed me that Harry and Liesel, his parents, had both
passed away, but that he and his wife Diana would be thrilled if I came and
stayed with them.

In late January 2003, I flew to Cape Town. Alfie and Diana were waiting
for me at the airport with big welcoming smiles and a sign larger than life
showing my name. We were delighted to meet one another. Their lovely
home was at the foot of the famous Table Mountain, South Africa's popular
tourist attraction and its landmark. They took me on the cable car up the
mountain for a breathtaking view of Cape Town and the harbor.

Alfie and Diana took me everywhere. The African coastline reminded
me of the California coast. We toured the wine country. Many vineyards,
restaurants and shops still bear the original French names that were given to
them by the Huguenots — French Protestants who fled to South Africa in the
late 1700s to escape a massacre. On our way we passed squalid shantytowns
that extended as far as the eye could see. My hosts took me to the penguin
colony in Boulders where we saw hundreds of penguins on the beach.

Eight days later, it was time to leave for my safari in Tanzania and it
was difficult to say goodbye, as neither of us knew when we would see each
other again.

The next thing I knew I was in Nairobi, Kenya where I boarded a tiny plane bound for the Kilimanjaro airport in Arusha, Tanzania. It was a 12-seater with only one pilot and five passengers. As much as I admired the stunning mountainous landscape and the imposing Mount Kilimanjaro below, I had only one thought: *What if this pilot has a heart attack or falls asleep?*

Forty minutes later, we landed safely. I was greeted by a smiling, handsome young African holding a sign bearing my name. For the next hour and a half, which seemed more like half a day. I was jostled, shaken and bounced over rocks and through potholes and puddles. By the time I saw some lights in the distance it was night. The driver took me to the entrance of a lodge and opened the wooden door. A group of six travelers from various parts of the United States were sitting comfortably in armchairs in front of a fireplace, chatting away.

"Eva, you made it! We've been waiting for you," Michael said, greeting me warmly. "You are the last one to arrive."

He got up and hugged me and introduced me to his friend Corbett, a nice looking young man in his early thirties, and to the rest of the group. The lodge was rustic, but comfortable.

The next morning at breakfast I asked Corbett, "How did you end up here in Tanzania?"

"I came to climb Mount Kilimanjaro when I was 19 and fell in love with the area, so I decided to leave Texas and move here for good," he said. "And now I organize safaris throughout Kenya and Tanzania for adventurous people like you. I did not have a wife or child at the time and was free to follow my heart and make my dream come true."

After breakfast Corbett and his assistant, Ali, loaded our luggage, food and water on the two Land Cruisers, and we left. We passed through Arusha, a busy township near Mount Kilimanjaro. Just one narrow, unpaved road lined with Indian shops ran through the village. It was packed with traffic — buses, cars, pushcarts and wheelbarrows. Pedestrians were walking in the middle of the road as there were no sidewalks. The cars and buses kicked up clouds of dust. That day we drove 160 miles, one third on paved roads, and two-thirds on *murram* through Maasai country and the Ngorongoro Conservation Area, northwest of Arusha.

Finally, by mid-afternoon, our group arrived at the Ngorongoro Serena Safari Lodge, a wonderful sight for our sore eyes, muscles and backs. It stood right on the rim of the Ngorongoro crater, and blended seamlessly and harmoniously into the landscape with its stacked, plant-covered roofs. We marveled at the stunning view over the plain below. The crater was home to more than 25,000 wild animals — lions, zebras, elephants, flamingos, gazelles, antelopes, leopards, herds of wildebeests and buffaloes.

The next morning, our group got into an open-roofed Land Cruiser. The driver loaded picnic baskets and drove us down into the crater, a large flat basin, 12 miles in diameter. We saw hyenas, jackals, elephants and elegant giraffes. Watching a group of giraffes run, with the mountains as a backdrop, gliding effortlessly, their long necks undulating, was incredible. It was like art in motion. *God created a beautiful world!* I thought. I fell in love with giraffes!

We spotted a cheetah waiting to catch a gazelle. The gazelles started running long before the cheetah did and the cheetah missed. Our group was grateful, not only to have witnessed this incident, but because the graceful gazelle had escaped. A lion and lioness were napping by the side of the road, looking very hot and tired. They did not seem to be bothered by the passing vehicle. A kori bustard, the heaviest bird in the world able to fly, weighing in at 44 pounds, stood in the grass, inflating himself and sending out a drum-like groan to attract a female. We saw hippos, a rhinoceros, two huge elephants and much more. The sun shone mercilessly and our vehicles brought up huge dust clouds. We were covered with dust from head to toe. My eyes were so dry I could hardly blink.

In the afternoon we drove to the Serengeti National Park, just northwest of the Ngorongoro Crater and south of the borders of Kenya and Uganda. There we saw ostriches and dik-diks (small antelopes). Vultures were feeding on the kill of the day while storks and herons were standing in line, waiting impatiently for their turn to feast on the remains. Two monkeys were swinging from branch to branch in an acacia tree. Birds of all rainbow colors sat everywhere in the few trees and flew off just when we were ready to photograph them.

We drove into the Loliondo Game Conservation area, Tanzania's best known Maasai community in the country's northeast. For the rest of the trip we would stay in brown dome-shaped tents. Corbett had hired three local Maasai–Matiko, Ali and Jagat–who would stay with us while we were in Maasai country. Matiko was the oldest. He was tall and slender, with very fine features and tightly-braided hair. Standing tall and proud, wrapped in his rust-colored cloth, he looked very aristocratic. In the afternoon we arrived at our first campsite. The Maasai had already set up khaki green and brown tents and camp beds with mosquito nets for us. They had dug a latrine and surrounded it with an opaque plastic structure for privacy. The shower was ready too — a structure held up by four wooden poles, which supported a hanging heavy plastic bag filled with water. The sun had warmed the water all day to a perfect temperature. The Maasai cooked a delicious dinner with lots of vegetables, meat, rice, plenty of fruit, including the sweetest pineapple slices I had ever tasted. We ate around the campfire. We talked, joked, laughed and had a great time. We were a friendly, boisterous group of Americans. I was by far the oldest. The others were all in their thirties and forties.

We changed camp again and the three Maasai traveled with us. Corbett gave our group a choice — to walk for five miles through the virgin bush or to ride with the camp equipment and our luggage. I decided to walk with the men while the women rode in the truck. I felt safe with Corbett who carried a big rifle, and Matiko, with his bow and poisonous arrows. The five-mile walk was not easy. We had to be careful where we stepped. Rocks and stones were everywhere and the grass was so tall it was hard to spot snakes or lizards. All of a sudden the sky turned black and for the next 30 minutes we trudged through a heavy hail and rain storm accompanied by thunder. Our waterproof jackets did not keep us from getting drenched to the skin. Corbett turned around.

"Eva, are you okay?" he asked.

"Yes," I said with a big grin as I was making my way through the wet grass. This was surely the experience of a lifetime.

Hungry, tired and happy, we arrived at the next camp. The sun came out again and dried us off. Although this was supposed to be the dry season, El Niño was playing havoc with the weather.

On day five, our group arrived at the third camp. After a meal we relaxed under a canopy in camping chairs in front of our tents with the Maasai, sheltered from the burning sun. Ali always held his bow in his hand while the other two kept a stick nearby just in case an animal got too close. Two women of our group gave each of the three Maasai pens and paper that they had brought from home. The three men's eyes lit up and they immediately began to draw animals with amazing skill and imagination. Then one of the women showed Matiko her little Mojo, a small stuffed monkey that she always carried in her backpack for good luck. He cradled it in his arms as if it were alive. Obviously he had never seen such a toy. The pure joy on Matiko's face brought tears to my eyes.

After dinner Corbett offered to take us on a night tour in his Jeep, which had two huge spotlights so animals could be easily seen in the dark.

"No one is allowed to get out of the vehicle," Corbett warned.

As we were driving through the darkness looking for animals with the spotlights lighting up the sides of the road, Corbett pointed at a huge spider in its impeccable web, some thirty feet from the road. It threw a thousand reflections in the light. It was so striking that two of the group members forgot all about the safety rules and without thinking jumped off the vehicle and rushed to photograph the web. As soon as they were back in the Jeep we spotted a lion in plain sight just a few feet away!

Exhausted, we came back to the camp. I had just crawled into my sleeping bag on the cot when I felt a tremendous jab on my left forearm. I reached for the flashlight, but I did not see anything. Yet my skin started hurting terribly. The pain shot down to my wrist and up to my armpit. It was pitch dark in the camp. Everyone was asleep. It was too dangerous to leave the tent among the rocks. Anxiously I waited for the morning light, never closing my eyes. All night I worried, not about what had happened to me, but that I would be sent to the hospital or straight back to California. As soon as there was some daylight, I got out of my tent and rushed to see the Maasai. They were already up, preparing breakfast.

"You must have been bitten by a scorpion," Matiko said casually. "One of the Maasai was also stung during the night."

He came to my tent and looked into my sleeping bag, but found nothing. When Corbett got up I told him what had happened.

"Scorpion," he said, agreeing with the Maasai. He gave me some Benadryl and said that I would be fine in 48 hours. He was right. I was relieved to be able to continue with our trip!

On our way back to Arusha, Matiko stopped by his village. The huts were arranged in a large circle, surrounded by shrubs, in the middle of a vast and dry landscape. We got off the van and followed Matiko inside through a small opening in the bushes. Here square mud-and-dung huts were arranged around a large corral, packed with cows and a few sheep and goats. Flies were everywhere, even on the eyes and lips of the children who rushed out to greet us. It was obvious that the Maasai's livelihood was centered around their animals. Their main food was cows' blood and milk.

The stench of manure was difficult to bear. I sank in with every step I took as I followed Matiko to his hut through the wet mud and dung.

At his hut, Matiko introduced us to his wife and his mother. His two children looked at us with big smiles. The entrance to the hut was no more than four feet high, so only a few of us went in. I decided to stay outside. This way of life seemed so primitive to me. From a Westerner's perspective they had nothing except some animals and a lot of dirt. Yet their faces radiated happiness and contentment. I watched the tall and slender Maasai men as they walked around gracefully in their bark cloth robes and their stick in one hand. They were handsome warriors who protected their families and their herds from predators with their simple handmade spears. Yet they were gentle and sweet. I can hardly think of the Maasai without getting emotional, seeing people who had practically nothing except each other and some cows, and who were happy with their way of life. The sculpture of the Maasai warrior Mel and I brought back from Africa over 40 years earlier meant even more to me now.

After our visit, a little plane took us back to Arusha and we said our goodbyes. My trip was over. After almost three beautiful weeks in Africa, it was hard to leave. I flew from the small Kilimanjaro airport to Dar es Salaam, where I changed planes for Amsterdam. Soon I was back in Los Angeles and the entire trip felt like a dream.

"My goodness!" Sharel, my neighbor, who had come to pick me up, exclaimed. "You look like you walked through the African bush!" My face was sunburnt and my hair dry and disheveled. She was right. I looked pretty awful!

I was very sad to hear, two or three years after our trip, that Corbett had died unexpectedly, leaving a young widow and two small children bereaved. He was only in his mid-thirties.

I had inherited a little money from my mother, and I wanted to make it last. David and I read a book about investing in real estate by Robert Kiyosaki, *Rich Dad Poor Dad*, which I found very interesting. I was ready to invest so I took a class.

I indicated on the form I was given that I was interested in Big Bear. Within two days I received a phone call from a realtor in Big Bear and I made an appointment to go see her.

"How much can you spend?" the realtor, a young affable woman, asked. "Up to $150,000," I replied.

We made an appointment for the following week. After a two and a half hour drive, I arrived in Big Bear and the realtor showed me four properties within my range. I fell in love with the fourth one. It was a pretty little house with French doors and a balcony that ran along the width of the house on the second floor. I made an offer and it was accepted. I became a proud real estate investor and started enjoying a little secondary income.

Three months later, I bought my second property, this time in Chesapeake, Virginia, and again I was able to rent it out immediately. I was happy as can be. The rents covered the mortgages!

I was told that, in time, rents would go up and the houses would appreciate. Another benefit was that all interest and expenses on those properties were tax deductible. I was off to a good start and enjoying my new status of property owner.

I attended investment meetings regularly and bought eight more properties with very little money down — in Idaho, Georgia and Oregon, two in Texas, and three in Florida. Because of my good credit I had no problem getting loans and I felt confident that these investments would give me a good return, especially since real estate values kept increasing.

In the summer of 2005, my eldest granddaughter announced that she was going to spend a year in Israel. Ilana and Mark's daughter, Diane, had been there once with her parents, and again for a semester in high school. She was next in our multi-generational attraction to Israel. My uncle Alfred and his wife had escaped to Palestine in 1934; my mother Charlotte had made thirty-three trips to Israel and raised money for this brave little country. Mel and I had wanted to live in Israel, but life had taken us on a different path. Mark and Ilana had both attended the Hebrew University in Jerusalem just as Mel had. Diane would be the 4th generation.

For Chanukah that year we all gathered together. My family had grown so big. Before dinner twenty-four adults and seventeen children gathered around the granite island in the kitchen, and each family placed their *chanukiah* in front of them. Our hostess Suzy, Mark's stepsister, welcomed us, and then each family lit its own candles. Together we chanted the blessings and sang *Maot Tsur*. As it was getting dark outside, the children's faces were lit by the many flickering candles. To see the wonder in their eyes moved me deeply. I thought of all the persecuted Jews throughout the ages and the

Holocaust, and of all the children who never had a chance at life. Here I was alive, standing in the middle of a large, beautiful, loving family. What a miracle that my family and I had survived the war! A few of us wiped away a furtive tear. Maman would have been so proud. I missed her and my son David and his children, who were still living in Canada. *Am Yisrael Chai*, I thought. The Jewish people is alive!

In 2006 I went to Costa Rica for three days. It was my first trip as a member of WorldVentures, a new networking company that I had joined. I was looking forward to this adventure. Among other activities, we prepared to take a zipline through a beautiful, lush, green forest. Once we arrived in the forest, an experienced employee gave us safety instructions before we were helped into our helmets and safety gear. I could not wait to zoom down the cable line, high above the ground. Some of the young people among us were scared of going, but when they saw me getting ready with such excitement, they decided, "If Eva has the guts to go on the zipline in her seventies, we have to go."

Zipping from tree to tree high up in the air in a foreign country was great fun. The last zip was as long as a football field. You had to be heavy enough to have sufficient momentum to make it all the way. Some young girls were so light that they stopped midway, and had to turn around and pull themselves up along the cable to the last tree.

After Costa Rica I went on several one-week cruises to Mexico, the Bahamas and the Caribbean Islands. I loved to be on a cruise ship, away from the hustle and bustle of city life. What could be better than filling my lungs with fresh marine air?

A trip to Hong Kong had been on my wish list for a long time, and I was fortunate to go there with a group. Fabulous sights, great shopping, British influence visible everywhere, it became my most memorable trip. There again, the quality of life varied tremendously, from people living in tall skyscrapers to the poorest boat-dwellers.

The most meaningful day for me was the day we went to Lantau, Hong Kong's largest island. After we had driven a good two hours partially along the coast of the island, we saw in the distance a gigantic statue of the Buddha sitting cross-legged and towering over the countryside. We climbed more than 250 steps to reach the round plateau on which the Buddha sat. I had never seen such a huge statue, 112 feet high, made of bronze. His left hand is open and turned up to the sky, symbolizing the fulfillment of wishes; his right hand is at a 90-degree angle, facing the climbers in a greeting gesture. The platform is so high that visitors, who were walking up the stairs, looked like ants from up there. From the top we enjoyed a 360-degree breathtaking view over the countryside. I had an overwhelming feeling of awe and gratitude to just stand there and take it all in.

When it was time to go home and our plane took off from the Hong Kong airport, I looked out of the window. Far away in the distance I spotted the giant Buddha waving goodbye with his right hand.

For the last four years, I had been a happy real estate investor. I was the proud owner of ten investment properties. All were rented, but unfortunately the rental income no longer covered my mortgages. Being an amateur investor, I kept holding on to the properties, thinking this was temporary and the market would correct itself — the mistake most amateurs make.

By the summer of 2008, home prices dropped by almost 30% and our country's real estate market was facing a major crisis. I sold my Encino condominium and moved into a two-bedroom apartment half a mile away. Now that I was renting, I no longer had to worry about repairs, clogged up sinks and toilets or leaking windows and ceilings. Once my furniture was set up, and I laid down my rugs and placed my treasures on shelves and walls, I felt at home again.

The market continued to fall and I had no choice but to sell more of my investment properties, one at a time. Over the next three years, I was forced to sell two of my properties in short sales and one went into foreclosure. Now I had only two properties left, one in Texas and one in Virginia. I continued with my business and my networking, and kept open to opportunities.

Another time I went to a four-day retreat with about sixty participants at a magnificent resort in Rancho Mirage, California. It was to be a silent retreat unless we were in class and called upon to speak.

That night I unpacked my suitcase next to a total stranger in complete silence. It felt so uncomfortable that my roommate and I avoided all eye contact. Once in a while, our eyes met accidentally and we exchanged an awkward glance or smile. I never put on my nightgown so quickly and went to bed so early.

At eight a.m. all sixty course participants gathered for breakfast in total silence: no coffee, no sugar, no alcohol, no smoking, and again, no talking. Some people experienced withdrawal symptoms and did not feel good. The rest of the day we spent in workshops, doing all sorts of exercises to examine our feelings, our failures and our dreams, and to think about what we were grateful for. Some students became very vulnerable. That endeared them to all of us. We cried. We laughed. We shared.

For lunch and dinner we gathered again silently. The servers did not know what to make of our behavior and looked at us in disbelief. They must have thought we were nuts! Again I spent the night in total silence with the same stranger. Soon, funnily enough, it became quite enjoyable not having to talk. Even couples had been separated for the night, and had to room with strangers.

"Tomorrow morning everyone will go on a four-mile walk alone," our seminar leader announced before we went to our rooms.

The next morning, I began my walk when it was dark outside. The world was still asleep. With the rising sun the birds began to sing. I heard a train in the distance. As it got brighter, I noticed the various types of trees and the colorful flowers along the meandering path. Subtle fragrances permeated the air. I was paying much more attention than usual to what I was hearing, seeing and smelling.

After breakfast we went to class. It was freezing cold because the heating system of the hotel had broken down. Thankfully a hotel employee walked in with a mountain of white down comforters. We wrapped ourselves up in them, looking like Eskimos in their igloos.

On our last evening, we piled up all the comforters against a wall. One of the participants started to run and threw himself into the pile, face down. Everybody laughed. I felt the urge to do the same, but did not dare. What would they think of a 79-year old woman who acted like a teenager? One of the young men seemed to read my thoughts and motioned to me, "Go for it!" That was all the encouragement I needed. I ran as fast as I could and jumped into the comforters face down, having the time of my life.

"Bravo, Eva!" someone yelled and everyone clapped.

On the last day, while having breakfast in silence again, two men broke out in laughter for no obvious reason. One by one everyone joined in until the entire group was laughing hysterically. The servers looked puzzled. For the last four days no one had said a word and now we were all laughing out of control. Even our leader laughed as hard and as loud as everyone else.

Every so often we managed to remain quiet for a few seconds and then we broke out again into irresistible laughter.

I drove back home, grateful and enriched by what I had experienced — the camaraderie, the silence, the self-discoveries. Spending time alone with my thoughts for long periods of time had taught me to feel comfortable being with myself, enjoying my own company and feeling good about myself. Silence is indeed golden. As they say in French, *La parole est d'argent, le silence est d'or.*

My six grandchildren in 2008

One morning in February 2009, I received an email from my cousin Judy in Haifa:

> *Eva, do you have the address or phone number of Robert Cohn? I met a German woman named Sigrun Marks, who is doing research about his grandparents, Ruben and Minna Riesenburger, who were taken from their home in Berlin by the Nazis and gassed in an extermination camp.*

I remembered Robert well. He lived in Kansas City with his parents and all three had come to my wedding. Maman had said to me: "His parents Betty and Bob Cohn fled to Shanghai where they survived the war. Betty and my mother were cousins." Now I understood that the Riesenburgers were his maternal grandparents. I immediately sent Judy his contact information.

Diane graduated from college and made *Aliyah*, bravely following her heart. She was determined to live and raise a family in the beating heart of the Jewish world.

Myra, Diane's younger sister, went to Israel for a year of study at the Hebrew University, just like her sister, her parents, and grandfather Mel had done before her. Mel and my mother would have been bursting with pride.

When Ilana invited me in 2010 to fly with her to Israel to go visit them, I jumped at the chance. I hadn't been there since 1990. With my granddaughters there as well, it would be a reunion of three generations of women in our family.

When we touched down at Ben Gurion Airport, just south of Tel Aviv, I noticed how modern the airport was. It no longer looked like the airport I remembered from 1990. So much had changed about Israel! I hardly recognized the place and was amazed by what had become of the mostly flat and dry desert landscape on my first trip to Israel in 1950. Now I was marveling at green fields with hundreds of tall trees on both sides of the freeway. I knew that every one of these trees had been planted by people from all over the world in remembrance of loved ones who had died or to mark a happy event such as a wedding, a birth or an anniversary. As the bus approached Jerusalem, the landscape became dry and rocky and the Holy City appeared in the distance, situated on inhospitable-looking hills.

Judy wanted us to meet this lady, Sigrun Marks, who researched Holocaust survivors. Although she lived in Berlin, she happened to be in Jerusalem at that time.

The next day, we went to meet Sigrun where she worked at the Great Synagogue in downtown Jerusalem. This was to be my first real encounter with a non-Jewish German. All my life I had hated everybody and everything German.

A charming, scholarly, middle-aged woman came to greet us. "I am so delighted to meet you," she said with a German accent and a genuine warm smile. "Please follow me!"

She led us into a huge empty room with a large table that was covered with documents.

"Have a seat, please," she said.

Sigrun looked through piles of papers and pulled out several sheets with family trees of both Maman's and Papa's families. I recognized them immediately. My mother had worked on these trees for years and she had shown them to me every time I visited her. I also saw my grandmother Else Lewin's handwritten memoir.

"How did you get these very personal documents?" Ilana and I asked almost in unison.

"From your cousin Judy," she answered. "My husband Wolfgang and I are working as volunteers on a project called *Stolpersteine* (stumbling stones) which commemorates victims of National Socialism. Jews were the largest group of victims. Most stumbling stones are laid for Holocaust victims. This project started in 1996 when the artist Gunter Demnig placed the first shiny brass plates into the sidewalk in Berlin Kreuzberg, a neighborhood where many Jewish families used to live. The Nazis rounded them up and later gassed them in concentration camps. Since these victims had no graves, this project is essential to honoring their memory. Every day more brass plates are being set into sidewalks in front of homes and stores where Jews and other victims once lived and worked, and from where they were picked up to be exterminated. Since Wolfgang and I got involved with this project four years ago, over 40,000 *Stolpersteine* have been placed in 18 countries (As of the beginning of 2019, 71,000 stumbling stones have been laid in 26 countries). All plaques are engraved with the victims' names, their year and place of birth, the date they were deported and when and where they died, in one of the many concentration and extermination camps in Germany or Poland. The letters are deliberately very small, so people who 'stumble' upon them have to bend down to read them, therefore paying homage at the same time. Every time a plaque is laid into a sidewalk there is a little ceremony. Germans who work for this project donate their time to help heal the Jewish-German relationship. The project is financed solely by donations from German citizens."

"This is incredible," I said. "How did you find the Riesenburgers?"

"We do our research street by street. While I was researching Jews whom the Nazis had taken from their homes on *Tierstrasse* in Berlin-Friedenau, I came across the names of Ruben and Minna Riesenburger. They used to live at number 20. Sadly, I learned they were gassed in Theresienstadt. Wolfgang and I found their names in the Schöneberg City Hall in an exhibition called *We Were Neighbors*. We then search for the victims' relatives who may still be alive, so we can invite them to the ceremony." she explained. "We have several sources, the *Memorial Book of Jewish Victims of National Socialism*, the *Memorial Book of Berlin*, and the *Federal Memorial Book* where all the victims are listed. In Berlin's "address books" of the twenties and thirties we then found out when exactly they lived on *Tierstrasse 20*. Once we knew that, we visited *Yad Vashem's* internet site, hoping that relatives of the Riesenburgers may have filled out a one-page testimonial form on which survivors recorded biographical information and photos of Jewish family members or friends who were killed. At the bottom, family members who wrote this page usually leave their contact information. Now we had the name of a person we could contact — Alfred Lewin. We had his address in Gedera and his phone number. Through his number we contacted his daughter Judy. The Riesenburgers' grandson Robert Cohn was also listed, but without contact information. If there had not been a testimonial page, we would have researched the deportation documents in the Potsdam archives and the documents about the restitution process in the Berlin archives."

I admired her dedication and asked her how she came to volunteer for Jewish causes.

"My father fought in the Wehrmacht. In May 1944, about a year before the end of the war, he was killed in Russia in the battle of Sebastopol, two and a half months after I was born. As a teenager I had read a lot about the *Shoah* (Holocaust) and the German crimes. My mother saved all the letters she had received from my father while he was fighting in Russia. When I was sixteen, I asked her if I could read them. I wanted to know if he had participated in all these crimes. I felt so ashamed about his racism and shocked about what he had written. His letters were full of hatred of the Jews, the Russians, the Poles and the French. I decided to go to Israel and work as a volunteer. I wanted to speak with German Jewish survivors as a representative of a new German generation. I did not feel guilty, but I wanted to show responsibility for the crimes my people had committed and start a process of reconciliation, and do whatever I could to make sure that such crimes would never happen again."

"In 1965," she continued, "I went to Israel for the first time. I attended meetings with political parties and youth organizations and worked in a kibbutz and a moshav as a volunteer. There I sought out German Holocaust survivors and recorded their stories. Three years later, I went back to Israel to study at the Hebrew University in Jerusalem and at Yad Vashem. When I lived in Berlin in 1964, I had asked around to see if anyone knew how I could contact former German Jews in Israel. Before long someone suggested that I should get in touch with a German Jew by the name of Ernst Oron of the Moshav Kfar Yedidya near Netanya, which he and other German Jews had founded in 1935. I wrote to him and he and his wife invited me to come live and work with them. It was twenty years after the *Shoah*. Flights to Israel were very expensive at the time and, being a student, I did not have much money, so I took a train to Marseille. From there I went by ship. Five days later I arrived in Haifa where Ernst picked me up. I interviewed quite a few survivors and recorded their histories. Then Ernst put me in touch with Kibbutz Hazoreah near Haifa, which was also founded by German Jews in 1936 and I worked there for another month."

"Many Germans feel guilty and ashamed for the Holocaust," Sigrun continued, "even if they were born after the war and had nothing to do with the killing of the Jews. So in 1958, some Germans founded an organization called *Action for Reconciliation and Services for Peace (ARSP) (Aktion Sühneze-ichen Friedensdienste)*. Its mission is to promote understanding and peace, defend human rights, and help nations and people to reconcile. For many years, my husband and I have dedicated our time to this organization. Every year it sends 18 to 27-year-olds to countries that suffered under the German occupation to work on projects supporting survivors of the Holocaust and their descendants. They work at memorial sites, take care of older and disabled people, and get involved in neighborhood projects and anti-racism initiatives."

Ilana and I were amazed and impressed. Meeting such a German gentile totally committed to Jewish causes was a first for us.

"In 1968, I went to Jerusalem again to study the Israel-Arab conflict at the Hebrew University and, at the same time, I worked on a kibbutz in the Golan Heights," Sigrun went on. "I decided to become a teacher so I could educate a new generation of Germans about tolerance, human rights, equality of all people and the abomination of racism and war. Several years later, in 1972, when I was 28, I started teaching history and political science in Berlin. In 1976, the senate of Israel and some Israeli kibbutzim sponsored a four-week trip for high school students to Israel. I took a group of 17 and

18-year-old students in their last year of high school there to meet political parties, youth organizations and to work on a kibbutz. Ernst Oron invited us to his moshav and my students, most of whom were Christian, stayed with different families there. These two days ended up being the most important of the entire trip. Since I am a direct descendant of the German generation who committed those horrific crimes, I feel responsible for what my country did and have decided to spend my life trying to help Jews. I want to make sure that the young generation understands the value of human rights. Since I retired from teaching in 2005, Wolfgang and I dedicate much of our time to the stumbling stones project."

Ilana and I thanked Sigrun for sharing her personal story with us. We were deeply moved by her work and commitment. Sigrun and I embraced and we left with a lingering feeling of awe and gratitude.

Later that week, we took Sigrun and her husband Wolfgang to dinner, and we invited Diane and Myra to join us.

Diane has written beautifully about what happened next, so I share this in her words (my grandchildren call me Mamie):

> ...what was important about that day for me, was that when Sigrun explained that she was researching our ancestors who were deported from Berlin, I realized that I myself didn't know my own family's history. I knew bits and pieces, I knew my grandmother was born in Germany and that her family survived the war in hiding in the south of France, but I didn't really know the details. How could it be, I wondered, that this stranger from Berlin knew more about my family history than I did? It was then and there in my Jerusalem apartment late that night that my sister and I told Mamie that we would like to learn more and know the whole story. That night we googled a map of France, and she pointed to Paris, to Le Vésinet, to Lyon and to Autrans, moving further south to avoid the Nazis.
>
> That night she started telling her story, remembering and making order out of the stories over time as we sat enthralled, asking many questions. As she went through the timeline, she mentioned family after family of non-Jewish French citizens who endangered their own lives to protect them. She was so glad that we were asking and were genuinely interested.

We walked to Jerusalem's main open-air fruit and vegetable market, to buy everything we needed to prepare the Shabbat dinner and the meals for the next day. Being in the midst of the most colorful fruit and vegetable stands, the bakeries, the curios and souvenirs, the butcher shops, the fish and flower stands, the noise, the unfamiliar sounds and smells, the vendors shouting out their wares, and the shoppers of all sizes, shapes and garbs felt like a dream. My thoughts were a swirling mixture of exhilaration and anguish as I remembered the suicide bombing that had taken place at the entrance to this very market a few years before, right where I was standing now.

For the next 25 hours, Jerusalem almost completely shut down. Shabbat had begun. Aside from an occasional taxi, the city had become engulfed in silence and we could even hear the birds sing. I was told that Tel Aviv is quite the opposite, and bustling on Shabbat.

On Sunday, Ilana and I walked to the Old City of Jerusalem, through all four quarters: Muslim, Christian, Armenian and Jewish. We walked down some stairs and arrived on a large esplanade. In front of us was the Western Wall (Wailing Wall or *Kotel* in Hebrew), the last remaining piece of the ancient Jewish Temple, the most holy site for Jews. To see that history was alive here was a very moving experience for me. As I walked up to the wall I noticed little white pieces of paper inscribed with prayers people had written, stuck in the crevices. I too touched the wall lightly and said a silent prayer of gratitude, thanking God for my precious family and my life. I thought about all the Jews that had come here to pray before me.

We went to the Hebrew University on Mount Scopus to visit Myra. The university, built in the champagne-colored Jerusalem stone, was modern, clean and elegant. During the tour, I suddenly found myself in front of a large framed photograph. Upon giving it a closer look I realized that this was a photo of the very first group of foreign students who had studied here over fifty years ago. Sure enough, I immediately spotted Mel in the last row, as he was the tallest and, of course, the most handsome.

"There's Mel!" I exclaimed excitedly. "I know this picture. It was taken in 1955, the year before we met!"

Our family has had a long history with the Hebrew University. Mel had studied there for a year, which profoundly impacted his life in more than one way. He became interested in social anthropology and realized he wanted to pursue this field. On his way home to Kansas City, he stopped in Paris to meet friends and tour Europe for three weeks. Instead he met me and we got married. Twenty years later Ilana attended this very same program where she met Mark, and her daughter Diane became the third generation to attend the university.

We had an amazing reunion with Hilde, who was indirectly responsible for my meeting Mel. Although we had stayed in touch, Hilde and I had not seen each other for almost sixty years.

"*Evchen!*" I heard Hilde exclaim as soon as I set foot into the *Max Brenner café*. I rushed over to the long table where she was sitting next to her children, Daniela and Michael, and their grandchildren, and I bent down to hug her. Even though many oceans had separated us for so many years, the connection between us was as strong as ever. It was hard to believe that she was already in her late eighties and I in my seventies.

She was as loving and effervescent as ever. I remembered Daniela and Michael running around as little six- and four-year-olds, and now they were grandparents! We laughed. We cried. We hugged. We reminisced while sipping hot chocolate and eating decadent chocolate crepes. What a miracle that we could be together after all this time! Hilde had aged gracefully. Beyond the wrinkles, she was the same bubbly, sweet and happy person.

Back home, I wrote to Yad Vashem and explained how Monsieur Plasseraud had helped us. He had employed my father immediately after he left Germany, he supported him and our entire family during all the time we were in hiding during the war, and he made him a partner of the firm after the war.

Eagerly I awaited the reply:

"Dear Mrs. Perlman," I read. "I apologize for not having answered right away. I am almost embarrassed to tell you that we cannot inscribe Mr. Plasseraud at Yad Vashem even though he has certainly done a lot of good for your family. He does not meet one of our main criteria — only Righteous Gentiles who saved Jews at the risk of their own lives are eligible."

I learned that the Menthonnex family had been inscribed because a young teacher who had lived at Clairfontaine had written to Yad Vashem in the 1960s. Sadly, all the other non-Jewish French families who helped to save us did not receive official Righteous Gentile status. In my heart, they definitely were Righteous Gentiles, and I am forever grateful to them.

CHAPTER 14

MARCH OF THE LIVING

If your plan is for 1 year, plant rice.
If your plan is for 10 years, plant trees.
If your plan is for 100 years, educate children.
Confucius

In the fall of 2010, I was invited to a Shabbat Service at Adat Ari El in Studio City. Craig Taubman, a Jewish singer my children knew and loved, was singing.

After the service we took our seats in the dining hall and a young lady walked up to the microphone.

"My twelfth grade class and I just came back from a two-week trip to Poland and Israel," she began. "High school seniors from around the world are privileged to go on this trip. In Poland we visited cemeteries and concentration camps, and on Remembrance Day we walked out of Auschwitz. It was a very educational trip and I am really glad I went."

Her speech sounded rehearsed. Then an 18-year-old young man stepped up to the microphone.

"I just came back from a two-week trip that has changed my life forever, The March of the Living," he began. "I was born into Judaism, so I took being a Jew for granted. Now that I have been on this trip, I realize how important it is to be a *conscious* Jew, and to stay connected to our heritage."

With these few words, this high school student had my full attention.

"I have become aware of the long history of persecutions we as a people have faced throughout history and yet, the Jewish people are still alive today. My grandparents experienced the Holocaust and many of my family members were killed in concentration camps. When I found the March of the Living, I felt an obligation to go see where it all happened. What I experienced during these two weeks was powerful, not just because being there made it all so real, but because we went with survivors and with other Jews. I was also moved by the optimism the survivors radiated as they went back to the worst place imaginable, out of their own free will. In Birkenau survivor Sidonia even showed us the planks she used to sleep on, and she did it while exuding incredible optimism. I want to raise my future children conscious of their heritage, and one day I want to take them to Poland so they too will learn about the Holocaust where it happened. An entire year of theoretical learning on university benches cannot impact a person as a week with survivors in Poland can. It is because of what I have learned during this trip, what *my* people have endured with such dignity, that I have returned proud of being a Jew. I am a changed person and I am so thankful."

As he finished his last sentence, this young man was so overcome with emotion he had tears in his eyes, which moved me to tears as well. His words had stirred something deep in my soul. I thought of all the people in my family I never had a chance to meet because they were murdered in the Holocaust and now I felt this inexplicable urge to go to Poland in their memory. It had never crossed my mind to go to Poland to visit a concentration camp or to go to Auschwitz. All my life I hated everything German. I did not buy anything German. I had no German friends. I avoided speaking German and I had even transmitted this hatred to my children. Yet, in that moment I said to Ilana, "Maybe I should go to Poland."

Ilana said, "I know the organizer, Monise Neumann. I will check with her."

"Maman, I have good news," she said excitedly a few days later. "Today, the definition of survivor is any Jew who came out of Europe alive after the war. You have a story that needs to be told. Monise wants to meet you."

Shortly thereafter, Monise came to my apartment, a lovely, slender lady in her fifties with a head full of little brown curls and an engaging smile. She wore a stylish, unconventional dress that was fashionably longer on one side. "Eva, I am so glad to meet you," Monise said with a charming South African accent.

I liked her immediately, but I felt intimidated because of the important position she held. Down in my core I was still shy.

"I heard you are interested in going on the March with us," she continued. "This annual trip is sponsored by the local Builders of Jewish Education (BJE), a department of the Jewish Federation. We take 12th graders to Poland to learn about the Holocaust where it happened. Then we fly to Israel," she explained. "What makes this trip so special is that survivors come along and tell how they survived. For the students to hear these stories from eyewitnesses is really special. The next generation will no longer have this privilege. The students become the eyewitnesses of the eyewitnesses."

She asked me about myself and said the next March would be in April after Passover. "We would be honored to have you join us, Eva."

As I closed the door, I marvelled at all the extraordinary opportunities that kept coming my way, regardless of my age. A new unknown horizon seemed to be appearing before me. In early 2011, the preparations for the March began. Our Los Angeles group consisted of 178 18-year-old students and nine survivors including Jack, Halina, Dorothy, Sidonia and Paula, who had been on the March several times. There were about twenty-seven staff members, including two doctors and a nurse. We all met twice before the March to get ready for the trip. It was a workshop designed to prepare us emotionally. We were shown two little movies about the Holocaust and we did some exercises.

"I would like to welcome all of you today," Monise began. "You are going to embark on an incredible journey. For many students who have gone on the March in the past, this trip has been a life-changing experience. We are so privileged to have nine survivors coming with us. They will share their stories with you."

Eighty-four-year-old Sidonia shared with us. "For me, returning to Poland with the March of the Living each year is not about death and darkness, but about life and the triumph of the human spirit over death," she said. "This is the history of *our* people. We must not forget it."

Our final meeting took place just two weeks before the trip, with the parents, staff, students and survivors, to go over all the rules and regulations and necessary travel details. We would be escorted by security guards everywhere.

The day of departure finally came. After crossing ten time zones, tired and bleary-eyed, we arrived in Warsaw. One of the survivors, who understood Polish, overheard someone say with a shrug of disdain, "Oh, here come the Jews!" It did not make us feel very welcome.

We boarded our buses and headed out. To my surprise the countryside was so green. I had always thought of Poland in black and white. That night we arrived in Lodz.

The next morning Monise introduced us to three very knowledgeable Holocaust historians.

Ronnie, a scholarly-looking man in his sixties with grey hair and beard, had come all the way from South Africa. Michal had flown in from Israel; she was dressed as a typical orthodox woman in a long skirt. Her hair was covered and she carried a pile of well-used papers under her arm. Jack, another survivor, joined us from Denver; he was clean-shaven and good-looking. He certainly did not look like he was in his eighties.

The first stop of the day was the Lodz Jewish Cemetery on Bracka Street in the northern part of Lodz. It was a gloomy day. After a short ride our buses stopped by an entrance gate. To the right was the old cemetery with all old tombstones. To the left, in stark contrast, was a huge grassy field with thousands of markers engraved with a name and a date. It seemed to go on forever.

Ronnie told us it was the biggest Jewish cemetery in Europe. Before the war, Poland had the largest Jewish community in the world. About 230,000 Jews are buried there, some of whom were the most influential minds in Jewish history. We walked among the tombstones and mausoleums. Some stones were still in good condition while others were partially overgrown with grass or had fallen over. Every so often Ronnie stopped in front of a particular tombstone and talked about the person who was buried there, usually a great rabbi, or an illustrious poet, scholar or artist.

We walked back to the entrance and followed Ronnie to the empty green field on the other side.

"This is where the ghetto was," Ronnie explained. "It's now a massive grave. 45,000 victims were buried here between 1940 and 1944. During the war, most Jews lived here behind barbed wire in horrendous conditions. They were forced to produce uniforms and ammunition in Nazi factories. So many people died here daily of disease, hunger and despair that there was no time to carve a stone for everyone. That's why you see only markers. Those who survived were deported in specially outfitted trucks that would gas them on the way to the Chelmno extermination camp where they were cremated."

To see all these markers here of innocent people who had suffered a terrible death was terrifying.

Our buses brought us to Radegast, a former train station, flanked by a tall memorial chimney, just north of the Jewish Cemetery. This chimney is now a memorial for the tens of thousands of Jews and other victims who were deported from this train station to Auschwitz-Birkenau.

We entered the station. Next to a platform, on the original rails, stood an old locomotive with two wooden cattle cars. *Deutsche Reichsbahn* was written on them.

Jack climbed into one of the cars and about twenty students followed, packing around him. "At first my father, my sister Esther and I were in a ghetto in Pabianice, about 12 miles north of here. In May 1942, the Pabianice ghetto was liquidated and we were transported to this Lodz ghetto as slave labor. In the summer of 1944, this ghetto was liquidated as well. Of the 300,000 people that had arrived here fewer than 68,000 of us were still alive. We were put onto these cattle cars at this Radegast station. After two days of unspeakable conditions without food or water, with just one pail in the corner for immediate needs, we ended up in Auschwitz. We were packed in so tight that we did not even have room to sit during the journey. There was only one small window and no fresh air. Can you imagine so many people jammed in such a small space under these conditions, traveling for 260 kilometers (156 miles). I was among those taken from the Lodz ghetto to the Birkenau death camp. As soon as we arrived, the Nazis sorted us into two groups — those who appeared strong enough to work were forced to step to the left. They would be marched to Auschwitz. Everybody else — the sick, the elderly, the women and children — were forced to step to the right and ended up in the gas chamber just a few hundred yards away. It is a miracle that I survived. My younger sister was not so fortunate. I was only fifteen when I was separated from my family. A prisoner advised me to 'look strong' so I might end up in the labor group."

Some students were crying as they stepped out of the cattle car. Others, also deeply affected, hugged Jack as they passed by him.

We walked through a long, dark hall back toward the chimney we had passed upon arrival. Along the walls of this hall, preserved in numerous glass cases, were letters, attendance lists, and memorabilia that the deportees had been forced to leave behind — photographs, identity cards, baby shoes — and more. The walls were covered with lists of names of the people who were transported from here. To see the meticulous records the Nazis had kept of everyone they had massacred was unbelievable. They had created a colossal and well-organized extermination machine. I remembered my parents talking about Otto Freundlich and Monsieur Weissmann, both betrayed by French people. The Nazis had picked them up in the middle of the night. Both were gassed — Monsieur Weissman in Auschwitz-Birkenau and Otto Freundlich in Majdanek. It became so vivid and real to me, having known these friends of my parents.

With solemn faces we boarded the buses quietly. We continued on to Pabianice, where Jack was born, a half hour drive southwest of Radegast and Lodz. He asked if we could stop by the cemetery where he was hoping to find his father's grave. Our group walked from tombstone to tombstone among tall grasses, looking for his father's name, but found only one tombstone with a name similar to his. Jack placed flowers on it.

During the three-hour ride to Krakow, Paula told her survival story.

"I was born in Poland and was only nine when the Nazis began to round up the Jews. I ended up in Auschwitz. Somehow I figured out that I needed to make myself invisible if I wanted to have a chance to survive. I was among a handful of children who were still alive in January 1945 when the Russians liberated us."

On Shabbat, the day of rest, we attended services at the *Kupa* Synagogue in Kazimierz, Krakow's Jewish quarter. On our way we walked through a beautiful park by Wawel Castle, which had been the residence of Polish kings when Krakow was the capital of Poland. When King Kazimierz ruled he welcomed many Jews as they were educated and could read. Inside the synagogue, well-restored paintings of biblical scenes and holy places decorated the walls. We took our seats and our counselors held the service. It is the only synagogue still being used for religious services to this day in Krakow. Hitler turned all the other synagogues into museums to prove that the Jews were extinguished for good. Some synagogues had been turned by the Nazis into stables for their horses!

"Every year we honor a righteous gentile who saved Jews during the Holocaust at the risk of his or her own life," Monise said after the service. "We have invited a Polish lady to share with us how her parents saved a Jewish family."

It was important to make the students understand that many non-Jews were instrumental in helping Jews survive. An elderly Polish lady with snow-white hair walked up to the *bimah*.

"During the war I was a teenager," she began in Polish. Our survivor, Halina, who was born in Poland, translated. "My mother and father saved six Jews, the Silverman family, by digging a huge hole in the yard and covering it with layers of straw. The Nazis came, looking for Jews. They began to remove the straw, but before they found the people who were hiding underneath, they miraculously received the order to retreat immediately. Had the Nazis found them, they would have surely killed not only them, but us as well. After the war the Silvermans had my parents inscribed at *Yad Vashem* in Israel as Righteous among the Nations."

That Saturday night, after dinner at our hotel, our entire group walked to a Jewish youth center to celebrate life with Klezmer music, dancing and singing. It was important to have a good time that evening because the next day we were going to Oswiecim, the town the Germans had renamed Auschwitz. Inside the youth center a large room was set up with rows of chairs. The front row was reserved for the survivors. Two students entertained us with guitar and singing. Jack told a joke.

> *A Jew passes by a storefront with a grandfather clock in the window. He goes in and asks, "Do you repair watches here?" "No," says the storekeeper, "we do not repair watches." "Do you repair clocks?" "No, we do not repair clocks." "So what do you do here?" "I am a mohel,"* (a person who performs circumcisions) *says the storekeeper. "So why do you have a grandfather clock in the window?" the visitor asks and the storekeeper replies, "So, what else do you want me to have in the window?"*

Everyone laughed. That inspired me to tell a joke as well, happy to have found my match.

> *A man brings his best buddy home for dinner unannounced at 5:30 after work. His wife screams, "My hair and makeup are not done. The house is a mess. The dishes are piled up in the kitchen sink. I am still in my pajamas and I can't be bothered with cooking tonight! Why the hell did you bring your friend home tonight?" And her husband answers sheepishly, "Because he's thinking of getting married."*

On our fourth day we visited Auschwitz. Sidonia, a sprightly 84 year-old, shared her story.

"I was born in a small town in the southeastern part of Poland where my parents owned a successful textile business before the war. I was a spoiled rotten kid.

In 1941, when I was eight years old, the Germans invaded our town and we were forced to move into a local ghetto. Food was so scarce that children risked their lives by digging holes under the ghetto's barbed wire fences and crawled out to trade whatever they could for extra food, which they brought back. Everyday people died in the ghetto and the coffins were used to smuggle in food and other things as well.

After about a year and a half, life in the ghetto got so bad that my parents and neighbors decided to build a bunker underneath our apartment building. For three months about thirty-five people lived there in hiding in darkness. There was no electricity, no water, no toilet, just a pail in the corner. The space was so small that we could barely stand or sit, let alone lie down. For three months I did not see the sun nor could we really wash ourselves. I had lice. Shortly thereafter, my mother was arrested.

My father worried about my health. Somehow he had found out that you could buy apples outside so he left the hiding place, hoping to find an apple for me. He was arrested as well. I never saw my parents again. I have never looked at an apple the same way. Now I was on my own. SS dogs found me and I ended up in jail. There I found out that my parents had been shot to death.

Adapted from "*March of the Living — Our Stories,*" by Jan Berlfein Burns

To hear firsthand how someone had managed to survive under such horrific conditions was very moving. I felt deeply grateful for not having been in such a situation. I was 9 years old in 1941. I doubt I could have survived.

We came to some railroad tracks and our buses drove parallel to them until we reached a few brick buildings with red tile roofs. We had arrived at Auschwitz. The complex was fenced in with double barbed wire.

There were thousands of people walking around.

Our group followed the guide through the metal entrance gate where we saw the now infamous words '*Arbeit macht frei.*' I had seen this sign in movies many times, but to walk through this gate knowing that *over one million people* never walked out was sickening.

Inside Building 5 on the first floor, we stopped at a small room with cement walls and a tiny window: the interrogation room.

In other rooms we saw statistics such as how many Jews, homosexuals, gypsies, communists and others had been killed here. Maps depicted the German invasion of various countries. There was a map of Auschwitz on the wall. It showed Auschwitz at the center of an immense train track network. Transports from all over Europe and even Russia, from as far as 1,300 miles, converged here. When I noticed Lyon on the map my heart almost stopped beating. Autrans was so close to Lyon. I reflected on how easily we could have ended up in Auschwitz if we had been found.

Routes of deportation to Auschwitz

Paula stopped in front of a huge photograph that covered the entire wall. It was a well-known black and white photo of children in Auschwitz behind barbed wire, taken at liberation. "This is me," she said, pointing to one of the girls. "I was twelve when the Russians liberated us in this camp on January 27, 1945. I had been here for a year and a half. Very few children had survived."

In another room prayer shawls, pajamas and Judaica that had been found in suitcases were displayed behind glass. In another display, mountains of pale looking hair that had lost its color over the years were piled up. Even brown and black hair had turned into a dull, sandy gray.

"As soon as the Jews arrived, the Nazis shaved off their hair and sent tons of hair to Germany. There it was used to fill mattresses and pillows," the guide explained. "What you see here is only a small remnant."

Behind other glass windows were mountains of eyeglasses and suitcases, shaving brushes, razors, toothbrushes, combs and rusty kitchen utensils the women had managed to bring along. Heaps of canes and prostheses were piled behind another glass window.

"So that those who arrived here went along without much protest, they were told by the Nazis that they were being relocated to a place where they would have a better life," the guide continued. "They had twenty minutes to pack their most precious belongings. In some cases they even had to pay for their own train tickets, and were glad that the tickets were fairly cheap. After days of travel in those infamous cattle cars without air, water, food or a place to sit, half of them were dead on arrival. One million one hundred thousand people died in Auschwitz-Birkenau. Ninety percent of them were Jews."

We continued walking from building to building and ended up in front of a flat stone block.

"This is an autopsy table," we were told. "Some Jews were forced to become *Sonderkommandos*. If they refused, they were shot on the spot. Their job was to take the dead naked bodies out of the gas chambers, put them onto the autopsy table, strip off wedding rings and gold teeth and check every cavity for valuables. Then they had to push the bodies into the ovens to be cremated. Twenty minutes later they had to remove the ashes from the ovens. Every four months or so the Sonderkommandos were murdered and replaced as the Nazis wanted no surviving witnesses. They collected about 15,000 pounds of gold from teeth. The contents of the suitcases — cameras, clothing, rugs, furs, sewing machines, silver candlesticks, jewelry, violins, prayer shawls — were also shipped to Germany. The clothes were disinfected in autoclaves before they were shipped."

We followed our guide to a room where two doctors had experimented on girls and women between the ages of 15 and 38 to find the best sterilization methods, performing surgery on them without anesthesia. Then most of them were disposed of.

Outside we passed by a wall where three people at a time were hanged because they had disobeyed or tried to escape. All inmates were forced to watch the hangings.

On our way out we went into a barrack with an actual gas chamber. Scratches covered the walls from desperate people trying to get out as they discovered there was no exit.

There were no words to describe our feelings. Most students were tearing up. I had a sob in my throat the whole time. The cold foggy weather added to the gloom.

From the Auschwitz museum we walked through a residential area to Birkenau. Across the street from the camp were several houses.

I couldn't understand how the people who lived so close to the camp could not know what was going on across the street. Michal told me the Poles who lived in these houses were forced to move out. Their homes were requisitioned by the Nazis who worked in the camp.

About twenty minutes later, we arrived at an elongated red brick building with a gate in the middle and a tower above. Railroad tracks went through the gate and continued on as far as the eye could see. We passed through the infamous gate of Birkenau.

"This is where the cattle cars arrived," Michal explained. To think that hundreds of thousands of Jews had gotten off the trains on this very platform with their suitcases and few belongings on their way to be exterminated, was a shock. We had seen many pictures at Auschwitz of people arriving on that platform. We walked to the end of this huge place to the ruins of the gas chamber and the crematorium. It started to rain.

"Toward the end of the war, when the Nazis knew that defeat was inevitable, they destroyed the gas chambers and the crematoria in an attempt to erase all traces of the hundreds of thousands of people they had murdered in Auschwitz and Birkenau at the rate of 18,000 per day," Michal continued.

We followed Jack across the sandy road to a smaller ruin, a pile of bricks and concrete blocks that lay strewn about like rubble, the remains of what was once the crematorium. It was windy and gray clouds crept across the sky.

Silently we watched as Jack took a few steps toward the rubble, holding a yellow rose in his hand. It was raining more heavily now. Our group gathered around him.

"I arrived here in Auschwitz on that platform with my father and my two sisters. The Nazis opened the heavy train doors. As soon as we stepped out we were sorted into groups — the fit and healthy men in one group, and whoever they considered useless, the old men, the women and the children — in another group. Peska ended up in a group with other children and women. My beautiful blond, blue-eyed little sister, who was only 12, took her last breath right here. It was a breath full of poison, pain and fear," Jack managed to say.

"I still see her today, looking at me with pleading eyes that said 'help me!' She must have been so frightened being alone." Tears were rolling down his cheeks as he brought the yellow rose up to his face and paused. "For sixty-seven years I have wondered and hoped that maybe someone held her hand as she was being herded to the gas chamber."

On our way to the exit, I followed Randy, one of our leaders, into one of the many barracks. Rows of wooden bunks were stacked on top of one another. Sidonia walked straight up to one of them. "This is where I used to sleep with nine other women when I was 16," she told us. "We were so cramped together we had to sleep on our side. When one turned, everybody had to turn at the same time. It was freezing cold and we had only one blanket..."

On the bus back to Krakow we were shown a Holocaust movie, but most of us slept. It had been a sad and emotionally exhausting day.

The next day was Holocaust Remembrance Day or Yom HaShoah, the actual day of The March of the Living. We arrived in Auschwitz and Monise and Maya, her second-in-command, handed out thin blank wooden markers and asked us to write a message on them in memory of someone who had perished here. I remembered Otto Freundlich who had been betrayed by villagers while hiding in the Pyrenees. I remembered Charles Weissman, the owner of Cabinet Plasseraud, whom the Nazis had picked up out of his bed at three in the morning because his stamp merchant had betrayed him. He was murdered here a few weeks later. Clara Goldschmidt died here; I had seen her name on Maman's family tree. I remembered Henri Bamberger, little Cathy's father, who enlisted in the underground army with my father. And Julius Blumenthal, my father's attorney friend. "I march in your memory," I wrote on my little board under their names.

Around 12:30 p.m. our delegation and 10,000 people from 40 different countries, mostly eighteen-year olds, gathered with flags and banners in the wide alleys between the red brick buildings. Many students were draped in blue and white Israeli flags. The March was about to begin.

Again I thought, "*Am Yisrael Chai*" (The Jewish people live).

When the shofar sounded, strong and clear, thousands of people became quiet in an instant and began to move slowly. Polish people were standing along the sides, handing out little notes that said 'thank you for coming.' We, too, thanked them for being here and supporting the Jews.

In silence, together, we walked out of Auschwitz. We marched in memory of the millions who had walked in and never walked out.

With two students   *Finally the March started*

Walking out of Auschwitz *together and alive* is the essence of The March of the Living. Two students locked arms with me as we marched.

When we arrived in Birkenau, thousands walked through the gate. We placed our markers with their messages into the ground between the rails along with the thousands of other markers placed by the marchers who had arrived before us. At the other end of a huge field, there was a platform set up for a ceremony. Several Israeli flags were swaying in the wind. Israeli soldiers stood guard. Everyone stood up to sing the *Hatikva*, the Jewish national anthem. Various people spoke including Israel's chief Rabbi, Meir

Lau. On two big screens we watched videos of the Holocaust and videos about how far Israel had come since its creation in 1948.

There were six huge gas torches, and one after the other, each torch was lit by a different Holocaust survivor. Each one was to remember one million Jews who were exterminated.

It had been another exhausting, emotionally-charged day. That night, after dinner at our hotel, students spoke of their experiences and their feelings and emotions.

"Shivers ran down my spine today as I walked side-by-side with survivors on the same route that led hundreds of thousands of my people to the gas chamber," one student began.

"Walking together in solidarity with thousands of young Jews from around the world in memory of the six million Jews who had died felt comforting, especially at a time when so many deny the Holocaust," another student added.

"I fear that the Jewish people may face a similar threat again in this day and age," someone else said.

"I haven't had much time to put *the March* into perspective, but I am confident that in the days, weeks and years ahead, I will look back at what I took part in today and be reminded of my obligation as a witness," another student commented.

As I lay in bed that night, many thoughts crossed my mind. *We must not forget,* I kept thinking. *It is the duty of the survivors to tell their stories to the young generation. We must keep history alive so this will never happen again.* Was this perhaps my purpose?

The following day would prove to be very draining emotionally as well. We left the hotel at 7:30 a.m. for the Zbylitowska Góra Forest near the little town of Tarnow in the south of Poland. It once was a flourishing Jewish community and an important center of Jewish learning. When we arrived, we walked along a path to a beautiful forest of tall and regal trees until we reached a monument and several fenced enclosures with toys and burnt-out candles. Attached to picket fences were pictures of children. We surrounded one of the enclosures. Ronnie stood in silence for a moment before he began to speak.

"Eight hundred Jewish children are buried in this mass grave," he began. "The Nazis took them away from their parents and transported them in trucks to this beautiful forest. They put them into sacks, so that they could not see their faces, and beat them to death with sticks and clubs in order to 'save bullets' that were too precious to waste."

Imagining the scene was unbearable.

Many of us were crying. What horrific crimes were committed here! Hearing the birds chirp happily all around us, it was hard to imagine these unfathomable atrocities. How could those murderers go home and play with their own children after doing such a thing?

Monise and Ronnie spread a huge *tallit* over the mass grave. We all held it up together and said *Kaddish*. It had been tough enough to hear about adults being murdered in horrific ways, but to imagine the murder of innocent children being beaten to death — some of the students broke down. Others sat speechless with tears rolling down their faces.

Back on the bus, we were unusually silent. We continued on to the Bełżec death camp. There were no barracks, just rails on top of a hill and a huge flat area with small black stones. An alley led down the hill to what looked like a white wall or a concrete building. Why were there no barracks?

"After Treblinka this was the second largest death camp," Ronnie began. "It operated from March 1942 to August 1943. Trains of forty to sixty cattle cars arrived with eighty to a hundred people crammed in each car. The people were let out of one cattle car at a time. They were ordered to take off all their clothes, regardless of the weather and to tie their shoes together. Once they were stark naked, they were forced to run down the hill so they would be out of breath and die faster. They were pushed into a small building without windows, the gas chamber. The guards packed as many people in as they could. Then a heavy steel door was bolted. They had no idea they would be ashes in about an hour. Six hundred thousand Jews were gassed here."

With horror I imagined all those people standing there naked and barefoot in the icy winter months, like a herd of animals, robbed of their humanity.

"Only two people survived this camp to tell the tale," Ronnie said.

We followed Ronnie and Michal down the path to the white memorial wall with Polish and Hebrew writing on it where the gas chamber once stood. There, Michal read to us a letter from an American soldier to his family in the U.S. after he had liberated one of the camps. The picture he painted was harrowing — mountains of corpses, dirt and vermin everywhere. It was horrible to hear this again and again. We said *Kaddish*.

The next morning, our last day in Poland, we arrived at the Majdanek death camp. A massive somber stone structure stands at the entrance of the camp, symbolizing the weight of memory. As we walked first down then up, as if through a valley, to this ominous structure I thought of Moses crossing the Red Sea. To others it felt like walking through the Valley of the Shadow of Death. In the far distance we saw barracks, a dome-like structure and a long building with a tall chimney. We took our seats on the steps for a moment.

"Majdanek was the worst of the camps," Ronnie began. "People here were killed on an industrial scale. The camp is so well preserved it looks like it could be back in running condition tomorrow. The Soviet Red Army advanced so fast the Nazis had no time to destroy the camp. Double-barbed wire and guard towers made it impossible to escape. The white house to your right was the doctor's house where the Nazis used to party at night after exterminating thousands of Jews during the day."

We followed Ronnie down the steps past the doctor's house. After a ten-minute walk we reached the first of many wooden barracks. Inside was a large room with rows of showerheads and windows on one side. Past the "shower room" was a glass case behind which mountains of empty cans, labeled Zyklon B, were piled up, neatly arranged. We continued on to two small, empty rooms with concrete walls and no windows. The heavy steel doors at the entrance to the rooms stood open and a waist-high glass wall kept the visitors from going in.

"These are the gas chambers," Ronnie explained. "Hundreds were crammed into these two small chambers. Once the heavy doors were bolted shut, it was pitch black inside. You see the hole in the ceiling? Through it the Nazis threw the deadly Zyklon B pellets, which released their poisonous gas through the warmth of the bodies. The old, the sick and the little children died quickly, while the fitter ones suffered longer."

We walked through an opening in the double-barbed wire and arrived at a massive dome, close to which stood another gas chamber and crematorium. It was raining.

"Under this dome are the ashes of 80,000 victims," Michal explained.

We boarded our buses, cold, soaked, exhausted. We would depart for Israel at midnight and were looking forward to some warmth and sunshine. An added privilege of this journey was the kindness and respect afforded the survivors. The first class seats on the flight from Warsaw to Tel Aviv made the arrival in Israel even more special.

A sea of flickering lights appeared in the distance. It was exhilarating to see this huge expanse of lights get nearer. What a large, thriving metropolis Tel Aviv had become and what a wonderful sight after all the death and darkness we had been exposed to in Poland.

We landed at Ben Gurion airport and boarded the buses. On every bus there were a tour guide and a soldier with a rifle for our protection. We passed through Tel Aviv with its towering skyscrapers and drove along the Mediterranean Sea to Caesarea, a former Roman town.

With the rising of the sun we reached Caesarea Beach. Tired but giddy with excitement, we took long breaths of our first fresh Israeli sea air. We felt free and alive. This was home.

We took off our shoes, formed a circle and sang the Shehecheyanu prayer.

"Who wants to make the Star of David in memory of Sigi?" Monise asked. Sigi, a Holocaust survivor and former participant, had died recently.

Six students stepped forward and reached for each others' hands and the Star of David was formed before our eyes.

Star of David

After several hours on the beach, we traveled to a youth hostel just below the Lebanon border. It was not without danger to be there, but we did not worry as our guards carried machine guns.

The next day we traveled to Jerusalem where we would stay at the Yitzhak Rabin youth hostel.

I was able to visit with Mark and Ilana who arrived that morning in Israel, and with Diane who lived there now. Diane had wonderful news.

"Mamie, guess what? I found Jean Menthonnex!" she said excitedly.

"My goodness, you found him! How?" I asked.

"On Facebook. I had unsuccessfully searched two years ago, but decided to try again after coming home from last week's Yom HaShoa ceremony." Ilana wrote him an email identifying herself and asking if he was the right Jean Menthonnex.

Two days later an amazing reply came:

Subject: famille Menthonnex
Date: Thursday, May 5, 2011, 12:54 PM
From: Geneviève Menthonnex
Thursday May 5, 2011

Hello Ilana,

I am Geneviève, the wife of Jean Menthonnex, of Clairfontaine in Autrans. We are thrilled to hear from you. Our family has always kept fond memories of your mother and her brothers, Ernest and Raymond, and we have spoken of them often. Jean would be very happy to see you when you come to France. Please tell your mother how much her memory is alive with us. We hope you receive this message and we send you hugs and kisses, dear Ilana along with your mother, Eva.

Jean and Geneviève Menthonnex

I was flabbergasted and thrilled beyond belief! We had not given my brothers' names and they replied with 'Ernest and Raymond'! This truly was my Jean! The memories of Jean and me guarding the two family cows together when we were eleven and ten years old were still strong. We loved each other in our own innocent way.

We called the Menthonnex immediately.

"Bonjour Geneviève. It's Eva Gutmann."

"Eva?"

"Yes, it's me. I am so happy my granddaughter found you. I have spoken of Clairfontaine and Autrans all my life and how much we owe Jean's parents for keeping us safe. How are you?"

"I am fine, but Jean is unfortunately very ill. He has lung cancer and he is almost blind."

"I am so sorry to hear that. May I speak to him?"

"Of course!"

"Bonjour, Eva," I heard a male voice say. "How wonderful to hear your voice after 69 long years! Remember Marquise and Piloune, the two cows we took to the hills together?"

"Of course I do. I am so thrilled to be in touch with you again."

"If you ever come to southern France I would be so happy to see you."

"I've wanted to thank you for many years for everything you and your family did for us. I'll plan to come next year with my daughter, Ilana."

"I can't wait, Eva," he said.

The next day, our first stop was Malon Chen, a hotel in Jerusalem the Israeli government had converted into a shelter for 195 Jewish survivors from Russia. I saw beautiful artwork on one of the walls.

The manager welcomed us warmly and showed us a video of the residents who lived here. An older lady in a simple blouse and long skirt walked in holding an old-fashioned doll close to her heart. With a strong Czech accent she said in English, "My name is Annika Tetzner. I am from Praha, Czechoslovakia. People call me Anna. When I was five, the Nazis came to our apartment and told my parents to pack up and be ready to leave in 20 minutes. My mother took my doll from my arms and handed it to our neighbor's little girl, who had always been jealous of me and my doll. 'You won't need this where you are going!' my mother said to me. My entire family was murdered in Birkenau and Theresienstadt. I was the only one who survived, in spite of being raped, beaten and experimented on by the infamous Dr. Josef Mengele. Many years after the war I went back to that town and apartment building. As I spoke to a neighbor, she suddenly exclaimed, 'Oh my God! You are little Anna! Wait here!' She rushed into her house and came back with a doll. She handed it to me with a smile. I recognized it immediately. It was *my* doll. She was still wearing the little cap that I had worn as a newborn and the clothes that my mother had sewn for her. The neighbor felt guilty all her life, having received the doll because 'little Anna had gone to her death.'"

Silently Annika stood there, hugging her doll. There was not a single dry eye among us.

Then she opened a little book and said, "I would like to read you a part of one of my poems from my book *Bloodflowers*. It is called *Mothers*."

It was written in the voice of a child. She called mothers stupid because they obey orders. They are helpless. They don't fight. They just go to the ovens obediently and abandon their children. Even after all these years she still sounded like that angry child of five. "I managed to live a fairly normal life after the war. I got married, had children and grandchildren. I am also a painter," she continued. "You can see some of my paintings on the walls here."

Some students hugged her and thanked her for sharing her story. Others told her how much her story had moved them. I also told her how touched I was by her story and her artwork.

In the evening, *Yom HaZikaron*, Israeli Memorial Day, began. The country remembers the soldiers who have died, leaving 5,000 widows behind since Israel's fight for independence in 1948. Israelis owe their independence and the existence of the state to those soldiers. We had a special memorial ceremony, followed at 8 p.m. by loud sirens wailing all over the country. We stood up in silence, respectfully, for two full minutes until the sirens stopped.

Early the next morning, on Memorial Day, our entire Los Angeles delegation was driven to *Gan HaBanim* (Garden of the Sons), a park in Tel Aviv. Many black granite pillars were standing everywhere. Inscribed on them were the names of all the sons and daughters of Israel who had lost their lives while helping to establish and defend this country since 1948. Several Israeli soldiers in regular combat uniform were waiting for us. They enthusiastically hugged Monise, who then addressed our group.

"We have asked these young soldiers to meet you here so you can ask them questions," she said. "They are originally from Los Angeles and have made Aliyah after having gone on *the March* in a previous year."

We broke up into groups, each with a soldier, and sat on the grass. First the soldier introduced him/herself briefly and told us a little about him/herself. Then our students asked many questions like, "Do you speak Hebrew fluently? Is it tough to be in the Israeli army? How do you feel living in Israel? Was it hard for you to get used to life here?"

Standing there in silence when all traffic stopped and the sirens went off again for two full minutes at 11a.m., I thought of how different this was from Memorial Day in the U.S. where many families enjoy spending the day together with a picnic. It was very powerful to see a whole nation remember its war heroes with dignity.

The transition from grief to joy was phenomenal. That night, we celebrated Israeli independence in the streets. Everyone was so happy. The highlight was the most extraordinary fireworks I have ever seen. Sparkles and explosions of all shapes and colors were being shot up at tremendous speed, illuminating the night sky. I was impressed by the incredibly advanced technology this tiny country had developed.

The next morning, we drove to Jerusalem early to march with thousands of people from Safra Square in downtown Jerusalem to the Old City and the Western Wall to celebrate Independence Day. On the square was joyous dancing and singing.

I want to meet someone from another country, I thought. As I looked around I spotted a young, clean-shaven man, in shorts and wearing a *kippah*. I planned to greet him, and tell him I'm from California. As I got close to him I read *Lewin* on his nametag — my mother's maiden name! In tiny letters it said, *Paul — Australia*.

"Are you a rabbi?" I blurted out without introducing myself.

He looked flabbergasted. "Yes, I am."

"And your parents are from Cape Town?"

"Yes," he replied. *Oh My*! He was Maman's cousin's grandson!

"I am Eva Gutmann-Perlman! My mother Charlotte flew from Paris to Cape Town to attend your *Bar Mitzvah* in 1985. We are related!"

"Of course! I am delighted to meet you, Eva," he said with a smile. "What a miracle that we should meet here among thousands of people! I can't wait to tell my parents." We could hardly believe our meeting! Had we both known that we would be here at the same time, we probably would never have found each other!

He had brought forty-seven students from Australia with him to the March. He invited me to come to his eldest son's *Bar Mitzvah* the following year.

The shofar blasted through the loudspeakers and the mass of people began to march, delegation after delegation, carrying little flags from their respective countries. We continued on up a hill along a narrow cobblestone path, climbing stairs every once in a while. We reached the big plaza, and arrived at the *Kotel*. Along two-thirds of the Western Wall men were davening (praying), and along the other third of the wall, the women were praying. Some kissed the wall while others were davening, holding a prayer book or stuffing little notes into the crevices. Even the tourists had covered their arms and legs and wrapped a black skirt over their shorts. You could feel the holiness of the place. I walked up to the Wall and touched it with reverence. I silently said a prayer of gratitude, thanking God for the extraordinary opportunity and privilege to be included in the March of the Living.

Meeting Paul Lewin

The next morning all two hundred of us met for breakfast one last time before half of our group would leave for the airport. Several students thanked me and hugged me goodbye. One of the students gave me a bracelet. They never ceased to amaze me. They showed the survivors so much love and appreciation. The trip had been such a bonding experience for all of us, an educational and spiritual journey. Tremendous grief was transformed into hope and exhilaration. We left strengthened in reverence and feeling proud of our country, Israel.

Passing through Paris on my way back to Los Angeles, I visited my brothers, and especially our parents' grave in Le Vésinet.

Back in LA, I was anxious to read the trip blog, which captured Monise's and students' comments. Monise wrote:

> *"As the surrogate mother of 178 students, I cannot tell you how much nachas (pleasure) I have experienced these past two weeks. The participants of the BJE March of the Living 2011 delegation are simply extraordinary young people. They have embraced the message of remembrance, of hope, of life and of Jewish peoplehood with vigor, passion and meaning. We traveled to Poland to learn from our nine incredible survivors not simply how their loved ones perished but also how they lived and learned and laughed. We met Jewish teens from around the world and marched together in the most profound understanding of Jewish heritage that you can imagine. We cried together, sang together and danced together in synagogues dating back to the 1600s. We are so blessed to be able to impart to all students how important their personal Jewish legacy is and will be, and we thank each parent for allowing his or her child to come with us and be a part of this journey."*

I had found a strong sense of purpose with the March of the Living. I could make a contribution to the lives of young people and help keep Jewish history alive. I returned with a renewed sense of looking toward the future since Monise invited me to come again the following year.

I wrote to Jean Menthonnex, asking him if he knew the Ravauds, our former landlords in the yellow house. All the families in Autrans knew one another because it was a small village. He wrote back saying that Colette Ravaud was still living not only in Autrans, but in the yellow house! He gave me her phone number. I called Colette and she remembered us. We made plans to visit them after my second March, the following April, 2012.

Soon the preparations for my second March in 2012 were in full swing. When I checked my mail there was a message from Monise.

Eva, please bring a memento of your life that has sentimental value for you to share with the students in a 3-5 minute talk.

After giving it some thought I decided to bring the hand-written note that Mel had written to me the day before I met him, to tell my love story, and how that handwritten note had changed my life forever in an instant. What could appeal more to a group of eighteen-year-olds than a story of love at first sight?

As part of our preparation we watched an amazing documentary film: *Swimming in Auschwitz, Survival Stories of Six Women*. One of them, Erika Jacoby, tells how it was so hot one day she could not bear it anymore; she dove into the swimming pool that was reserved for the Nazis, who lived in luxury in the surrounding area and came here to swim.

"I knew they would shoot me and I couldn't have cared less," she said. "Lo and behold no one shot at me and I survived to tell my story." I was very impressed by her courage and the miracle she told us about.

Shortly after we arrived in Poland, a young man greeted me shyly and introduced himself.

"Eva, I am Bryan. One of my friends who was on the March last year told me to make sure I meet you." I liked him right away. There was a very attractive sensitivity about him.

With Bryan and Shoshana

I loved his company. During the trip, he was always close by, always offering help. We had many conversations together. He was a delightful young man.

On this trip each survivor had brought a memento that had great sentimental value.

Natalie, a survivor joining us for the first time, held up a picture of a teapot.

"When the Nazis came to our village they stole this teapot. It meant a lot to my family. Years later, on one of my trips to Israel, I visited a little museum in the north and what did I see? My precious, old and fragile porcelain teapot, intact! Somehow it had found a home in the museum. The staff gladly returned it to me."

Gabriella showed us a purse.

"My mother made this purse in needle point," she said. "I am very attached to it."

When it was my turn I showed the students the letter Mel had written to me when we first met.

"This is a letter that a stranger wrote to me and within five weeks we were married! Ever since I turned sixteen I hoped to find my soul mate," I began, holding Mel's note close to my heart.

"We had 32 wonderful years together and, although he died at 55, I am confident I will see my beloved again." I showed the students a photograph of our wedding.

"Eva, you look just like you did then," one of the students remarked. The students clapped with excitement.

Just like the previous year we visited Auschwitz again the day before the March. As we followed the staff through the camp, looking for a place to sit for lunch, we came to a pool.

"This must be the pool Erika Jacoby jumped into," I said, remembering the documentary.

"It is," Randy said. "Let's have lunch here." We all sat around it and ate our sandwiches.

I felt I had finally found my purpose and was coming into my own. I would go on the March of the Living as long as I was able to walk. It had become very important to me with its goal of always remembering, and helping the students understand the Holocaust. The students and staff showered me with the love and appreciation I had craved my whole life, and

I realized that I too was a woman of substance, different from Maman, and that I had indeed something important to contribute in my own special way.

Ilana, Diane and I had made plans to fly to France together to visit the family in Paris and Jean Menthonnex and his wife in Vence. On the way back from Vence, we would stop by the Ravauds in Autrans. I was really looking forward to this reunion and sharing an important part of my past with my daughter and granddaughter.

When we arrived at Jean's doorstep he opened the door. "Eva!" "Who would have thought that we would ever see each other again." His hug was so special, and despite his illness, still strong. What a reunion! It was very moving for me that Jean was so happy to see me. He opened a bottle of champagne to toast our reunion. Over a delicious dinner at a French restaurant we caught up on the 70 years that had gone by. His wife Geneviève was charming.

After dinner, we returned to their apartment where they showed us the thick folder of documents they had about Jean's parents who had been inscribed as Righteous Gentiles at *Yad Vashem*.

Menthonnex Recognition at Yad Vashem

"I feel like I know you and your brothers very well," Geneviève said. "I have heard about you and your family all my life."

Thank God we were able to have this amazing reunion. It was hard to say goodbye. Jean died a year later, and what a precious memory it became to have seen him again after all these years!

Ilana, Diane and I drove back up north to visit Georgette and Colette, the daughters of our former landlords, the Ravauds. After an hour drive up a curvy mountain road from Grenoble, we reached Autrans and Ilana pulled up in front of the familiar yellow house that now belonged to them, both in their eighties. I had not seen them since we lived upstairs. "Eva! We are so delighted to see you," Georgette exclaimed when she saw the three of us at the door. It certainly did not feel like a lifetime had passed since we'd last seen one another.

Ravaud 1943

"Were you as scared as we were when the Nazis slept upstairs and ate with you and your parents?" I asked.

"No," Georgette replied. "We actually felt safer because we knew no other Nazis would bother us as long as those two were here."

"But we were terrified they might burn the house down before leaving," Colette added.

We wanted to pay our respects to their parents so we visited their graves and also the graves of the Menthonnex, my "Parrain" and "Marraine," of *Clairfontaine*.

Ravaud 2012

The following December, I was delighted to meet my whole Australian family, to attend Paul and Talya Lewin's son's *Bar Mitzvah* and to tour Sydney, and its gorgeous Opera House, with Paul's parents from Cape Town.

April 2013 came. I felt immensely grateful to the Builders of Jewish Education for making it possible for me to go on the March again. It had become the highlight of my life.

Four years had passed since I had first met Sigrun in Jerusalem. When she found out I was going on the March again, she suggested we march out of Auschwitz together.

At the preparatory workshop, we were shown a different movie. An old Jewish man is waiting on a train platform. The train arrives, he boards it and finds a seat next to a beautiful, elegant gentile woman. When the Nazis pass through the train, asking to see identification, the old man fumbles in his pockets. It is obvious that he has no card, so the elegant lady next to him pretends to be his wife and scolds him angrily, "I told you not to forget your card. You left it on the kitchen table, you good-for-nothing!" The Germans left. She had risked her life to save his.

We arrived in Warsaw on Friday, April 5th.

On the day of the March, I looked around to see if I could find Sigrun. I saw a woman with smiling eyes coming toward me.

"Eva!" she shouted.

Never in a million years would I have thought that I would walk out of Auschwitz with a German. I started to think about the hatred I had lived with my whole life. Sigrun was so dedicated to helping heal the past that I felt my hatred slowly disappearing. I knew, of course, that not all Germans were Nazis and that their descendants were not responsible for their fathers' and grandfathers' actions, but hatred is long lasting. This German woman had dedicated her life to healing the German-Jewish relationship. She and her husband, Wolfgang, were extraordinary people. Sigrun shared with me that after having a daughter of their own, they traveled to Latin America, Africa and Asia and, upon seeing how many children lived in orphanages, decided to adopt. Over the following twelve years they adopted five children from Peru and Brazil, all of whom are now grown, and have good jobs and children of their own.

There was a long line for the women's restroom before the March was to begin. One of them told us to go into the men's room, which was empty. I met a young beautiful German journalist, Olga, as we were washing our hands. We became instant friends! Imagine: a Jewish woman meeting a German woman in the men's room in Auschwitz!

On that trip we visited one of the many memorials to Dr. Janusz Korczak. Dr. Korczak was a Polish educator and writer of children's books whose real name was Henrik Goldszmit. He directed a large orphanage for Jewish children. Even though he was Jewish, the Nazis gave him the chance to escape because he was very well-known and respected. Instead he chose to stay with his 200 children. "You do not leave a sick child in the night, and you do not leave children at a time like this," he said. Dr. Korczak's mission was to create a better world by educating the children. He was transported with them to Treblinka where he was murdered in August 1942, along with all "his" orphans. He was 64. Everytime I hear this story, I am devastated.

Dr. Janusz Korczak with "his" orphans

This Holcaust Remembrance Day story appeared in an Israeli newspaper:

In 1942 the Nazis came to the apartment of a young Jewish woman. They told her that she had twenty minutes to pack her most precious belongings. Among the items she took was an expensive fur coat to protect her from the cold weather. When she arrived at the entrance to Auschwitz, two Polish women took the coat from her. The coat was very heavy and the two women wondered why. When they got home they searched its pockets. They found several pieces of gold and some jewelry. But even after they had taken out these items, the coat was still heavy, so they kept searching and, to their utmost surprise, found a tiny baby girl in the lining."

"What?" one woman exclaimed. "How could she stay alive without any food? She never cried?"

"I don't know," said the other woman, "but you know what? I have children of my own and you don't have any. Why don't you take the baby and I will take the jewelry." And so 'Paulina' was raised in the Christian faith and eventually became a pediatrician. When her mother died, the other woman came to see Paulina. "I have to tell you something," she said. "The person who just died was not your real mother. Let me tell you how she became your mother."

"How do I know that you are telling me the truth?" Paulina asked, confused.

"When we took you, you were wearing this little gold necklace with a pendant. A name is inscribed on it, and we could not read it, but for what it's worth, here it is. It's yours now."

Suspecting that the writing on the necklace was in Hebrew, the young woman went to see a Rabbi and told him her story. She showed him the necklace.

"Rosa," he read. "That's the name you were given at birth."

"Does that mean that I am Jewish?" Paulina asked, surprised.

"I think so. I suggest that you write a letter to the great Lubavitcher Rabbi in New York. He is the highest authority for Hassidic Jews and he can advise you."

It did not take long before she received an answer. He confirmed that she was Jewish and advised her to go settle in Israel to take care of Jewish children there."

Paulina followed the rabbi's advice. She changed her name to Shoshana (Rose in Hebrew) and started working as a doctor at a hospital in Israel. She got married and had two children, and grandchildren.

One day, while she was taking a walk with her husband in Jerusalem, she heard an explosion nearby. It happened at the Sbarro Café in August 2001.

"Go home immediately!" she told her husband and check on the family. "I must go to the hospital right away. There will be casualties."

As she arrived at the hospital, an elderly man came to her in great distress.

"Please, help me find my granddaughter!" he pleaded. "When the bomb exploded I lost her in the smoke."

Shoshana went looking for the child, found her and brought her back to her anxious grandfather. As she watched this reunion, she noticed that the little girl was wearing a necklace that looked just like hers.

"Where can I buy such a necklace?" she asked the old man. "I would like to get one for my granddaughter."

"I am sorry to tell you that you cannot buy such a necklace anywhere," he replied. "I am a goldsmith and I only made two like this in my life — one for my granddaughter, and another one for my baby girl who died in Auschwitz a long time ago."

Shoshana pulled out the necklace from underneath her blouse and showed it to the old man. You can just imagine that reunion!

This is how a man and his daughter were miraculously reunited 59 years after the war.

In Israel we visited the most incredible place, the Ayalon Institute, an hour's drive south of Tel Aviv, past the city of Rechovot. A long, single-story house stands in the middle of a grassy area. As we walked inside, our tour guide, a young Israeli woman with a warm smile, welcomed us into a room with a large industrial-size washing machine.

"About thirty feet below the ground you are standing on, there used to be a bullet factory," she began in excellent English. "In 1945, a group of young resistance fighters, members of the *Haganah* (the underground army of the Jews of Palestine during the British mandate) decided to build a bullet factory to manufacture enough ammunition to gain their independence from the British. Above ground, it was a quiet kibbutz where the people grew vegetables and had babies. Thirty feet below, they secretly built a factory as big as a tennis court. They went to Poland where they found some cheap, rusty bullet-making machines and managed to bring them here without being detected by the British stationed nearby in Rechovot. They rebuilt the machines. It was a top-secret undertaking. Nobody else who lived above knew what they were doing underground. Our guide pointed to the huge washing machine.

"The machine you see here had to be operated 24/7 to cover up the noise of the factory below, and because the kibbutz did not have enough laundry to justify operating the washing machine around the clock, they offered laundry service to all the inhabitants of Rechovot, and even to the British stationed there. Forty thousand bullets were manufactured here daily. The British never figured out that the money they paid for their laundry was being used to fund the production of the very bullets that would eventually lead to their demise and the establishment of the state of Israel."

I listened in amazement. Our guide swiveled the washing machine to the side revealing a steep, spiral staircase that led underground.

"Do you really want to go down there?" Monise asked me, worried that I might fall.

"Of course I do," I answered.

One by one we went down the narrow staircase, very carefully, and we ended up in a long room with various machines and a blue light at the very end of the room.

"Because the workers never saw the light of day they grew pale and weak," the guide explained, "so the doctor advised them to sit under this quartz light for five minutes every day as it has a similar effect on people as sunlight."

We walked past the machines and several small rooms to the other side of this elongated basement, passing by the gunpowder storage room. In another room food was kept, in case the British showed up and the workers got stuck down here. Then our group climbed up a steep staircase at the other end of the building, and we came out in a room with a huge oven. The guide swiveled the oven back into place over the opening and the exit was cleverly hidden.

"To conceal the smell of gunpowder and to justify baking 24/7 the Jews baked cookies and bread around the clock, again not only for the kibbutz, but for the town — and for the British officers. Had the British found out, they would have destroyed the factory and executed all the workers," the guide said. I was so impressed by the bravery, the creativity, the courage and the ingenuity those people had demonstrated. I had never heard of this place, yet I wished every tourist would see it. It blew my mind. Of everything I have seen in Israel, this was for me one of the most amazing.

I spent Shabbat with my family. I was happy to meet Diane's fiancé

Gilad, I rejoiced when I learned they would marry in August and I returned to Israel for the wedding. Guests flew in from various parts of the world. Even Sigrun, who had become part of our family, joined us from Berlin to attend her first Jewish wedding.

It was a beautiful celebration and I had a chance to spend some time with Sigrun while everyone was dancing. "Come visit me in Berlin," she suggested as we said our goodbyes.

Maybe it's time I went back, I thought.

In preparation for my fifth March, Monise asked me to say a few words and perhaps tell a joke to lighten the mood and reassure the parents who were sending their children across the globe to learn about a dark part of their history. But when I heard Monise say, "I have asked Eva to tell a joke," I felt a little jittery, having to address an audience of about five hundred people. Fearful memories of speaking in front of any group, no matter how small, flashed before me for a split second, but the anticipation of making them laugh made me forget my fear. I began:

"The Chinese emperor is looking for a new chief Samurai. After two months of advertising, three men come forward applying for the job — a Chinese Samurai, a Japanese Samurai and a Jewish Samurai." Immediately the audience began to chuckle. "He calls all three men to his court and asks one after the other to perform for him. The Chinese Samurai is first. He opens a little wooden box and lets out a fly. Then he takes his sword and goes swish, swish, swish." I gesticulated with wide arm movements. "The fly is on the floor, cut in two. The emperor is very impressed and says, 'That's quite a feat.' Then he turns to the Japanese Samurai and says, 'Can you do better than that?' The Japanese Samurai opens a little silver box, lets out a fly, goes swish, swish, swish with his sword and the fly is dead on the floor, cut into quarters. So the emperor says, 'That is fantastic!' He turns to the Jewish Samurai and says, 'How can you possibly top that?' The Jewish Samurai opens a little gold box, lets out a fly, and goes swish, swish, swish ten times and the fly flies away. The emperor says, 'Your fly is not even dead!' 'Dead is easy,' says the Jewish Samurai. 'Circumcision, that's the trick!'" The audience burst out laughing and clapping. I glanced at Monise, "Should I tell another one?"

"Yes, by all means," she replied. I continued.

"On the first day at the new senior complex, the manager addresses all the new seniors, pointing out some of the rules: 'The female sleeping quarters will be out-of-bounds for all males, and the male dormitory for the females. Anybody caught breaking this rule will be fined $20 the first time. Anybody caught breaking this rule the second time will be fined $60. Being caught a third time will cost you $180. Are there any questions?' At this point an older gentleman stood up in the crowd and inquired, 'How much for a season pass?'"

Back in Auschwitz, while I was waiting for the March to begin, I looked around to find some Polish people so I could thank them for supporting us. Three grey-haired ladies were standing together; they did not look Jewish.

"Excuse me, ladies, are you Polish?" I asked.

"No, we are German," one of them replied. "We came to march with the Jewish people."

"We love the Jewish people and we love Israel," another one of the ladies added.

The third lady stretched out her arms to hug me and said: "I thank the God of Israel for having kept you alive to this day! I am Rose," she said, "What is your name?"

"Eva," I replied, with tears in my eyes.

I was stunned. These simple words from a German woman I had never met in my life will stay engraved in my heart forever.

"We are here with the ICEJ, the International Christian Embassy Jerusalem," she said. "It's a global ministry that represents millions of Christians worldwide who share a love for Israel. We came to march with the Jewish people, to show our solidarity, to show you that you are not alone."

It was an extraordinary meeting, and I am moved to tears every time I think of it. I had never met Germans because I avoided them and now I had met Sigrun, Olga, Rose, and of course my primary editor, Martina! I was profoundly shaken and in awe. Every one of these ladies helped to end my old hatred.

After visiting Majdanek, our team leaders handed each student a letter from his/her parents.

"This is for you, Eva," Monise said.

"For me?" I asked, surprised.

Inside the envelope were various letters — several from my family and one from Bryan, the student who had been on the March with me in 2012, who had adopted me as his third grandmother and whom I viewed as my third grandson.

Dear Eva,

Over the last three years you and I have reminisced about our experiences on the March of the Living. There are a few things I should tell you that I never said before. Prior to leaving for Poland in April 2012, I turned to my friends, who were at the time freshmen in college, and asked them for advice as they had participated in the March of the Living the year before. Many said, "Keep an open mind!" Some said, "Experience and learn from everything you see." But one friend repeated, "Get to know Eva Perlman! She will transform your life."

But how was I going to get to know Eva Perlman? There were 200 other students trying to learn and grow from the stories of these amazing survivors. But that first day in Krakow, I approached you and said hello. Whether I came off as awkward, weird, or unusual, it didn't matter because that single "Hello" was about to change my entire life. It took me only one day to understand that March of the Living was only the beginning of an exciting new friendship.

I cannot begin to recall every conversation throughout the two weeks in Poland and Israel with you, but I can tell you that you truly captured my heart. Not only is your story so inspiring, but your genuine love of life is amazing. Every day was exciting from breakfast to bedtime. Your jokes kept me laughing when I needed to feel good. Your conversation kept me listening when I needed to be inspired, and your story kept me learning when I needed to gain perspective.

You adopted me as one of your own. I look forward to coming home from college and getting the chance to see you, and I look forward to our email conversations while I am in Washington, DC.

Thank you for your love, support and guidance over the last three years. I will never again take for granted an opportunity I am given.

With love always,
Bryan G.

I was deeply moved. My friends at BJE and the students don't believe me when I tell them that I have always been shy and unsure of myself. Their love, sincere care and respect have helped me to be proud of what

I'm doing, and to feel grateful for my life every single day. I may give a lot to the students, but I receive more. The March continues to change my life every year.

In addition, I received several letters from my children and grandchildren telling me how much they love me and how proud they are of me. My grandaughter Myra, who would soon become a rabbi, wrote:

Dear Mamie,

Let me first say how proud I am of you and how proud I am to be your granddaughter. You are helping a whole new generation understand and connect to a sense of Jewish peoplehood, of what it means to belong to something bigger than themselves, and the responsibility that comes with that.

On my own recent trip to Poland, I found myself asking the very basic question of why it is we feel compelled to visit a place where such atrocities were committed against our people. Of course the immediate answer is to "Never Forget." But I felt that this reason wasn't compelling enough for me – that, although the magnitude of the Holocaust is unparalleled, we should be vigilant not to forget any of the persecutions and destruction that we have survived.

My next attempt to answer the question of why we go, is simply the idea of showing up for one another, that we have the desire to be there for the ones we loved, and for our kin, to be witnesses to their lives, and to somehow show them that we still love and care for them even after they are gone. And although I felt better about this answer, I found yet one more.

On my recent trip, as I sat at the mass grave for 800 children in Zbylitowska Gora, I realized that our greatest weakness as a people is our belief in the unquestionable sanctity of human life. As I sat there I began to think of all those children, and how different the world might be if they had lived – not just in the sense of how many Jews might live in the world as their descendants, but of the contributions to our people and to the world that they and their descendants could have made. Then suddenly I realized that what is missing from the world, the distance we often feel from our task of perfecting a world that is still so troubled, stems from the fact that they and so many others were never able to fulfill their missions in the world. It seemed clear to me why I had come: I must live for those who could not take on the values and missions of theirs that I am capable of, I must bring them to fruition - that their lives and their souls might be raised through me, and that our world might be that much closer to the dream we have for what it could be.

And so, each person that you accompany to that place each year, each one who commits to remembering those who were never given the chance to fully live out their purpose on this earth – they each bring us that much closer to the work of repairing our world – indeed a holy mission.

May God continue to bless you with the strength and courage to continue this holy work, and may we all merit to see the incredible impact that your life and your story continue to have on our family and our community.

Je t'aime,
Myra

As I put the letters back into the envelope, I was so moved as I had not consciously realized the magnitude, the impact I, and the other survivors, had made in our own right and what responsibility came along with it. BJE has helped me to grow and be able to touch the current generation of young minds, and perhaps the next — after I am gone.

I shared another story with the students:

The brand new rabbi and his wife were assigned to their first congregation and were tasked with reopening a Shul in suburban Brooklyn. They arrived in early February, excited about the opportunity. The shul was very run down and needed much work. They set a goal to have everything done in time to have their first service on Erev Purim, the eve of Purim. They worked hard repairing aged pews, plastering walls, painting, etc. On the 8th of Adar, they were ahead of schedule and just about finished. But a terrible snowstorm that lasted two days hit the area. When the rabbi went to the shul, his heart sank. A leak in the roof had caused a large area of plaster, about twenty feet by eight feet, to fall off the front wall of the sanctuary, just

317

behind the pulpit. He cleaned up the mess, postponed the Erev Purim service, and headed home.

On the way home he passed a local business that was having a sale for charity, so he stopped by. Among the items that were for sale was a beautiful, handmade, ivory-colored, crocheted tablecloth with exquisite work, fine colors and a Magen David embroidered in the center. It was just the right size to cover the hole in the front wall of the sanctuary. He bought it and headed back to the shul. It started snowing again. An older woman was trying to catch the bus. She missed it, so the rabbi invited her to wait in the warm shul. While she sat in a pew the rabbi got on a ladder to hang the tablecloth. He could hardly believe how beautiful it looked and how perfectly it covered the problem area.

Just as he had finished hanging up the tablecloth, he noticed the woman. She was walking down the center aisle. Her face was as white as a sheet. "Rabbi, where did you get that tablecloth?" she asked. The rabbi explained. The woman asked him to check the lower right corner to see if the initials E.B.J. were crocheted into it there. They were. These were her initials. She had made this tablecloth thirty-five years ago in Poland. The rabbi told her how he had just gotten the tablecloth and the woman explained that before the war she and her husband lived in Poland and were well-to-do. When the Nazis came she was forced to leave. Her husband was going to follow her the next week. He was captured, sent to a camp and she never saw him or her home again. The rabbi wanted to give her the tablecloth but she made the rabbi keep it for the shul. The rabbi insisted on driving her home. That was the least he could do. She lived on the other side of Staten Island and was only in Brooklyn for the day for a housecleaning job.

What a wonderful service they had on Erev Purim. The Shul was almost full. At the end of the service the rabbi and his wife greeted everyone at the door and many said that they would return. One older man, whom the rabbi recognized from the neighborhood, continued to sit in one of the pews and stare. The rabbi wondered why he wasn't leaving. "Where did you get this tablecloth?" he asked. "It looks just like the one my wife made years ago in Poland before the war."

He told the rabbi how the Nazis had come, how he forced his wife to flee, and how he planned to follow her, but was arrested and put in a camp. He never saw his wife or home again.

"May I take you for a little ride?" the rabbi then asked. They drove to Staten Island, to the same house where he had taken the woman three days before. He helped the man climb the three flights of stairs to the woman's apartment, knocked on the door and saw the greatest Erev Purim reunion he could have ever imagined.

I had a hard time reading the last paragraph through my tears. When I lifted my eyes from the paper, I saw that the students were crying too.

Some people say this is God at work. Others, who don't believe in God, say, "Oh! these are just coincidences." This convinced me there are no coincidences. I believe that there are only miracles and that the universe brings people together.

CHAPTER 15

RETURN TO BERLIN

Darkness cannot drive out Darkness. Only Light can do that.
Hate cannot drive out Hate. Only Love can do that.

Martin Luther King Jr.

In May 2015, as our delegation flew home from Tel Aviv, I boarded a plane to Berlin. I had never wanted to go back to my place of birth — yet, here I was on my way to Berlin to visit Sigrun, eighty years after Papa, Maman and I left Germany. All my life I had hated speaking German, or hearing someone speak German. When my accent revealed my origin, people exclaimed, "Oh! I love Germany! It is SO beautiful!" It made my heart cringe. I decided to keep an open mind. It is funny how I vow never to do certain things, then life changes my mind. I never thought I would go to Poland either, or God forbid, to a concentration camp. Yet, I had just completed my fifth March of the Living. How would I feel among Germans? What would it be like to speak German again?

As I exited the Berlin Tegel airport, I immediately spotted Sigrun with her loving smile and a man with a huge head of hair next to her. It had to be Wolfgang, her husband. He reminded me of the Flying Dutchman in Wagner's opera. Their warm welcome made all the difference. Wolfgang immediately took my suitcase and placed it in their van. We were on the way to their apartment in Berlin Friedenau, driving through streets that looked familiar — after all, I lived in Europe for many years.

Wolfgang and Sigrun were wonderful hosts. For the next few days Sigrun took me around Berlin and showed me many things of interest from a Jewish point of view. Jews had lived in Berlin since the late 1600s.

There was construction everywhere. A sophisticated transportation system allowed us to hop from bus to streetcar to subway in seconds. I was surprised to see that Berlin was quite cosmopolitan and that I did not find the Aryan-looking crowd I had imagined. I saw people of all ethnic groups, all colors, all manner of dress. As I walked through the streets with Sigrun, a funny thought crossed my mind. *'With my blond hair, blue eyes and fair complexion I look more German than most of the people around me!'*

In their immediate neighborhood, there were *Stolpersteine* (stumbling stones) in almost every block. Sigrun and Wolfgang had helped place many of them. Information about the Holocaust was displayed on the sidewalk behind broken glass.

"Vandals broke the glass," Sigrun explained. "Many people are thinking of ways to heal the past, but unfortunately there are also still those who are anti-Semitic. Many Germans feel responsible for the Holocaust, even the young generations born years after the war."

Sigrun showed me the *Stolpersteine* of Minna and Ruben Riesenburger, the relatives of my grandmother who were taken from their home by the Nazis and murdered.

Riesenburger stumbling stones

Myra, visiting Berlin, with Sigrun

We walked a lot. With each passing day I felt a little more comfortable speaking German. We passed Humboldt University, once known as the Friedrich Wilhelm University, where Maman had studied medicine.

"This is *Friedrich Strasse 158*," Sigrun said as she stopped in front of a tall office building, "where your father used to work."

It was so interesting to see the places that I heard my parents talk about for many years!

From here Sigrun took me to *Grosse Hamburger Strasse 27*.

"This is the Moses Mendelssohn Boys School and Teachers Training college," Sigrun explained, "which your Grossvater directed and where he lived." I could hardly believe that I was seeing that building with my own eyes! "Grossvater (Josef Gutmann) was the principal until he retired in 1931," I said.

Just around the corner, on Oranienburger Strasse, my eyes were drawn to a *Stolperstein* that was gleaming in the sunshine. I truly stumbled on it. Bending down, I read:

HIER ARBEITETE (Here worked)
RECHTSANWALT (Attorney)
DR. JULIUS BLUMENTHAL (Dr. Julius Blumenthal)
GB. 1900 (born in 1900)
ALS GEISEL INHAFTIERT (imprisoned as hostage)
SACHSENHAUSEN (Sachsenhausen)
ERMORDET 3.12.1942 (murdered on Dec. 3, 1942)

Julius Blumenthal stumbling stone

"Dr. Julius Blumenthal!" I exclaimed. "Papa's best friend!" I remembered Papa telling me how he had begged his friends Arthur Bursch and Julius Blumenthal to leave Germany, but unfortunately they decided to stay, and neither of them survived. I was very moved.

A few weeks later, Sigrun would write to me: "I researched Dr. Blumenthal on the Internet and found out that he was born in March 1900," Sigrun said. "He was just two years older than your father. When Jews were no longer allowed to work in Germany in 1933, he became very active in Berlin's Jewish community. By 1939 he was the legal advisor for a Jewish newspaper. Two years later the Gestapo forced the Jewish community to give them a list of their coworkers and they picked up all the Jews. Those who had not left the country by then were taken. Dr. Blumenthal ended up in the Sachsenhausen concentration camp where he was shot to death." My heart cried for him.

Sigrun brought me to a garden.

"This is *Hansa Ufer 8* where you used to live," she said. "Unfortunately the apartment building has been torn down."

We walked on the sandy path along the Spree River where Grossmutter Bertha must have taken me for outings in my baby carriage.

Sigrun took me to the Holocaust Memorial. Just south of the Brandenburg Gate, on *Cora-Berliner Strasse*, thousands of thin concrete blocks of varying heights are standing, separated by pathways, commemorating the murdered Jews of Europe. It felt like a cemetery which invites you to remember. As we walked between them I thought I was losing my balance. This had been done on purpose while constructing the pathways.

Sigrun took me to the Memorials for the Sinti and the Roma that had been built to commemorate the homosexuals and gypsies of Central Europe who were murdered. It is a large pond with a stone in the middle, on which a fresh flower is placed daily. Panels on the wall give information on the persecution of those two minorities under the National Socialist regime of terror.

On my third day in Germany, Wolfgang drove us to Driesen, which was now called Dresdenko and part of Poland. I wanted to see where Maman was born and had grown up. Just before reaching Driesen, we passed the small railway station where Maman used to board the train to go to high school in Lansberg. In town, we took a walk through the streets and next to one of the schools stood a statue of Dr. Janusz Korczak. Around the corner, as I stood on the pretty central square of the little town with benches amidst the flowers, I was overcome with emotion.

Driesen in 1910

Driesen in 2015

This was where Grosspapa (Adolf Lewin) once used to have his jewelry and watch store. This was where Maman lived and played as a child! As I lifted my eyes, I saw the tower with the clock that Grosspapa had come to repair during the First World War. I could hardly believe that I was in Driesen!

The visit to Berlin had been quite an event for me. When upon my return I was asked repeatedly how it felt going back to Berlin, I was embarrassed to say that I actually had a good time! I felt so fortunate and blessed to have had the chance to get to know Sigrun and Wolfgang in their community. They helped me erase bad memories and create new positive ones about Germans and Germany.

I received an email from Rose, my other new German friend.

"There were times when I was ashamed of being German," she wrote. "Still in the last few years, our society has undergone some change, and we are facing our tragic history, hoping to atone for it. Especially now, in 2015, we often see commemorations of '70 years since WWII' brought to attention in exhibitions and events, and I am very happy that our government now openly recognizes the responsibility of Germany, and does not try to hide it. Remembrance is necessary, important and right. These 70 years and the March of the Living made me want to participate in that trip to Auschwitz, so as to witness there – with 10,000 young Jews—the triumph of life over the Nazis' plans of annihilation.

And then, I was allowed to meet you. I still cannot believe what happened to us when we met. My heart is so deeply moved when I think of you, and the fact that our hug and my prayer also moved your heart and soul is for me a great gift. That place (Auschwitz) is so horrible, and it was my greatest wish that people could feel that there are also 'other Germans,' different from those of the war generation."

Dear Rose, I wrote back.

"I agree with you that this hug in Auschwitz between a Jew and a German was extraordinary and a sign of reconciliation. Rabbi Artson, Dean of the Ziegler School of Rabbinic Studies has said, 'The only people who can heal the Germans are the Jews, and the only people who can heal the Jews are the Germans.'"

Dear Eva, came the reply.

"Reading your email, understanding your attitude and your understanding that Jews and Germans 'need each other' to find healing, has touched me to tears. From the bottom of my heart I want to be a part of this movement, to bring healing to relationships that have been so terribly destroyed by the Nazis.

But now, the Holy One has made this encounter with you 'beshert.' I will be thankful for the rest of my life, as you are one of the most wonderful and extraordinary persons I have ever met. Thank God for His mercy and great love.

My dear Eva, let me hug you again and bless you in the Name of the Almighty, who kept you alive!"

This five-minute encounter in Auschwitz turned out to be one of the most meaningful events in my life, one that has moved me greatly and helped me to put the past where it belongs, in the past. Our friendship developed. One more miracle, and not the least! There are good people in this world, and we are fortunate when we meet them. We must be forever grateful.

With every German I met, my bitterness eroded more. These relationships I formed with a new generation of non-Jewish Germans has finally put all those years of hatred behind me. A few months before my sixth March, I received another email from Rose in which she expressed the desire to meet me in Auschwitz, the place of death where our friendship had begun. She wanted to walk with me out of Auschwitz. When I replied that I loved the idea, Rose was overjoyed.

On our fourth day in Poland on the next March in May 2016, I was looking for Rose in Auschwitz. Soon I saw her, draped in a German flag, walking towards me. We hugged like old friends.

"Come, walk with me and all the survivors in the front of our U.S. group," I said and I took her by the hand. "This is such an honor for me to walk beside you out of this place of death," Rose said, deeply moved. Hand-in-hand we walked to Birkenau. During the walk Rose shared with our students the mission of ICEJ.

Eventually, I went to Berlin a second time, and Rose came to see me and met Sigrun.

With Rose and Sigrun in Berlin

After the March, we returned to Warsaw to spend Shabbat before flying to Israel. After the Shabbat ceremony in the Nozyk synagogue, two Klezmer musicians arrived, one with a guitar and one with a violin, and set up their instruments on the *bimah*. The adult group with Monise had joined us. Everybody started dancing in a circle in the center aisle. It was so crowded that there was hardly any room to move. The music and the noise were deafening. Then six or seven students picked up Gabriella and pushed her into the air. *'Oh my God, are they going to do that to me too?'* I thought as I watched from the sidelines. Next they took Bob. Then I felt hands picking me up and lifting me in the air. Before I knew it I was being carried by many hands, floating in horizontal position above the crowd. I lifted my hands and waved and blew kisses to everyone with a huge smile on my face. People clapped, shouting, "Eva, Eva!" Some people took videos. After me they lifted the staff, one by one. The students were drowning in sweat at the end! From then on, we would do this again every year. This crowd of young and old dancing and singing and having raucous fun was always one of the highlights of every trip for me. I invariably thought, *Am Yisrael Chai! We'll show you, Hitler! You can turn in your grave forever!*

The happiness in the synagogue blew me away!

By the time everyone had crowd-surfed, it was late. Exhausted and in a great mood we walked back to our hotel. It had been a long, exciting, rewarding day.

The following Shabbat we were in Israel. I had been impatient to get there. My great-granddaughter Aviv was born in March in Jerusalem. I finally got to hold my first great-grandchild in my arms. She was, of course, the cutest baby I had ever seen. While Diane and Gilad napped, I sang to Aviv. And I sang my gratitude to the Lord.

Soon after we returned, it was graduation day at the Milken high school and the survivors were given seats near the front. The synagogue was filled by proud parents, siblings and grandparents. With pomp and circumstance, the graduates filed into the synagogue and took their seats on the steps next to the *bimah*. There were several speeches by the President and other dignitaries of the school. Then it was time for the valedictorian speech. I was so delighted to see Aviva, one of the students who was on the March a month earlier! I was surprised when she started speaking:

A couple of weeks ago, I was walking with a friend back to my room in our Jerusalem hostel when I spotted Eva, a survivor traveling with us on March of the Living, struggling to open her door a few rooms down. I offered to help, and soon after, asked if she would be willing to tell us a couple of jokes before we went to bed. Seeing that she and I were both clearly very tired, I quickly added an "oh, well it's actually pretty late, maybe it would be better if we waited until morning."

She took a few moments, deliberating internally, and decided she could carve out a few minutes of sleep to share a couple of jokes. Those few minutes extended to nearly an hour, most of which had all three of us laughing hysterically at Eva's private joke collection, some of which she even refused to share with the rest of the group.

Eva Perlman, a particularly giggly, bubbly, and vivacious woman, preached to us about the conscious choice she's made to be happy. While the concept of "choosing to be happy" sounds great, it confounded me. How could someone simply choose what emotion to feel in a given moment? However, I soon came to realize that this choice was not a mere switch of affect, but a shift in mentality that allowed for happiness to permeate a person's life.

Her humor brought happiness not just to herself, but to everyone around her. She used it to heal, to entertain, and to transition us to a theme of celebration. After a sad Yom Hazikaron ceremony, she could heal the sadness of those around her with a spontaneous joke.

Her focus was outward, and this allowed her to stay positive. What I mean by that is when something obstructed her mood, her first thought was always about how to make things better for everyone else. She also found her happiness by seeing the world as a place of miracles. She told me with dire conviction, quoting Deepak Chopra, that "the world is full of miracles. They bubble up from their hidden source, surround us with opportunities, and disappear. They are the shooting stars of everyday life; there are no coincidences; everything happens for a reason. Each day these miracles provide us with the opportunity to do something new or meaningful in our lives. It is a person's choice, though, to seize those opportunities in order to propel his or her self forward."

I wanted to find some way to carry Eva's impact with me everyday, but nothing seemed right. I knew that what I had learned from her wasn't about mastery or application. Every action or practical application I thought of felt wooden or forced.

AND THEN I FOUND THIS STORY BY ELIE WIESEL...

When the Baal Shem-Tov, a great Chasidic rabbi, saw misfortune threatening the Jews, he would go into a specific spot in this specific forest to meditate. There he would light a fire, say a special prayer, and the miracle would be accomplished. Years later this responsibility fell on his disciple. He would go to the same place in the same forest and say: "Master of the Universe, listen! I do not know how to light the fire, but I am still able to say the prayer, and this must be enough" and again a miracle would happen. Still later, the responsibility fell to another rabbi. He went into the forest, looked at the sky, and said "Master of the universe, I do not know how to light the fire. I do not know the prayer, but I'm here, I know the spot, and that has to be enough." For this man too, it was enough. Eventually, it fell to this one final rabbi to beg for a miracle. Sitting in his armchair, his head in his hands, he said, "God, I am unable to light the fire, and I do not know the prayer, and I cannot even find the place in the forest. All I can do is tell the story, and this must be enough." And it was enough. Just like this last Rabbi, I don't know the proper steps to take to make Eva's example my own. All I can do is tell the story with awe and gratitude, and this must be enough.

When Aviva finished speaking, I was astounded, proud, embarrassed, grateful... and more astounded and grateful! I was also impressed by Aviva's maturity and by her ability to write and express herself.

On my seventh March, Randy said something in Treblinka, when a sudden wind made the trees sway from side to side, which has stayed with me: "It looks like even the trees are davening." It was such a moving image. Those trees witnessed atrocities that occurred there over 70 years ago, and they were still grieving.

On my ninth March in May 2019 my friend and main editor Martina Gruber — my first real non-Jewish German friend — met me in Auschwitz to march out of the camp with all of us. She had learned so much about it from editing my book that she wanted to experience it for herself. She wanted us to march hand in hand.

And we did.

AFTERWORD

Looking back over 87 years, I am awed and truly grateful for all the miracles that have guided my life. Of the many miracles, two stand out. First, as a child in hiding in Nazi-occupied France, my immediate family survived, allowing me to finally find my purpose in transmitting testimony to almost 2,000 young people over the last decade, who will bear witness for generations to come. Surviving is both a privilege and a responsibility. I am doing my best to carry this responsibility. Although, along the way, I faced breast cancer, radiation treatments, and five eye surgeries, I have not missed a March in the last decade.

Meeting Mel was the second miracle above all others that decided my life. As soon as I could read, fairy tales shaped my ideas of love, fidelity, kindness, and integrity and I grew into a hopeless romantic. I waited impatiently for my prince to arrive — and he did. I was willing to follow him all over the world. And I did.

I count my blessings every single day. I have three wonderful, loving and caring children, six beautiful grandchildren, and two gorgeous great-grandchildren! Three of my grandchildren are happily married — and I pray that I will witness the weddings of the other three! I love each of them deeply and they fill me with pride and joy, but I am not the gushing, adoring type of grandmother that other women are. My mother was never affectionate with me, and I do not remember my two grandmothers ever swooning over me either. I know they all loved me, but I did not learn from them to show love and to live in gratitude. I learned those attitudes much later.

I am blessed to have many friends, and relatives in France, Canada, Israel, Australia, South Africa, and now even in Germany.

What have I learned in 87 years ? Above all, I am grateful for my wonderful life.

I believe in enjoying the little things, never taking anything or anybody for granted, staying positive, and weathering to the best of my ability the small and not-so-small problems, which make up the stuff of life. Mel was right; there are always problems! We are on this earth only for a little while, so let us try to be our best, and make the best of life.

I have also learned to be alone without feeling lonely. After a busy week, I love the quiet of a Sunday afternoon, in my armchair with a good book. I believe in always being myself. I hate secrecy and lies, as they never work for long. I love entertaining my friends by sharing one of my favorite movies or telling a good joke. I have often been told that I missed my calling as a comedian.

Even though I've experienced many miracles, life has not always been easy. My dream was to grow old with my husband. We had a beautiful relationship for 32 years and would have stayed married forever. Redesigning my life after losing him taught me painful lessons. I had to learn to become a whole person in my own right rather than being just one half of a couple. I became more confident, and I believe that Mel is watching me from above and is proud of me. When I face hardships, I've learned to seek the silver lining. I've learned that you should not wait for something good to happen for you to be happy. Decide first to be happy, and then good things will happen to you. Happiness is a choice.

ABOUT THE AUTHOR

Eva was born in Berlin, Germany in 1932. Soon, to escape Hitler, her parents emigrated to France where she grew up. The family added two more children, and miraculously survived the war by hiding in the mountains of southern France.

She had several careers: pediatric nursing, accounting, real estate investing and travel. She has been active in network marketing for over 40 years, and her latest, and best business is distributing Organo Gold coffee. Health has always been a great interest of hers, and her passion is to help people maintain their health or improve it.

She was married for 32 years to Mel Perlman, a wonderful man who died prematurely at the age of 55. She has three children, six grandchildren, and two great-grandchildren. Maintaining a positive outlook and an attitude of gratitude has helped her deal with the challenges in her life.

Her passion and purpose are to accompany Jewish teens as a survivor on the annual March of the Living, led by the Builders of Jewish Education of Los Angeles, and she has participated in the March nine consecutive times beginning in 2011. She is looking forward to joining the March in 2020 for the tenth time.

Following her childhood in Germany and France, she lived in Israel, Switzerland, England, Uganda, Canada, and now the U.S. She is a wonderful storyteller, and is now publishing her autobiography: *Eva's Uncommon Life, Guided by Miracles.*